6-9-80

Changing to a drastically different career in midlife—between the ages of thirty-five and fifty-five—has quietly become a new social phenomenon. Studies find that midlife crises bring career crises 80 percent of the time. Forty percent of working people over forty have seriously thought of changing careers. One-third of all workers do change in a five-year period. No longer is staying put the only choice in a decade that emphasized self-analysis, opened up career options, and deepened concern with the quality of life.

Many reasons prompt this traumatic step. Some people are seizing control over their lives. Others are switching to careers where they can see the day-to-day results of their work. Some are top-level executives who have experienced the "Is-that-all-there-is?" feeling. For others, changing is a long-incubated rebellion against other people's expectations. Readers will recognize themselves among the Diverted, the Renewers, and the Seekers as Jones reveals their different, yet related, motivations through fascinating interviews and anecdotes.

Personal crises don't happen in a vacuum. Jones asked the wives, husbands and children of career changers how they survived the upheaval and uncovered some extraordinary stories of adaptation and love in action.

This book shows some of the best benefits of midlife stocktaking in these compelling portraits of ordinary people in the workaday world finding the right impetus to make the world work for them.

THE BIG SWITCH

New Careers, New Lives after 35

by Rochelle Jones

McGraw-Hill Book Company

NEW YORK • ST. LOUIS • SAN FRANCISCO
DÜSSELDORF • MEXICO • TORONTO

For Peter Woll

1 2 3 4 5 6 7 8 9 D O D O 8 7 6 5 4 3 2 1 0

LIBRARY OF CONGRESS CATALOGING IN PUBLICATION DATA
Jones, Rochelle.
    The big switch.
    Bibliography: p.
    Includes index.
    1. Vocational guidance—Case studies.   2. Job
satisfaction—Case studies.   3. Age and employ-
ment—
Case studies.   I. Title.
HF5381.J66   650'.14   79-24200
ISBN 0-07-032810-2

Book design by ROBERTA REZK.

Other books by Rochelle Jones

The Other Generation:
The New Power of Older People

The Private World of Congress, with Peter Woll

Blessed be he who has found his work,
he needs no further blessing.

THOMAS CARLYLE

Contents

Acknowledgments

Without Rick Gore I might have seized upon the idea for this book but I often wonder how. Rick implanted the idea and my agents Katinka Matson and John Brockman helped to bring it to maturity. To each of them I owe a debt of gratitude.

My editor Peggy Tsukahira has been superb. She was unfailingly encouraging and supportive and her many fine suggestions have helped to give this manuscript its final shape. Her cheerfulness in the face of repeated delays will never be forgotten. I owe her many, many thanks.

In my initial stages of thinking about this book, Lew Howland was enormously helpful. That Lew, a fine editor, has left publishing in order to make a career change of his own is a loss to us all.

Obviously this book could not have been written without the life stories of the people who enthusiastically supplied them. The substance and details of their career changes and their lives were offered by them. The interpretations were mine. I can only hope that I did them justice. All of the people I interviewed were willing to spend with me as much time as I needed and to each of them I offer an individual thank you. I am especially indebted to Ely and Nancy Callaway who welcomed me time and again in my quest of their stories.

There is one account of a career change that should have been included but was not because of the untimely death of Gene Tubbs. Gene was a fine doctor and an outstanding member of the Florida House of Representatives. He would have made a distinguished attorney. That he did not have an opportunity to realize his career change is tragic.

I wish to thank several career counselors who went out of their way to help me. Robert Foulkes and John Landgraf stood ready to inform me. The staff of Mainstream Associates shared with me their experiences and the unpublished results of their inquiry into some 500 career changes.

Of the many friends who offered shelter or support along the way I am particularly grateful to: Pam Greene, Rae and Harry Gumaer, Kent Pollock, Criss Green Rogers and Mary Gore for her fine pictures.

Billie Jones ran her clipping service with inspired efficiency as usual. It uncovered one of the most interesting career changes in this book. And to her I am more than appreciative.

Natalie Neviaser was a formidable typist but beyond that her unflagging interest in the manuscript and my progress helped to nudge the book toward completion.

There really is no way that I can acknowledge my debt to Peter Woll. He has lived, hoped and dreamed these pages along with me. Without his logistical, intellectual and moral support, there would be no book.

August 1979   ROCHELLE JONES
Washington, D.C.

Part
ONE

One
Out of Three 1

The first official bulletin on the subject of career change was issued in February, 1977. There were rumblings beforehand, of course, but the statisticians who document and record such transformations in our national life had largely ignored them. It wasn't until the scribes at the Bureau of Labor Statistics in Washington, D.C. got around to analyzing some of the data which was compiled during the 1970 census that confirmation came. The fact was that Americans were shedding careers in unprecedented numbers and with surprising frequency.

The *Wall Street Journal*, the house organ of the business and financial community, played the story on page one. "Career changes are made by a striking number of U.S. workers," read the boldface type which introduced it.

"Nearly a third of all American workers may change their careers over a five-year period, according to the Labor Department's first major survey of career-switching, based on the 1970 census," the article stated. "The new report shows career-switching was the greatest single reason for workers' resignations between 1965 and 1970, even though most earlier government studies overlooked it. More recent data show the trend continues.

"Federal projections of future job opportunities will have to be revised to incorporate the 'tremendous volume' of career changing, the study suggests."

Out in Temecula, California, which is two hours south
of Los Angeles and an hour east of San Diego, Ely Callaway
no doubt snorted when his secretary bought him that February
8 edition of the *Wall Street Journal*. Callaway has a short
terrier bark of a laugh which manages to combine rapacity
and glee. Callaway laughs a lot but most often when he thinks
he has beaten the competition. Ely is a man who relishes
winning and likes to be first. Once again he was. When the
article appeared, Ely Callaway was already four years into his
career switch.

Ely Callaway was born in LaGrange, Georgia, some fifty-
eight years ago and he left there as quickly as he could. That
drowsy Southern town was too small to contain his ambition.
Even then he was intensely competitive, highly ambitious. A
small town in the midst of a predominantly rural area of the
Deep South was too confining for him. There were too many
strictures of birth and class in the 1940s. Ely needed to go
where the only constraints would be the limits of his talents
and drive. His high school diploma was his passport out. He
fled first to Emory University in Atlanta and then into the
Army in World War II and finally into the corporate sphere.
Like his colleagues in the New York business world of the
1950s, Ely played fast and to win. He never looked back to
LaGrange.

In time Ely rose to be president of Burlington Industries,
the largest textile company in the Western world. Still that
was not enough. Unexpectedly he left Burlington Industries
to start a vineyard that would bear his name.

Almost four decades after Ely left Georgia he still drops
the endings of his words. His softly drawling sibilants betray
the Georgia origins that he has tried so hard to put behind
him. They also belie the consuming energy and motivation
that drove him to become president of a major corporation.
Sometimes competitors misjudge him because of that drawl
and think he is easygoing. That is a mistake they make only
once and to their lasting regret. Ely is no man's fool.

On that February morning Ely was restless. As he looked

out his office window, he could see the barbed wire strung out across the fields tracing fine black lines in the dust toward Rainbow Gap. In the spring the grape vines would wrap their tendrils around the treillages and in the summer they would drip Pinot Chardonnay and Zinfandel grapes but in the midst of the slight drop in temperature that passes for winter in Southern California, they were bare. No need in February to worry if the rains would wait until after the harvest or if there were sufficient sun.

Which left Ely free to brood about something else. Ely wanted to grow and produce fine wines. He also wanted his efforts to be recognized and praised. He wanted to be taken seriously. The summer before he had basked in the publicity that followed the selection of one of his white wines for a Bicentennial luncheon in honor of the Queen of England. The publicity was useful but even more helpful would be the attention of the men who were respected in the wine industry. That and the extra distributorships and listings on wine cards in restaurants which would enable him to turn a profit and survive were on Ely's mind.

A continent away George and Eleanor Pavloff didn't read the *Wall Street Journal* that day. It was probably just as well. If they had seen the article, they might have cried, not laughed. At the start of 1977 everything seemed to be going wrong for them.

A year earlier they had quit their jobs in Washington, D.C. and moved to Maine. George had resigned a secure civil service job at the Department of Health, Education and Welfare and Ellie had abandoned a less-settled life as a self-employed potter and teacher of crafts. They were in their middle forties. They had married late in life and had a daughter later still. To look at them, they seemed a perfect example of opposites who attract. Ellie is a tramper through life. She has a hearty laugh and a robust figure that reveals her love of cooking and eating. She likes to talk often and listen sometimes and although she owns a lot of books, she generates the feeling that she really prefers to learn about life firsthand. At the very least she would like the author to be there in her living room weaving his story aloud. George has spent a great deal of his life in one kind of cloister or another. Before he worked at HEW, he had been a Roman Catholic priest. He is calm and reflective and in a room full of boisterous people he seems to actually hear the slow rolls of "Trumpet Voluntary" in the background.

For all their apparent differences they shared one important thing. Both of them had the same goal in mind. Their objective was to own and operate a small country inn and they wanted to live in Maine. When they left to pursue their new life, they never anticipated they would spend so much time looking for an inn that they wanted to buy, that they could afford to buy. Reconciling their aspirations and their means seemed impossible for a long while. The trouble more often than not was the latter. Capital, they agreed, was too grandiose a term for the small horde of money they had managed to assemble. And so it happened that in February, 1977, they were just beginning to embark on their new careers.

They envisioned a cozy lodge where they and their guests could huddle together in front of the fire. They got the fireplaces but they hadn't anticipated that the wind would whistle down the chimneys. The day they moved into the eighteenth-century house that was to become the Pilgrim's Inn the biggest blizzard of the winter struck Maine. In the best of times Deer Isle is an isolated spot, a good hour and a half drive from the nearest town that can claim a population in five figures. Now they were completely isolated, alone in an empty house, without any furnishings, cut off by snow drifts from supplies. Only ninety days hence they had planned to open for their first paying guests. (They hoped there would be paying guests.) They looked at each other and panicked.

What, they wondered silently, each alone with his or her thoughts, had they let themselves in for? They couldn't visualize then that the time would come when every bedroom would be occupied and they would have more requests for dinner reservations than they could handle. Instead, they watched helplessly as the snow blotted out the road and obliterated the shoreline and listened to the wind breathing down the chimneys all night long.

In Miami, Florida, such problems don't exist. In February the only uncertainty about the weather is if the mercury will rise into the high eighties or snag in the mid-eighties. And the Tuesday the article appeared was again an advertisement for Coppertone Lotion. Iver Brook looks as if he might buy it in gallon jugs. But Iver Brook doesn't swab on suntan oil to loll on the beach at Crandon Park. Brook earned his tan working although some people might argue that spending the day on a boat in Biscayne Bay hardly classifies as toil.

Once the *Wall Street Journal*, Midwest edition, was as much a part of Iver Brook's life as his morning orange juice. When he was a commodities stockbroker in Chicago, buying and trading, wheeling and dealing at the Chicago Board of Trade, the *Wall Street Journal* was essential reading. He rarely glances at it these days. Now he is more apt to pick up the *Bulletin of Marine Science* or *Transactions of the American Fish Society* for a little light reading before dinner.

If his superiors had predicted Iver Brook's future back when he was a neophyte employee of Bache & Company, they would have been certain of his activities on the afternoon of February 8 and they certainly would have been wrong. He was supposed to be waiting for the market to close, to check the final figures and hop an early commuter train home where his wife might already have the vermouth uncorked and waiting. He seemed that predictable. He had been to war and that was enough insecurity and threat. When he returned he wanted predictability in his life. In fact, Iver Brook had envisioned a similar fate. Twenty-five years ago Iver Brook might have suspected that on February 8 he would be looking forward to an early retirement. After all he would then be fifty-four.

Instead Brook was reviewing the first draft of a paper that he was to present at the end of March at the University of Georgia. The title he had selected was "Some problems in determining the primary food sources of the benthic fauna in a coastal lagoon." By February, 1977, Brook had earned his Ph.D. and was spending his days on the second floor of the University of Miami marine biology lab. Retirement was the last thing on his mind.

His doctorate was two years old. The hardships of entering graduate school as a fifty-three-year-old first-year student in a rigorous field that he had never before studied were behind him. He had served his stint on graduate assistantships and postdoctoral fellowships. All that was past and he could begin now to hope to emerge as a full-fledged scientist. A few months before in October, 1976, he had received his first grant. The Energy Research and Development Administration in Washington, D.C. awarded $52,281 for the study of the food sources for marine animals in southeast Florida. The paper would report on some of his initial findings which made it even more important to Iver Brook. He hoped that it would be well received, that it would begin to build his reputation among the people whose opinions mattered in his field.

Ely Callaway, the Pavloffs and Iver Brook are four of the "workers" in the Department of Labor's study of career switching. At first glance they have little in common. They come from varied parts of the country. Their backgrounds are not the same and their interests differ drastically. Their upbringings were springboards to different directions and they had diverse life experiences. They achieved various levels of success in their careers before they decided to change. As dinner partners they would be hard pressed to find conversational topics of mutual concern.

But they share one characteristic which is more important than all of these differences combined. If they had been born twenty-five years earlier, none of them would have been likely to contemplate changing careers. They symbolize a new group of career changers who switch careers because they want to, not because they are forced to. They were not fired. Their jobs were not eliminated by their employers. They changed careers simply because they discovered something they would prefer to do. And that is a drastic departure from the recent past.

Restlessness and the propensity for mobility may be in

our genes. Very few of us are more than a generation or so removed from a passport that carries a different official seal on it. Dissatisfaction may be a national trait. After all, our forefathers and foremothers did not leave wherever they were to come to the United States because they were happy with their lot in life. And once they arrived, a goodly number kept right on moving around, spreading out from the Atlantic Seaboard to the Midwest and the Southwest and farther on to the Far West and the Northwest until the land ended and there was no place left to go. They were a peripatetic lot.

But of late their inclination to stay on the move has been borne along on our national chromosomes as something of a recessive trait. The equally human need to conserve and consolidate what we have already acquired has tended to dominate. The impulse to root can be as strong as the urge to repot ourselves when we are no longer able to grow in our present circumstances. The dictum "shirt sleeves to shirt sleeves in three generations" testifies to the fact that we are often more like our grandparents than our parents. In fact, there is a psychiatrist in Washington, D.C. who treats his patients by asking them to draw psychological family trees. Often his patients find that they are reenacting family dramas that have skipped a generation. In this case the sins of the father are visited on the grandsons.

If our grandparents forsook their careers and lives to come to these shores, our parents were the conservators. They tended the family flame and displayed a remarkable willingness to stay put. That probably would have happened anyway. Such proclivities tend to run in generational cycles. But the predisposition to remain in place was hurried along by the Depression. The Depression was the central fact of their lives. Their lives were shaped by it and it was a powerful persuader. People who have watched banks close, seen homes repossessed because mortgage payments can't be met and known men who commit suicide when they lose their jobs are not inclined to take risks. They stayed where they were.

The people who are currently running the command posts of the country learned about the Depression through their American history textbooks rather than personal experience. Still enough of their parents' attitudes were ingrained in them that they became the Silent Generation of the 1950s. A good job and security were important to them. If they had that, they were not ones to complain. Senator Joseph McCarthy molded them as the Depression had formed their parents. They learned early on that there was danger in speaking out, in being different. They toed the mark and thought they were wise to do so. Let's not have any trouble was their motto. They were the gray flannel men and were happy to be so. Until Sloan Wilson came along with his *The Man in the Gray Flannel Suit*, they never balked at corporate conformity.

Now in the midst of their mid-life crises they appear to be reverting to the archetype. "Go where you want to go; do what you want to do," sang one of the most popular groups of the 1960s, the Mamas and the Papas. A lot of people who are now changing careers listened to that song on their drives to and from work. The message seems to have seeped into the national consciousness. In their late thirties and forties and into their fifties people are once again beginning to move on, going where they want to go, doing what they want to do. One out of every three Americans will change jobs in the next five years. One out of every five Americans will change their zip code in the next twelve months. But history never repeats itself precisely.

Since the start of this century a simple fact has been transforming our lives. We live longer than ever before. In 1900, the average life expectancy was forty-seven years. In 1973 it was seventy-one years. More people are surviving to ages over sixty-five than ever before. The changes that have occurred as a result have engineered a revolution in life styles. A profusion of options has been created which we are just now beginning to explore.

Tom Wolfe, the new journalist and social commentator, baptized it "the me generation." A career counselor I interviewed called the same syndrome "the Schlitz (you only go around once) generation." Whatever label is pinned on, the phenomenon is the same. It is a rejection of the one life–one marriage–one career concept.

In the early 1960s Shirley Polykoff, a copy writer at the Foote, Cone & Belding advertising agency, dreamed up the slogan "If I've only one life, let me live it as a blonde" for Clairol. It became wildly popular and sold millions of bottles of hair dye. The slogan was a smash, Tom Wolfe hypothesized, because it perfectly captured the spirit of the decade to come. People seized on the slogan and filled in their own blanks. "If I have only one life, let me live it as a _____." For women this becomes, "If I've only one life, let me live it as . . . a free spirit." Instead of as a "household slave, cleaning woman, a cook, a nursemaid, a stationwagon hacker and an occasional household sex aid." For men this translates as, "If I've only one life, let me live it as a . . . Casanova or Henry VIII . . . instead of a humdrum workadaddy, eternally faithful, except for a mean little skulking episode here and there . . ."[1]

Both men and women claimed the right to shed their mates whenever they pleased. As average life expectancy has gone up so has the divorce rate. In California, which is supposed to be the harbinger of things to come in the rest of the country, the marriages and divorces are beginning to cancel each other out. The largest number of divorces still occur in the early years of marriage but the divorce rate is going up the fastest among those who have been married twenty years or more. To be sure, the majority of the couples who pledge "to honor and obey" still expect to make it to the finish line but fewer of us who are their witnesses expect to be able to celebrate their Golden Wedding anniversaries. Only some 16 percent of us in the 1980s live in the traditional nuclear family of two children, a daddy who works and a mommy who tends house. The revised *Book of Common Prayer* of the Episcopal Church contains a *Prayer for Those Who Live Alone*.

People who will cast their first votes in the 1980s might find it hard to believe that divorce was once such a stigma that it is widely credited with ruining two men's political careers. Adlai Stevenson's divorce helped to bring about his defeat in the 1952 presidential race and Nelson Rockefeller's scandal-tinged divorce hurt his chances of winning the Republican presidential nomination in 1964 and again in 1968. That voters once worried about a divorced man in the White House or that the Republican Party assumed a divorce would cost them enough votes to lose the presidency seems foolish in the wake of the marital and sexual changes that have taken place over the last few decades.

"Serial monogamy," sociologists call this practice of acquiring a new spouse who will be an empathetic companion for the various seasons of our lives. Where we once mated for life, we now divorce for our passages. Serial monogamy is a challenge to the age-old belief in serial immortality.

Tom Wolfe writes:

> Most people historically have not lived their lives as if thinking, "I have only one life to live." Instead they have lived as if they are living their ancestors' lives and their offsprings' lives and perhaps their neighbors' lives as well. They have seen themselves as inseparable from the great tide of chromosomes of which they are created and which they pass on. The mere fact that you were only going to be here a short time and would be dead soon enough did not give you the license to try to climb out of the stream and change the natural order of things. ... Hence the wicked feeling—the excitement!—of "If I've only one life, let me live it as a _____." Fill in the blank if you dare.

Our attention spans seem to have shortened. Unlike our parents, we are unwilling to lock ourselves in. We want the escape hatches unbolted in case we decide on a quick exit and increasing numbers of us are managing to find them. More is the key word.

The underlying message of the Clairol slogan is if I have only one life to live, let me live it for *me*. After all, Clairol was not selling bottles of bleach to natural blondes. Life has come to resemble a multiple choice question with numerous right answers that are apt to change over time. If one man or one woman can no longer capture our imagination for life and hold us fast, neither can one job. Along with the freedom to change spouses has come the permission to change careers. Eugene Jennings, professor of business administration at Michigan State University, has said, "We have broken down the ethic that a successful life must be spent in one enterprise or corporation. . . . We don't believe any longer in the gold watch theory." Perhaps one marriage and one career never guaranteed life-long happiness but now in the new hedonism we are unwilling to endure the tedium of past choices gone wrong.

A dilemma of the twenties is the terrifying belief that our decisions are forever. So many potential partners, so many possible careers—how will we ever choose? Psychologists call this an approach-approach conflict. We are attracted to so many different things that our very attraction is paralyzing. Faced with a smorgasbord of alternatives, we can't make the first selection. We rush to choose and just as quickly dash back in a frenzy of indecision. Everything seems so awesomely final. Our thirties teach us differently and by our forties we know better. Few commitments can't be broken, redefined, altered in time—or for that matter won't be in spite of us. Whether we crave these changes, relishing the variety they bring to our lives or shrink from them out of fear of the unknown, there is one thing we can consistently count on. As we grow older, our lives will vibrate to a different tempo. Around forty we may even be ready to begin again in the middle.

Work, like our gender and our biology, is a powerful shaper of our identities and almost as many myths have sprung up around our offices as our bedrooms. The number of people who are leaving careers that they were trained for, in some cases even born to, is a clue that these myths have changed.

Back in the cocoon of the 1950s these values and attitudes toward work were as clear-cut and unquestioned as they were toward marriage. Everybody knew more or less what was demanded of them and for the most part they acquiesced. A woman was expected to stay home after she was married unless she was forced to go to work. Talent, ambition, personal desires and inclinations were surrendered on her wedding night. Her identity was the newly acquired Mrs. in front of her name. That was all the definition she was supposed to need. A man whose wife worked was diminished in front of his friends and family because no man would "let" his wife work if he could afford to support her. The man as the breadwinner and good provider was the flip side of the cultural coin. In order to confirm that role and enhance that self-image, a man submerged his individual personality in his work. It might be a job or it might be a career but either way work became the major source of a man's identity. If a company offered a man a decent living and economic security, nothing more was to be required. The Saturday mornings on the golf course were not to clinch the sale that would help the family to move to the bigger house in the more expensive suburb even though he might lie and say it was. What he was really doing out there at the nineteenth hole was building his self-image and self-esteem. The puzzle is that he had to discard so much of himself in order to do so. Most conflicting personal desires which threatened to slip between him and his work were discarded. The more of his eccentricities and whimsies he suppressed to fit into the corporate cookie cutter, the more he was forced to rely on the corporation's evaluation of his worth. Their standards became his standards. If he were fired or retired prematurely, he would find he had little self to fall back on. The more he rated himself by his corporation's measures, the more he was inclined to empha- size those aspects of his personality that would be rewarded by the company. He became tied to and dependent on this source of ego sustenance even while his work gave him ulcers and jangled his nerves and kept him awake at night. In the end he was the perfect company man tied to his job not just by necessity but by an umbilical cord of personal loyalty to his bosses.

If a job was not all that satisfying or if it required tasks that were repugnant or boring, that was too bad but it was certainly no cause to quit. In that respect most jobs were assumed to be interchangeable. Work was a means to an end which was not happiness. Pragmatic was the approach. "For all practical purposes," writes social researcher Daniel Yankelovich, "a job was defined as a paid activity that provided steady full-time work to the male breadwinner with compensation adequate to provide at least the necessities, and, with luck, some luxuries, for an intact nuclear family."[2]

The new attitudes about work are less well defined, still generalized. They have had a shorter period of time in which to solidify. They have not calcified at all. From the 1950s to the 1980s is long enough to raise several generations of children but in terms of cultural myths it is short indeed. The most succinct summary of these attitudes was offered by *Psychology Today* after they queried their readers on their feelings about work. After examining some 23,000 questionnaires, the magazine said, "It seems to us that the best term to describe our respondents' approach to work is 'self-oriented.' The phrase expresses a turning inward that is taking place in the nation as a whole."[3] A self-oriented disposition to work means: more psychological satisfactions, more opportunities to learn and grow, more chance to exercise talents to the fullest and more occasions to accomplish something meaningful. It also means that work should be fun. If we only go around once, we should be sure we have a good time on the one loop allotted us. When Thomas Jefferson penned the Declaration of Independence, he listed "the pursuit of happiness" as an "inalienable right" of man. Little likelihood, however, that he dreamed of just how ferociously his descendents would claim this right.

In many ways Paul Hadley is not at all typical of the people in this book.* He lacks their intensity and drive, their all-out push to accomplish one single, meaningful thing, their

* In the case of Paul Hadley the name and some of the identifying characteristics have been changed.

certainty about their pursuits. Most of the career changers I studied were prone to view the obstacles they encountered as hurdles to leap over. Paul Hadley seems to have responded as if they were roadblocks to further progress. In their self-definition and individuality they resembled Polaroid close-ups. Hadley approximates a photographic negative that was snapped at the wrong *f* stop. "Most of my life," he said, "has been spent in a restless search for meaning." Meeting him or listening to him talk leaves little doubt this is true or that the search still goes on. The rest of the career changers had fueled meaning into their life early on—sometimes several meanings and more than once.

Nevertheless, I offer the story of Paul Hadley to clarify some of the distinctive aspects of the self-oriented work style. He illustrates the evolution from the 1950s attitude to the 1980s values. No one would accuse Paul Hadley who is approaching forty-nine and has the thinning hair and the wrinkles to vouch for it of not being a card-carrying member of the me generation. It took some four decades for him to pay his dues. In the extremeness of his life, he illustrates some abiding generalities.

Hadley was the middle of three sons of a New Orleans family. His father was rich, respected and thoroughly authoritarian, a product of the Victorian era in which he was born and the South in which he grew up. The accidents of place and time produced a man who longed to start a dynasty or at the very least a clan. His sons never had any doubts about his expectations for them. All of them would enter his oil-refining business and they would not only work together but also live together. He purchased enough land out in the bayou country for three spacious houses. It would be the Hadley compound.

Paul saw things differently. "My father was someone who spent his health getting wealth and then spent his wealth gaining health. The picture I have of him as a kid is that of a man who was always looking and never finding." Paul was determined to live his life in direct contrast to his father's.

And, of course, in time was to offer the same description of himself in almost identical words.

When Paul got to Princeton, he took an aptitude test. His guidance counselor told him he was innately suited to science and engineering. That sounded too much like the oil-refining business and Paul said thanks but no thanks for the advice and proceeded as if he had heard nothing. "I started looking more in a spiritual direction because business and my parents' life didn't seem to satisfy them."

Two years into Hadley's college career, Sam School-maker, the rector at Grace Church in New York City, came to preach in the vaulted nave of the Gothic chapel at Princeton. Paul was spellbound. "I really came under his influence. He was a charismatic figure who was out to recruit for the ministry and picked the Ivy League as the hunting ground. I was very much smitten by the idea."

There was only one thing wrong with the idea. Scientists and engineers and people who are suited for those professions like things. Ministers must sincerely like people if they are to handle the inevitable frustration that springs from the constant contact with human fallibilities. Nowhere in Paul's aptitude tests had the slighest fondness for people shown up. The omens were not auspicious.

After graduation Paul declared a moratorium on further study and trundled off to gather experiences. His was the familiar story of the young man who wants to experiment, to explore, to seek truths and to be free to wander the byways of life before settling down. Paul thought it had never been written before. He wanted to see the world as it looked to people who hadn't grown up with servants padding softly across the terrace or had the advantages of an Ivy League education.

His graduation present became the down payment on his brother's 1948 Pontiac. "I'll never forget driving off by myself and ending up in a boarding house in Griffin, Georgia. I went there on a lark. I knew no one in the town. It was just a place to go. I had a desire to get a job on my own and I was also tired of being Charles Hadley's son." The job he landed by himself was night janitor in a casket factory. He worked sixteen hours on the third shift and by the end of the year he had been promoted to inserting the linings in the caskets.

All of this was rebellion pure and simple. A refusal to go along with the Hadley destiny and the cultural imperatives of his background. The year at the casket factory was Hadley's way of postponing commitment. He called it education but it was really the adult equivalent of a foot-stomping temper tantrum. The fact that his father could barely conceal his impatience with the course he had chosen strengthened his conviction that he was on the correct track. If his father was against it, it must be right.

There was one important difference between Paul and his fellow workers at the casket factory which he blithely chose to ignore. He could leave. They were stuck. By the time his first anniversary rolled around, Paul was ready to quit. He enrolled at Virginia Theological Seminary in Alexandria, Virginia. Another blow against father.

"My father was very upset when I entered VTS. Up to then he had always thought that I would come around and in the end I would wind up in the family business. My father was definitely used to getting what he wanted and he was sure he would this time, too."

And mother?

"Well, my mother was a Southern lady and nice young Southern ladies have always been attracted to ministers. I sort of had the notion that she viewed my entering the seminary as sort of her gift to God. Which is not very healthy."

Paul again returned to Georgia following graduation. His first assignments in New Brunswick and Valdosta were successful. He built a mission church subsidized by the diocese into a self-supporting parish. The rector for whom he worked, who supervised his work as an associate, praised his flair for administration. In both cases he was dealing with things, not people and as his Princeton guidance counselor had forecast, he progressed happily.

Paul Hadley was now in his early thirties. At that age the success glands in most men are pumping overtime to produce adrenalin for the spurt to the top. Not Hadley's. There was no place he particularly wanted to go.

"I really wasn't very ambitious in the stereotypical sense. I was more interested in the kinds of things I was doing, not in getting an ever-larger parish. I never really had that sort of zeal. I never really aspired to be the rector in a large parish or to be a bishop. I wanted more to do my own thing and be good at it."

If he had stayed in Valdosta, if he had remained with a safe and secure parish, if he had played his life on that small arena, everything might have worked out. But Hadley had performed so well there that he was offered a position as the rector of a church in the suburbs of Atlanta. The parish was bigger and more demanding. Hadley blundered and accepted. In his new post he was required to demonstrate the facility in human relations that he woefully lacked. He was completely miscast. He did not excel in Decatur.

The turning point arrived in the mid-sixties, four years after Hadley became rector. Congress was in the process of enacting the landmark civil rights legislation of that decade and Hadley was swept up in the movement. One Christmas Eve when the choir director was called out of town, Hadley invited the organist from a nearby black church to substitute at the midnight service. The parish leaders hadn't cared when their rector was appointed chairman of the local civil rights commission but they didn't want him to practice in their church what he was preaching outside of it. A delegation visited his office and demanded that he rescind the invitation. Hadley might have refused resolutely and hoped to shame his congregation into acceptance of his decision. He might have knuckled under and withdrawn the invitation which would have silenced the outcries. He did neither and as it turned out, either would have been a better choice.

"The vestry, all but one man, said the invitation would tear the church apart. I had a stake in the parish. We were in the midst of a building drive and I didn't want to destroy all that I had worked for. I left the meeting saying I wouldn't have the organist. I found in talking to parishioners that there was more support for my decision than I had been led to believe. It was just a sticky situation. I finally decided that I had to go ahead with it or I couldn't live with myself.

"That January there was a vestry election and we had a progressive slate and a conservative slate. The election became a ratification of my decision. The progressive slate won. But in a sense I felt I had won the battle but lost the war because from then on everything went downhill. The vestry felt that I had been wishy-washy and, in fact, I had vacillated.

"I thought about leaving the ministry then but something in me wanted to see it through. I did go into a deep depression and I seemed to lose my effectiveness."

A year later he resigned. Hadley moved his wife and four children to Washington, D.C. where he eventually landed a position as an associate rector in one of the city's most prestigious parishes. This was a second chance and a more promising one than he had any right to expect. He was now in his mid-thirties and the future still beckoned. But the lure that the ministry once held for him had been buried with the past in Decatur. "The position was a holding operation and I knew it." Another year and a half and he quit. "I just wanted out. I had gone into the ministry to be a good guy and when it didn't seem to be working out, I quit."

In this ending Paul Hadley found his beginnings. He was through trying to be something other than what he was. He was old enough to break his ties to his father. (Rebellion against a parent is as much a knot as conformity to parental wishes.) He broke out and into a self-oriented work style.

"I came to realize that it was valid to be self-oriented. I had spent my entire life trying to do what others wanted me to do. I was completely other-oriented. Shit, I even saw it in those terms. I had this version of the world divided into people who were self-oriented and people who were other-oriented. I was in the other-oriented group and almost everybody else was in the self-oriented group. This, of course, was completely phony. Everybody else was not thinking about themselves first and I was not thinking about myself last. I was completely caught up in the false altruism of 'doing God's will,' quote and unquote. I finally owned up to the fact that this was a disguised selfishness and I was getting the short end of the stick. I decided to accept it for what it was."

Today Hadley works at the Department of Transportation in Washington, D.C. He is at the middle-management level and makes about $30,000 a year. By civil service standards that is not very high on the pay scale and at his age there is not very much chance that he will rise into the upper level of the bureaucracy. In Washington, which has one of the highest median incomes in the country, he supports his family and sends his sons and daughters to the Ivy League schools he once attended by dipping into his trust fund.

He says he realizes he has not reached his top career potential and will not now. "Jobwise I feel that I am under-employed." But Hadley says he is happy.

"I am really content with my life. My brothers are more successful than I am. One of them is vice president of the family business and the other is vice president of an auto-mobile manufacturing company, but I feel that I enjoy life and have a happier family life than they do. I feel that I have fun whereas they do not. Right now I wouldn't trade places with anybody. That is an unusual feeling for me because most of my life I have been jealous of others.

"It is the same way with people at the Department of Transportation. Some of them want to talk shop all the time but I don't need that. If I'm happy with what I am doing, that is sufficient in itself."

In Hadley all the generalizations come together. He was born into the conforming 1950s and he matured in the free flowing 1970s. He is a transitional figure whose story spins webs between the new values and the old. When I interviewed Paul, a friend who had come of age in the fifties went along. As we walked out of the house and down the steps to the street, he shook his head and breathed deeply. "What a pathetic figure." I told Paul's story to other friends and got some completely different responses. "He is doing what he wants to do. Nothing wrong with that." I found that the reactions to the histories of individuals often revealed a lot about the people who read them. (A male college professor who subscribes to conventions was appalled by the case of a male college professor who left teaching computer science for nursing.) So it was with Paul Hadley. The people who espoused the old values were puzzled by his life. The people who embraced the new values resonated to him instinctively.

In the new scheme we soar above our jobs. We are more important than the sum of our parts. We may sell houses but the person who sells real estate is not the same individual as the person who is a real estate salesman. It is the difference between a person of many complex pieces and a person who is supported by a single component. The people who know they are the total of their parts and a little bit extra, who see themselves as filling many roles simultaneously (and more still to come), who have an independent image of themselves are most likely to pick up that identity and carry it into a new life. If people don't require constant feedback from a single source, they will more readily relinquish it. They will be cheered by the notion that if they have only one life to live, they can spend their allotted three score and ten in a variety of pursuits.

This should not imply that work is less significant in our lives although like a kaleidoscope it may have rearranged itself in new shapes. In fact, we may value work more now than ever before. A few years ago Congress raised the age of mandatory retirement for most workers. The action was taken in part because legislators recognized that a majority of people say they prefer to work as long as they are physically able. In 1978 the number of people who held jobs hit an all time high. An estimated 24 to 27 million people, primarily women, young people and those now retired, would like to work full time but are unable to find jobs.

The unsettling discovery is that as much as we value our work we often do not take pleasure in it. Significance and satisfaction may not move in concert. Quite to the contrary. Of the young professionals who answered *Psychology Today's* questionnaire, well paid and highly educated, some 60 percent said that work was not the major source of their satisfaction. Some 44 percent replied that they felt trapped in their present jobs. A broad sampling of 3,000 businessmen who responded to an American Management Association survey spotlighted their discontent. Fully 40 percent of all middle managers and 52 percent of supervisory managers said they found their work, *at best*, unsatisfactory. (If they are so unhappy, one shudders to think of the dissatisfaction of the men and women who call them boss.)[4] Ronald E. Barnes, a former associate at the Menninger Clinic, says that on the basis of his clinical experience he would estimate that 50 percent of people are unhappy with their careers and as many as 90 percent may be working at jobs that are at odds with their real goals in life.[5] They are well on their way to swelling that scant 50 percent into a clear majority. Up to 40 percent of engineers are so unhappy in their professions that they say they would now choose a different career if they could start over.[6] And half of all Episcopal parish priests have become disenchanted enough that they have seriously considered leaving the ministry.[7]

Can the statistics be right? Is there really such unhappiness lurking in those glass and concrete office buildings? Do that many people port desperation in their briefcases? The answer is yes. (The reasons for this dissatisfaction are explored at length in chapter four.) And perhaps there are even more that the surveys and questionnaires have failed to turn up.

The centrality of work and the discontent with specific jobs leads to the impulse to leap into a new career and to try again. The census bureau may have underestimated the numbers. The census figures do not include the people who

changed occupations more than once between 1965 and 1970.
In some professions, due to economic shifts and changing
cultural expectations, the exodus had already reached near-
epidemic proportions when the census bureau started to
gather its statistics. In the late sixties some 800 Protestant
ministers a month were deserting their congregations. By the
mid-seventies there was one former Roman Catholic priest
for every six priests who remained in the church. The sudden
withdrawal of government support for the space program left
a whole generation of engineers without jobs or prospects for
future employment in their fields. The growing up of the
post-World War II baby boom had a similar effect on teachers.
And of the 3,000 businessmen reported on by the American
Management Association nearly 50 percent had changed or
considered changing careers.

   This longing to switch has intensified in the last decade.
What Color Is Your Parachute?, subtitled *A Practical Manual
for Job Hunters & Career Changers*, has sold over 650,000
copies since 1972. Its author, Richard Bolles, who found a
new career in guidance counseling after he was fired from
the pastorate of a San Francisco church, has estimated that
the typical worker will switch careers three to five times over
the course of a lifespan. In a two-year period toward the end
of the seventies some 500 people in New York City and its
environs were so eager to change careers that they were
willing to pay $2,000 and up to Mainstream Associates which
promised to pilot their career switches for them. And, perhaps
most significantly of all, some two-thirds of *Psychology Today*
readers who have the education and kinds of skills that can
readily be transferred to new fields say there is a chance they
will change occupations in the next five years.

   Who are these people and why are they changing careers?

   The bare statistics of the census report reveal some of
the subterranean discontent. When the census bureau conducted its 1970 census, people were asked to report their job
status and occupation for that year and for 1965. By plotting
the occupational transfers, the census bureau fashioned a

composite picture of people who stayed in their jobs and who did not. Excavations in those findings can begin to reconstruct some of the patterns of career change.[8]

Some of it is scarcely surprising. Common sense says that people in low-paying jobs which hold out little chance of advancement leave as rapidly as they can. If their new jobs fail to pay better or to promise more, they at least assure a new variety of drudgery. Little wonder 61 percent of busboys or 53 percent of stockroom workers or 50 percent of warehouse laborers found other ways of earning a living between 1965 and 1970. That 58 percent of gas station attendants or 42 percent of parking lot attendants or 48 percent of newspaper vendors decided to try a new line of work should furrow few brows.

The intriguing aspect of the study is that the rate of career change among professionals is highly inconsistent. In general the higher up we go on the career ladder the more attached we are to our jobs and the less inclined we are to change. The time and money invested in training for those careers alone tends to cement those attachments. The one out of three figure is decidedly misleading. Overall one out of every three people may have changed careers in those five years but professional people were much more disposed to leave some jobs than others. Some 37 percent of surveyors left their jobs but only 12 percent of registered nurses did. College administrators were over two times as likely to switch careers as elementary and high school principals. Twice as many painters and sculptors stayed with their careers despite the financial hazards as radio and television announcers remained in theirs. Only 5 percent of doctors and 6 percent of judges and lawyers switched careers but 33 percent of economists and 40 percent of social workers found new occupations. Half as many funeral directors changed careers as computer programmers and advertising salesmen.

A way of explaining who these career changers are is by defining what they are not. The trouble with talk about the me generation and the Schlitz life style and the "If I have only one life, let me live it as a blonde" concept is that it implies something which is emphatically wrong. It connotates a frivolity of purpose that is totally absent among the people whom I researched and who brought their life stories to this book. The people I met were not middle-aged dropouts. They are not the linear descendents of those who read *The Greening of America* a decade ago and found in author Charles Reich a Peter Pan to follow into the counterculture. Quite to the contrary. Even when it seems that they have hugged an alternative life style, they have not. Often these differences are subtle and easy to confuse. Sometimes the distinction may lie in the personal meaning of the career change and that is not quickly or readily divined. Jack Davies resigned a position as vice president of a fairly large Los Angeles-based warehousing company to start a small vineyard in the Napa Valley north of San Francisco. Jack may appear to be the perfect embodiment of a career changer who has disowned the rat race. Nothing could be further from the truth. For one thing he is working harder than ever. For another he never thought that his business career was a rodent maze that he should strive to escape. When he is asked about changing life styles, real anger seeps through his normally placid facade. "Talk about changing life styles makes me sick. I did not do this to escape from the rat race as I was once quoted in a newsletter. I hope that when you write your book, you make that clear."

This difference was emphasized in a study which Mainstream Associates commissioned on their clients. After examining their files on some 500 career changes, the author of the unpublished report concluded, "Changing careers appears to be late-70s chic. What dropping out was to the 60s, starting over is to the 70s. But, while it was the very young who led the movement away from the professions and into the counterculture, now it is people in their thirties, forties, even fifties, who are giving up the security of their accumulated work experience to seek new challenges and new meaning in new careers."

An exasperation with the demands of the working world and rejection of most of its basic values was an underlying theme in the conversations that Betty Holroyd Roberts conducted with forty middle-aged career dropouts.[9] Typically these men and women were thirty-nine years old when they dropped out. They included educators, engineers, advertising copywriters, business managers, real estate salesmen, social workers, the vice president of a bank and an international interpreter. When they made their breaks, their incomes varied between $8,000 and $40,000 a year. Afterward they survived on savings or the incomes of their employed spouses and hustled odd jobs and occasional consulting contracts to pay the rent. Characteristically their incomes had dropped, ranging from $2,000 to $25,000 annually although some were now higher. They were deeply affected by the anti-establishment rhetoric of the sixties which extolled the virtue of the unfettered individual and the demeaning nature of corporate hierarchies of all sorts. Most had left their careers behind between 1969 and 1973. Roberts discovered, "The ideology which is humanistic, noncompetitive, hedonistic and emphasizing interpersonal relationships pervaded much of their comments or their perspective on the world of the dropout compared to what they had experienced before." They were frustrated in their careers, disenchanted with their lives. They said things like this:

"As a chemist, I dislike both the technical aspect and the immorality of the chemical industry."

"Dropping out was a reaction to a bad job experience. Though I was making $18,000 (a year) as a Madison Avenue advertising account executive, I couldn't justify the purpose."

"I was not enjoying the academic horseshit and pretense where one intellectualizes his life away around theory rather than reality."

"I disliked the focus of my work. The advertising of bad products is damaging the country. . . . I couldn't hack the fact that people bought (useless things) which I so cleverly wrote ads for. The whole idea of advertising seemed wrong."

"From readings I began to develop new values. Suddenly, I became angry. Although I oversaw 60 million dollars in common stocks, I began to see the economy as incompatible with the environment."

"As a college president, I began to have a decreasing belief in the thing I was fronting for. I had to leave—the ingrown problem of class distinction, dealing with people as symbols rather than people, I could no longer justify."

By contrast the people in this book were not in rebellion against the establishment. Many, in fact, were from the establishment and proud of it. They were not angry. No private guerrilla actions were being waged. They had no reason to lash out. The biggest difference between the career dropouts in Roberts' research and the career changers who people the following pages is this: The career dropouts were running away; the career changers were running toward. Dropping out was a negative act. Switching careers was a positive shift. When the dropouts decided to leave their lives, they had no clearly defined goals. They knew only that they wanted to escape. The career changers had a distinct vision. They had already formulated the kind of life they wanted and the career that would lead to its achievement. A hallmark of the people who dropped out was a change of locale. They thought a new environment was the secret of a more satisfying life. The people who changed careers were forced sometimes to move in order to accomplish their goals but moving on was a by-product of a decision that had been reached before. They did not see relocating as an end in itself, simply a means to their personal objectives.

When I began my research, I deliberately shunned the dropouts. As I pointed out, none of the people in these pages had to change careers, but for my study I wanted to go beyond this. I pursued people who had been successful in one career and were again a success in their second career. Success, of course, is highly subjective. Aspirations may differ, there are various levels of achievement and where the starting line is drawn by the accident of birth affects both.

The career changers here reflect all these gradients. Basically I sought out people who could be called achievers. By the standards of their chosen professions they were "on track" and by their own individual standards they had generally gone far. Some of them were even ahead of their time schedules. In a few cases they held higher positions and were making more money than they had ever anticipated.

At the start I thought that the trend toward second careers was a social phenomenon. It *is* a reflection of a societal transformation, but as I progressed, I saw career shifts in a different way. For the people I was interviewing, the cultural changes were merely a backdrop which made their career changes possible. I had settled at the outset on an arbitrary definition of career change—a change after the age of thirty-five—because I wanted to study people who had been committed to one career and then switched. Before that age career switching tends to be a reflection of vacillating interests. I wanted people who had already found themselves. A book editor who was in the process of changing careers summed this up best. He said, "The mid-career change represents a nexus of personal and social forces. The way one's personal needs and desires are expressed has implications for society. And, of course, society will influence needs and desires. The way in which people are acting out their needs at mid-life says something about society. It is really a fore-runner of things to come and an indication of more powerful social changes ahead." The more I progressed in my research, the more I found he was right. Mid-life and mid-career changes had as much to do with adult development as it did with cultural revolutions. In my conversations people talked about growth, not rebellion.

I interviewed individuals who were thinking about chang-ing careers, some in the process of doing so and a few who had considered a switch but rejected the idea. In the end I settled on two dozen men and women for intensive study. They ranged in age from thirty-four to fifty-four at the time they decided to switch careers. (The one exception to my age thirty-five guideline was a woman who had pursued the same career for twelve years before she decided to switch at thirty-four.) All of them made radical changes. They veered off their career trajectories in unpredictable ways which often dismayed and shocked their former colleagues. They were librarians, housewives, Army officers, newspaper reporters, life insurance salesmen, artists, potters, presidents and vice presidents of corporations, film-makers, craft workers, college deans, government bureaucrats, social workers, teachers, ministers, hospital administrators and stockbrokers. They went on to be ministers, real estate salesmen, vineyard owners, proprietors of restaurants, lawyers, civil servants, chimney sweeps, nurses, inn owners, marine biologists, educators and entrepreneurs of all stripes.

In short, they were a diversified lot. Their upbringings confirmed it. All sections of the United States were represented in their background but by the time I talked to them most had gravitated to one coast or another. They were situated in Boston, New York City and environs, Washington, D.C. and its Virginia and Maryland suburbs, Denver, Portland, Seattle, the Napa Valley and Southern California, Miami and West Palm Beach, Florida. They had been lured to these urban centers from a host of other, usually less-populated places. A few lived in small towns in Maine, West Virginia and Virginia.

I knew a few of the career changers in their previous incarnations. Some were recommended by mutual friends. Occasionally I found myself unexpectedly in a strange town and asked the people I encountered if they could suggest people who had switched careers. Once while I was chatting with a career counselor, her secretary turned around and said, "My brother changed careers. You should really talk to him." So I did.

I also talked to the families of people who changed careers, both their spouses and their children, and sometimes to their colleagues, present and former, as well. In the beginning I made a lot of appointments with career counselors

but with a few notable exceptions I found they were looking
at career changes from the wrong end of the telescope. More
and more as I proceeded, I relied on the stories of people
who had made changes and drew my own conclusions.

We talked in homes and offices, over dinners and lunches,
in courtrooms and labs that smelled of formaldehyde, in grape
fields and over gas burners in the kitchen of inns as I tried to
grasp the tenor of the lives of people who switched careers.
The hours often stretched into days as I hung around and
sometimes I returned more than once.

None of the people requested anonymity. In two instances I chose to provide it either because of my interpretations of the material I was provided or because I felt their
comments might be embarrassing in retrospect. Otherwise,
the names and details are of real people and of real lives.
There is no editing; no characters appear here as composites.

This book was conceived at a dinner party. My friend
Rick is a keen player of such games as Murder and Dictionary
but when there aren't enough of us around to form a group,
he tends to invent his own. He did that night.

"If you had to do it over again and could do anything
you wanted," he quizzed us, "what would it be?"

The question quivered in the candlelight. We lapsed into
silence, tantalized by the transformations Rick had suddenly
evoked. Peter spoke first. Twirling his wine glass, he said, "I
think I would like to run a vineyard in Northern California.
Developing new wines, running my own business. I love
Northern California."

That was a surprise. Peter, the college professor who
taught political science and always claimed that he loved the
sovereign immunity of a tenured faculty position, secreted a
desire to be an entrepreneur which entailed nothing but risks
and endless demands. But his reply turned out to be no more
of an astonishment than the others. As each of us answered,
I was struck again by the realization that no matter how well

we think we know people, in some ways we never know them at all.

Rick, a science writer for a national magazine who spends his time peering into the mouths of crocodiles in East Africa and chasing killer bees in South America, always conjured up for me visions of the swashbuckling correspondents of World War II movies. He would drape himself in peat moss and experiment with fertilizer formulas. He wanted to be a horticulturist.

Mary, a wife, mother and an exceptionally talented photographer of gazelle-like gentleness and charm, craved the applause of Broadway crowds. "I'd like to be a musical comedy star. To dance and sing and make people happy. I think it would be wonderful to entertain people."

As for me, well, I fancied myself as a Julia Child type of owner of a small country inn in New England, an auberge of sorts, where I would never again curdle a Béarnaise sauce. It was a life as physical as the one I had chosen was mental.

The answers and particularly the question haunted me. It took possession and would not let go. Since it would not be exorcised, I used it. I asked it of everybody I met and listened, really listened, to the answers. It was a great party game and the fall this book was being born, it enlivened a number of otherwise dreary cocktail parties. That season there was a hyperbole of discontent among the people I knew, a condition which I later learned was associated with the fact that most of them were approaching their mid-life and mid-career turnings. I heard in those answers a not-so-buried longing to start over. Almost everybody it appeared harbored a desire to be something other than what they had become.

"If you had to do it over again and could do anything you wanted, what would it be?"

Along the way I discovered that quite a few people had already asked themselves that question and acted on their answers. In the end this is a book about private dreams and their public attainments.

Patterns

There is no single mold into which people who make mid-life career changes easily fit. The decision to change careers is as individual as fingerprints. Even the dropouts, those urban refugees camped out in the nation's backyards, are, I suspect, more diverse than writers of newspaper and magazine articles allow. Stereotypes are comforting but reality tends to be perversely, confoundedly complicated.

Nevertheless, certain themes and common codas appear and reappear in the lives of the people I talked with and several patterns emerged among those I studied. They were:

THE RENEWERS. Frustrated and often disillusioned, these individuals no longer believe in their jobs. In the midst of their mid-career crisis, they reaffirm their original goals by changing careers.

THE SEEKERS. These people find at mid-life that the goals and values of their youth have changed. They seek to express their new objectives and ideals by switching careers.

THE DIVERTED. These people never had an opportunity to pursue the careers they really wanted. At mid-life they set out to act on long-suppressed desires.

THE RENEWERS

Of all the people who elect to change careers at mid-life the pattern of the renewer is the simplest and easiest to understand.

The renewers have always known where they were going and what they wanted to do when they got there. Their trajectories are straight and sure. Many are hot-shot businessmen who were running for president of their companies from the day they were graduated from Harvard Business School. Others are ministers, social workers, assorted people in the helping professions who knew they always wanted "to work with people." The mid-life crisis which sends less-sure people spinning into unexplored back roads of their lives is a mere bump along the way for many of these people. In fact, many deny that they have encountered a mid-life crisis at all.

Halfway through, however, all of us face a crucial issue: to reaffirm our original career decisions or to choose again. Not even the most self-possessed and self-assured escape such confrontations. The renewers are people who found that they chose correctly but that their jobs now threaten their goals. In order to revalidate their earlier decisions they must start second careers. This happens in different ways. The minister who envisioned bringing people to God and comforting the afflicted is brought up short at mid-life. Twenty years out of the seminary, he realizes that his ministry consists of heading the annual fund drive and administering a small army of church employees. Still wanting to help and comfort, he salvages his original goals by switching to a new career in social work or counseling. The businessman who spends his days trudging through a corporate bureaucracy slashes through the red tape that inhibits innovation and creativity and renews his career choice by launching his own business.

My friend Joe Jordan became a newspaper reporter, as young idealists often do, because he thought the typewriter was a powerful weapon for changing society. After nearly two decades of writing about the victims of social injustices and a slew of by-lines on front-page stories, he had changed very little. Today he works directly with many of the same kind of people he once wrote about. He is a lawyer who specializes in representing clients who are fighting the establishment.

None of the people I talked to, however, fit the pattern
of the renewer better than a man named Ely Callaway. Five
years ago he ran Burlington Industries. Now he is the owner
of a small vineyard and winery in the unlikely desert dot of
Temecula, California.

Ely shoved an article immortalizing the moment I had
missed across the Parson's table that serves as his desk.

"You can read it," he said.

Callaway has the knack of turning the simplest declarative
sentence into a command. Naturally enough, I read.

The author of the article which appeared in *San Diego*
magazine happened to be hanging around Callaway Vineyards
when a representative of NBC Entertainment arrived for a
meeting with the man whose name it bears.[1] That encounter
superbly captures the essential Ely:

> *The thin man had his arm outstretched, his business card
> thrust toward Ely and a sincere, practiced smile in place. Mr.
> NBC was cool, one of those Madison Avenue types who gets
> private shoeshines on the 23rd floor. The way Ely was standing,
> though, and something about the look in his eyes, killed the
> power in the thin man's smile. Ely just stood and waited.*
>
> *"Mr. Callaway, I'm with NBC Entertainment. . . ."*
>
> *"What the hell is that?" Ely smiled and took the card.*
>
> *"We're an affiliate of NBC. . . . We include such things as
> Disney on Parade. It's not a Disney production; it's an NBC
> production. . . ."*
>
> *"Ah'm glad to meet ya," drawled Ely. Ely's voice is smooth
> as Chenin Blanc, but something way down has the bite of raw
> whiskey.*
>
> *Mr. NBC cleared his throat. "NBC is just now completing
> construction on what we call the K-House over the hill there,
> and we thought, or I thought, we might be able to cooperate
> with Callaway wines . . ."*
>
> *"What the hell is the K-House?"*
>
> *"Well it's a model house where NBC employees get to
> vacation, and it has samples from all the major industries, you
> know, including Burlington Industries. . . ."*
>
> *Ely, the former president of Burlington Industries, the*

largest textile manufacturer in the (Western) world, rubbed his nose and squinted at the thin man. "Just what kind of cooperatin' you got in mind?"

"We figured you'd like to donate some wine over there and help promote your wine. . . . "

Ely was silent. The thin man grinned expectantly.

"Nope. We've got a policy. No free wine."

The article continued on in that same profane, irreverent fashion. At one point Callaway reportedly refers to Prince Charles as "the goddamn son" of Queen Elizabeth II.

Ely waited expectantly while I read. He tried to seem relaxed. The heel of a black Gucci loafer was propped on top of a stack of opened mail and the *Wall Street Journal* on the Parson's table desk. He played with the tip of a letter opener. Coiled in his chair, he was as relaxed as a rattle snake.

"Well," he barked as I finished reading and glanced up. "What do you think?"

"I like it. I think he describes you."

"Now, Rochelle," he drawled in the same Chenin Blanc cut with raw whiskey voice, "how much time have you spent with me now?" The question was purely rhetorical as he charged on. "Quite a bit, right? Have you ever known me to be that profane? Why, I've never said 'goddamn' in my entire life!"

Well, maybe not, and no, I had never heard him *that* profane but profanity and irreverence are somehow expected. They seem appropriate. It is something in those brown eyes flashing in that Jason Robards face, something in the relentless gaze, something in the intensity of his uncompromising directness of manner, something in the way he carries the few grudging pounds that cling to his lean frame. One thing comes across above all: don't mess with me. Even in baggy, too-short corduroys and a tee shirt, Callaway projects authority. Ely Callaway is obviously a man who has never willingly accepted no for an answer in his entire life.

Ely has always been fortune's child. He was born into a very old, very distinguished Georgia family, the Callaways of

Callaway Mills and later on Callaway Gardens. Ely was born to privilege and affluence, to a place in the Georgia aristocracy and a nice comfortable niche in the Callaway Mills. For most people that would have been sufficient. For Ely "sufficient" was not nearly good enough. Nowhere in the country is more emphasis placed on family and place than in the South. Ely was *a* Callaway. He was not one of *the* Callaways. His father worked in the family business but his uncle owned it. In the Callaway Mills, in LaGrange, in Georgia he would always be of the best but never quite the best.

His background instilled a sense of self and a gnawing need to test himself in a world not contained by the narrow limits of LaGrange. His father helped. "My father was very good at instilling independence in his three children—my sisters and me." The family destiny was there if they chose to embrace it. They were also free to choose their own.

Ely started early. Before he was eight, he was ringing door bells in LaGrange, selling housewives subscriptions to the *Literary Digest*. When he had $800 in savings, his father gave him a bit of advice that he followed ever after: take your capital and invest it. By the time he was nine, Ely had a peach tree orchard and $1,500 worth of indebtedness to the LaGrange National Bank.

"The peach trees grew and the peaches were good and I made some money."

Ely learned a valuable lesson. In risk lies opportunity. With his father's backing, the risk was small but it was a risk nonetheless. Ely gambled and succeeded. A pattern was established early on that extended into adulthood. Ely played to win and winning meant taking risks. A certain mental framework was the basis for this pattern. Success was presumed. Each time he won his confidence grew and his belief in a successful outcome was strengthened.

Ely, the super achiever. When other boys his age were playing sandlot baseball, Ely was out making money. There was never any doubt in his mind that he would go into business, never any doubts that he would rise to the top. Ely

Callaway was running for president when he was eight years old.

Ely explains his success in a slightly different way. "Success comes from the interplay of foresight, luck and courage. All of these things are relatively rare but rarest of all is the combination. Number one is luck and I've always been lucky. Number two, I've been lucky enough to have foresight. And number three, I've had the courage to act on my vision."

The first time this combination appeared was in June, 1940. Ely was just graduated from Emory University in Atlanta. "To me it was obvious that there was going to be a war and I was concerned about the likelihood of war. I wanted to get my active duty out of the way. I took a twenty-one–day correspondence course and got my commission. By July I went on active duty." He was assigned to the quartermaster corps in Philadelphia. As his one-year tour of duty was ending, the officer in charge talked Ely into re-enlisting. By the time he was twenty-one, he was responsible for negotiating and administering contracts for the purchase of cotton garments for the U.S. Army. Wheeling and dealing, wheedling and cajoling, Ely learned to take only yeses from the seasoned businessmen who headed the big clothing manufacturing companies.

"From the age of twenty-one to twenty-six I was in the position of dealing with people who were head of Levi Strauss, the Arrow Shirt Company and others. Officially I was the only one empowered in the whole United States to buy these garments for the U.S. Army. I got accustomed to dealing under a great deal of stress with older businessmen. The problem was to convince them to give their production to the military instead of to the consumer. That was the issue every day and night for four solid years."

Ely knew when the war ended that he could go further, faster if he left LaGrange behind forever.

"After the war, having spent a lot of time in textiles and liking it, I said, hell, I might as well remain in it. I didn't want to go with my own family. Since my father didn't own the mills—his brother did—I felt it would be a disadvantage for me to be there. By the time I got through the military I felt I had something to offer on my own."

Callaway joined Deering Milliken, a large family-owned textile company, instead. He moved steadily through the ranks from the regional offices in Atlanta to the executive suite in New York. In 1953 at the age of thirty-three he was earning $50,000 a year. Ely was on an express train to the top—or so he thought. One day he went to work and came home without a job.

"There was a series of reorganizations and I was fired by Roger Milliken's brother-in-law. Why? I don't really know. Who ever does? We had a few clashes over policy but basically when people are fired, it's a matter of personality differences. I suppose it was in this case, too." Ely was a casualty in an undeclared corporate war.

Ely possessed a boundless capacity to spring back. His abrupt dismissal was simply a goad that spurred him to further heights. The happenstance of his birth propelled him into the higher reaches of American business. Just so, this career setback stiffened his resolve to succeed. Turn minuses into pluses was his motto. If you have a lemon, make lemonade. There was no shortage of job offers.

"I was the highest paid person in merchandising of my age in the country. I was making $50,000 a year at age thirty-three. There wasn't much of a problem in finding another job. I admitted I had been fired which was pretty unusual. People appreciated my honesty."

Callaway went to work, still in textiles, for Royal Little Textron and once again fortune tapped on his shoulder. In 1956 Royal Little sold its textile division of Raeford-Worsted to Burlington Industries. Shortly afterward Callaway was named president of one of Burlington's largest divisions which merged the newly acquired Raeford-Worsted with its old-line Pacific Mills.

The president of Burlington Industries in those days was

a legendary businessman, Spencer Love, who was single-handedly responsible for the growth of the company. "Mr. Spencer J. Love" is the way that Ely refers to him. Love was a hard-driving executive who had only one interest in life—Burlington Industries. "He ran the company through fear." He walked through the executive offices as a hunter stalked prey in a forest. He was the kind of fickle executive who fell in and out of love with his employees regularly but demanded constant devotion in return. His employees were generally terrorized—all except Ely Callaway.

Spencer Love recognized in Ely Callaway something of his former, younger self. Ely Callaway saw in Spencer Love a model of what he could one day become. Love draped his protective mantle around Callaway and in exchange Callaway supplied unstinting loyalty.

> *Love was one of the great geniuses of American industry, a brilliant and extremely complex man. He was one of the great influences of my life. I learned a lot from him. Total dedication. The need to be extremely involved and absorbed in the company. The necessity of knowing everything about your own company and your competition. The importance of having good, sound judgment and the guts to back it up.*
>
> *He was my mentor and we worked very closely together until he died in 1962. I doubt that I would have risen as high and as fast as I did without him. I always knew he wanted me on his very top management team.*

Callaway was advancing rapidly through the upper echelons of Burlington Industries. "I didn't have a timetable. I didn't really need one. I was moving awfully fast and the responsibility and compensation to match was coming at me as fast as I could handle it." His destination was clearly visible. Love told Callaway that he should become president and then chief executive officer of the company. Before Love died in 1962, Callaway was named executive vice president of Burlington Industries. Six years later he became president of a company that grossed $2 billion annually and had 85,000 employees. By the time he left, his salary and fringe benefits would be worth $300,000 a year.

Ely loved Burlington as he loved himself. Burlington Industries was simply a further extension of Ely Callaway. He was totally and completely dedicated. Spencer Love had known everything there was to know about Burlington because he had been its midwife and its nurse. Callaway was equally determined to know all. Six months of his first year as president were spent on airplanes visiting the various companies, sometimes three plants in one day, that composed his new far-flung empire. After a while, when mealtime came, Ely automatically reached to pull down a tray.

Burlington Industries was the hub around which Ely's world revolved. He kept an apartment in New York City on West 58th Street only two blocks from his office. That made it easier to get to work by 7:45 A.M. and easier to get home after the twice weekly dinners that lasted well into the evening with his division heads. He traveled constantly, not as much after the first year but still more than many people do in a lifetime. Eventually his second wife tired of rattling around the $395,000 house on the nine-acre estate in New Canaan, Connecticut, by herself and left. Without a wife who occasionally demanded to see the man she married, Ely could work even harder. He knew four months in advance where he would be and what he would be doing at any hour of any day.

People like Ely who run through twelve-hour days and spend their vacations reading corporate reports are often called workaholics but the psychologists and sociologists who attach such labels miss the point. They presume an arbitrary distinction between work and play. On the one hand there is work and on the other hand there is play. For men and women such as Ely, work and play are one and the same. Their life is an integrated whole. Ely found in his work a continuing exhilaration that brought with it a constant renewal. He had no need to chase after tennis balls to escape from his work. Ely discovered himself in his work. Through his work he managed to expand and to grow, to create something he could be proud of and in the process to be proud of Ely Callaway.

"Sure, it was stressful. I was dealing with a lot of uncertainties, dealing with things over which I had little control. But I coped with the stress."

As president of Burlington Industries, Callaway was a major mover and shaker in the mesosphere of American business. He lived in the rarefied world of people whose names automatically command the best tables at The Four Seasons. (Owner Paul Kovi is a personal friend and one of the first promoters of Callaway wines.) He was consulted by the top policy-makers in the country and a host to presidents such as John F. Kennedy.

In many ways Ely had left LaGrange, Georgia, far, far behind. He had risen further than he ever would have if he had gone to work in the family business. Burlington Industries was fifty times the size of Callaway Mills and Ely was president of it. In other ways Ely was a functionary, a $300,000-a-year functionary, a functionary at levels that most people do not even dare to dream of, but a functionary nonetheless. Even the president of a corporation like Burlington Industries must take orders from those who are higher up.

Between himself and the top stood the chief executive officer and the chairman of the board. "I was never the final boss—only president. I always wanted to be chief executive officer of Burlington." Love had been both president and chief executive officer. Ely dreamed of following in his footsteps. He had done so to a certain extent. He had the presidency. He had reason to expect that someday he would become chief executive officer. That was the ultimate. "For a long, long time I had the ambition to be chief executive officer."

In 1973, five years after Callaway became president, Burlington Industries began to play musical chairs. The corporate officers were being shuffled. A committee was appointed to choose a new chief executive officer. Callaway was an obvious candidate. One day Charles Meyers, the chief executive officer and chairman of the board, strolled into Ely Callaway's office. A decision had been reached. A new chief executive officer had been chosen. It was not Ely Callaway.

Ely's life screeched to a stop.

They appointed one of my top executives instead. A younger man, but not a hell of a lot younger, who had been in the company before I got in. He owned a big part of one of the divisions. I think it was a personal thing based on personality differences. These things always are personal. Of course, I was disappointed and with not a little anger thrown in. It was a form of rejection; there's always disappointment and hurt then unless you don't like the person who is doing the rejecting. I loved Burlington.

But I was very, very fortunate and very, very lucky to have been in the right place at the right time to become president of Burlington. I was extremely successful to be president for five years. I have no regrets. I don't sit around and say "Oh, how I wish."

Three months later Callaway quit.

"If I couldn't be in control of Burlington, I'd be in control of my own company. I'd create it and I'd control it."

He could have stayed. His responsibilities were undiminished and he collected a handsome salary in return. There was, however, nothing to stay for. Some of the opportunity, the challenge, the excitement and the possibilities of his job had vanished. Money alone was not enough of a motivation. For Ely it was chief executive officer of Burlington or nothing. As president of Burlington he already had more responsibility and earned more money than he could have as chief executive officer of smaller companies.

"Burlington is awfully big. Even as corporate executive vice president I had responsibility for about half of the company and a lot of money. My responsibilities and title and compensation as president were much bigger than any other company to which I could have gone. As chief executive officer of another company I would not have as much responsibility as president of Burlington."

Many businessmen and women capitalize on their work experiences and go off to create their own companies. Nothing at all is unusual about that but when Ely Callaway elected to leave Burlington Industries, he made a drastic departure. He did not start his own textile company. He turned to an entirely new field. All he knew about wine at the time was that he enjoyed drinking it.

Such radical career switches, however, are surprisingly common among *outstandingly* successful men like Ely Callaway. All twenty subjects in a University of Michigan study of such individuals either made radical career changes which increased their responsibilities or channeled their energies into political and social causes in middle life.[2]

The men included executives of major corporations and banks, lawyers, academicians, business entrepreneurs, a physician and a university administrator but they shared certain traits. Their work was the source of their identity while the task to which they lent themselves was relatively unimportant. Instead, they sought certain intrinsic characteristics in their work. They looked for opportunity and challenge, the potential for change and creativity and these can be found in a variety of endeavors.

These men shared certain characteristics. Whether or not they were actually in business, they possessed an entrepreneurial spirit. An element of risk and uncertainty in their work was essential to them. In fact, the more the outcome was in doubt the better they liked it. They welcomed change for its own sake. "Good feelings accompany change [for these men] and the possibility of change," wrote Bardwick, "as though learning, coping and creating are ways of growing." They loved solving problems and took pride in their ability to reach decisions. They were confident to the point of arrogance and totally lacking in introspection. All denied a mid-life crisis but the breaks in their lives betrayed the inner reality.

Success often provoked a crisis in these men's lives. In the wake of achievement floated an end to the striving and a certain stability, which was exactly what these men didn't want. Instead of savoring the rewards of their hard-won success, they dashed off in entirely new directions. A physician abandoned a thriving middle-class practice to open a ghetto clinic. A respected academician was working to change national social policy. In short, they were not just risk takers. They were risk creators above all else. "In general," concluded Bardwick, "these are people who need to feel the emotional exhilaration and anxiety accompanying risk, who need to create it in the work sector of their lives." Changing careers or adopting causes injected new excitement into their lives. When other men might have acquired mistresses, they took on major responsibilities. "Theirs," Bardwick stated, "is a reaching, an extending style of life. Especially the most prestigious men in the sample are trying to create excitement, to grab opportunity and to create it."

Ely threw himself into the creation of Callaway Vineyard and Winery. He had acquired the land in 1968 before he became president of Burlington and with the help of John Moramarco, a tenth-generation viniculturist, the grape vines were planted in 1969.

"I started thinking about retirement at a very early age. Most people don't get to the top until later but I had a top position at age forty-five. I achieved certain things that people look for in careers early on. Burlington was always the pinnacle for me. I'd already recognized that being anywhere near the position of president involved tremendous pressure. I hoped to have the good sense to retire young."

But Ely Callaway would never be content merely to sit in the sun. Ely's version of retirement entailed hard work. "I've always been involved in farming since I was a kid. I love it. Whenever I've had some money, I've put a little in farming. Even textiles are related because if you care, you're involved in cotton and wool. I figured if I could retire and still have some involvement in agriculture, I would be happy."

He sold his Burlington Industries stock and invested the $1.8 million into his new project of growing, vinifying and bottling fine premium wines.

"I didn't want to sit down and do nothing when I retired. It was a question of not working for somebody else. I could have gone to work for someone else but I didn't want to. I wanted to create something of my own."

Up in Northern California the wine barons of the Napa and Sonoma Valleys scoffed. Everybody knew that fine wines couldn't be produced in Southern California. Ely's folly, they called it.

"Hell, yes, I'm a gambler. I've always been. I'm a calculated gambler though."

Ely was no fool. Decades before, grapes had been grown briefly in the area, a fact that Ely discovered on one of his frequent vacations in Palm Springs. The question was: could good wines that would compete with the best that Northern California had to offer be created from Southern California grapes? Supposedly knowledgeable people said it couldn't be done. Which made the doing of it so much more fun. "I consulted with some of the local people and the enology department at the University of California at Davis. It was reasonably well researched but it turned out to be much better from a climate and soil standpoint than I had anticipated."

Amid the cactus and boulder-strewn hills of Southern California, Callaway had chanced upon a micro-climate that happened to be exactly right for growing premium varietal grapes. In nearby Palm Springs the temperature in the summer peaks in the 100s. In nearby Riverside the smog is the color of chicken noodle soup. Callaway Vineyard, 1,400 feet above and 23 miles due east of the Pacific Ocean, is a cool and sunny haven. Around 1 P.M. each day the ocean breezes are pulled through Rainbow Gap to the southwest and are funneled over the grape vines. The grapes mature slowly and evenly. So while the so-called experts laughed, Ely just continued clipping his grape vines and crushing his grapes.

All of the lessons he had learned from Love were now applied to the Callaway Vineyard and Winery. No detail was too small to escape his attention. He paid the employees who pruned and thinned the vines by the hour, instead of by the piece rate, to encourage careful pruning. He selected oak staves for his barrels and casks from 200-year-old white oak trees grown on Germany's Spessart Mountain and air-dried for three years. He commanded and demanded the finest. All his grapes were hand-picked. His viniculturist, John Moramarco, makes the final decision on pruning the vines on an individual basis and then does the pruning himself. Ely rejected synthetic fertilizers and dumped 7,500 tons of manure on his fields. He ages his white wines from twelve to sixteen weeks which is an unusually long time. He hired the ablest people he could find and set about instilling in them a sense of dedication to producing a superior product. Along with the United States and California flags, the flag of Mexico flies over the vineyard in recognition of the numerous Mexican employees.

Ely was determined to have the best and he bided his time. The first wines came on the market in 1975. There were five then. Today, depending on the harvest and the way the wines are classified, he produces up to nine. Wine writers consider his wines some of the best that are produced in this country and are generous with their praise.

At Burlington Ely had been a merchandising genius. That was his real strength and under his general direction the annual net sales grew in size in eleven years from $850 million to a sum of $2 billion. Ely turned all of that skill onto his wines.

When the first wines were ready to be sold, it was not a good time. "The whole economy was going into a depression. It was an awful period." Instead of bemoaning his fates, Ely went off to New York. "We went with some samples. We went to the top wine stores. I knew who they were. I went to Sherry-Lehman, for instance. Anyone knows if you want to sell in New York City that you must be in Sherry-Lehman. And I went to see Paul Kovi at The Four Seasons whom I had known for years."

Ely, the super salesman, managed to get his wines accepted and business began to take off. One of his luckier breaks occurred when his 1974 White Riesling was selected by the Pilgrim's Society and the English Speaking Union for their joint luncheon for Queen Elizabeth during her Bicentennial tour of the United States. "It was a very, very tremendous break. It was about the best thing that could have happened to us. It was at the start when no one, broadly speaking, had heard of us and the event was one of the most special kind in the world. If I could have picked one event for my wine to be at, that is the one I would have selected." It was the only wine served the Queen. "And she asked for a second glass." Ely reaped the rewards of the resulting publicity.

Ely once estimated that five years were required before a corporation the size of Burlington Industries could react to a new leadership. He was president for just five years. As owner of a small vineyard and winery his imprint is stamped on every bottle of wine that is sold.

As Ely and I talked during my third visit, the telephone rang. An executive at Aetna Life Insurance which has helped to finance his venture was returning Ely's phone call. Ely had a new project and that required more capital. Ely wanted the executive to come visit and hear all about it. The executive resisted. He had a full schedule. Perhaps he could send an assistant. Ely, as usual, was not taking no for an answer. Pulling a bulky ledger that is his appointment calendar across his desk, Ely ruffled the pages.

"Now you just tell me when you can come," he drawled, "and I'll clear the decks."

On the other end of the telephone the executive succumbed. Ely Callaway was at it again.

THE SEEKERS

These are the people who come most readily to mind when mid-life career changes are spoken of. Work and values, both

social and personal, are so closely tied together that it is
scarcely surprising that people who change once are apt to
change the other.

Pollster Louis Harris has reported that "a value revolution
of significant magnitude" has taken place in the last decade.
In a broad-based national survey Harris found that Americans
are no longer content to live by bread alone. Rather there
was a deep sense of the value of the individual experience
and an aversion to the competitive rat race that has characterized much of twentieth-century America. He found that
the idea of "voluntary simplicity," a return to basics and a
distrust of too many material possessions, has captured the
public imagination. "Psychological, even existential values
are rapidly coming to dominate the thinking of people on a
mass basis," Harris wrote.[3]

Many of the seekers could have been interviewed by
Harris. They are the career changers who have switched to
alternative occupations. They have tired of the struggle and
chosen to lower the volume in their lives by leaving the city
to earn their living with their own hands. The carpenters in
Vermont, the ski instructors in Aspen and the inn owners
everywhere belong here.

But there are others. I talked to artists and free-lancers
in all fields who were compelled at mid-life by their shifting
values to go into business. They were eager to make money
and lots of it. Off to a late start, they knew they had to run
just that much harder to get ahead. They embraced the work
ethic and its material rewards with gusto. The story of David
Goldstein, a documentary film maker who started selling
commercial real estate, appears later.

The common denominator among all these people is the
need to find careers that are consistent with their current
perceptions of who and what they are. The challenge such
people face is to find an occupation that will reflect their
grown-up selves.

Carol Anderson is a seeker.

The crabmeat quiche is delicious as well it should be.

The Alaskan King Crab was bought fresh that morning at Pike Place Market which overlooks Puget Sound.

Carol is the hostess for this repast on Capital Hill in Seattle, Washington. She is also one half of the August West chimney sweep business. Her friendly urchin looks fit right in. With us are Carol's eight-year-old daughter Gillian and her partner Belize Brother. Also sharing the last of the second crabmeat quiche are Belize's lover and her lover's son. The three women live—and some of them love—together in this cheerful, rambling house in a middle-class neighborhood of tree-lined streets. It's remarkably ordinary except for the three-foot-tall paper mannequin which lies on its side in a corner of the dining room. The cut-out was carried by the women recently in a gay rights march.

Four years ago Carol slipped into pantyhose in the morning, kissed her husband goodbye and went to work in the county juvenile probation office. Now she is a lesbian, a feminist and when she goes to work she puts on a black top hat and carries a broom. From juvenile probation officer to chimney sweep, from married lady to gay activist. Outwardly the transformation could not be more complete. Inwardly, the change has been just as great.

Carol is thirty-seven. Hers is an in-between generation. She was twenty-one when Betty Friedan stated a commonplace in *The Feminine Mystique* and startled the country. Women could be more than wives and mothers. She was twenty-seven when the flower children smiled back from the covers of *Time* and *Newsweek*. "I've always thought of myself as ten years behind," said Carol. No more. Carol has come of middle age at exactly the right time. Her career change and the reasons behind it fit right in.

Carol was raised in the middle-class traditions of the 1950s. There were two shoulds. Women snared husbands and had children. The End. People who worked, and they were mainly men, found jobs, were loyal to their employers and eventually collected gold watches. The End.

Her mother, a Smith College graduate, taught briefly

before her marriage and then devoted herself to her children. She assumed that Carol would do the same.

"Most of the women who went to school with me were husband hunting. The dropout rate was high. My parents' expectations were the same: find someone and get married. But I was eccentric. I always assumed I would work. I always wanted to have a career."

In 1963 when Carol was graduated from Tulsa University with a B.A. in math, a professional woman was still regarded as an eccentricity. And Carol was still trapped, more than she knew, in her parental shoulds. She collected a Master's in social work from Washington University in St. Louis. Social work was a safe occupational choice for a woman.

"I was a real do-gooder. I felt I was going out to cure the ills of the world. It was a very romantic notion, completely unrealistic. I grew up in a very middle-class, sheltered environment. When I actually got into social work I couldn't believe what I found."

She married a man she had known as an undergraduate at Tulsa. Marriage was the thing to do.

Don* was transferred to Seattle in 1969. Carol, the good wife, tagged along. She landed a job in the county juvenile probation office. She had a child. All was well. If she had not followed in her mother's footsteps exactly, at least she had walked a similar path.

One night in 1973 Don announced he wanted out. The marriage was not ideal, Carol knew that, but she had accepted its imperfections. To do otherwise would have demanded more than Carol was ready for. She was not prepared to fly in the face of her parents' expectations. Her own self-image also required that she stay.

The separation aroused mixed emotions. She would not have chosen to terminate the marriage, at least not then. "His decision was quite a blow to me. I was very depressed. I felt I had failed." But her feelings were directed more toward

* The name of Carol's husband has been changed.

the loss of a way of life than toward the loss of a love object. By the time Don left, she had little emotional involvement with him. It was the idea of marriage that she cared about, not Don himself.

"I rather enjoyed being married. It was a very steady, sort of stable and easy way to live. We had a very egalitarian life together. I was not uncomfortable in the marriage even though we were not very intimate and did not have a good sex life. We were, however, very compatible in the kinds of things we liked to do. It would have been okay with me if we had continued on as roommates but I suppose that would not really have been fair to him."

Carol suggested marriage counseling. "We did go to see a marriage counselor a couple of times but neither of us really had the energy to work it out. We had a very amiable marriage and in the end we had a very amiable divorce."

Don's leaving showed Carol the way out as well but she didn't know that yet. The nights at the opera and the Saturday night dinners with Seattle's young married set were over. Carol retreated. Weekdays she concentrated on her work. Weekends when there was no work to preoccupy her, Carol and Gillian wandered for hours through Capitol Hill park.

Carol had never fully accepted all of her parents' values. The doubts which had simmered below the surface now bubbled up. On those long walks through the park, she began to question the one true way of her upbringing.

Although work was a safety zone in the midst of the turmoil of her life, she was becoming increasingly disillusioned with her social work. Without juvenile crime, she would not have a job. It was a depressing thought.

"I became increasingly dissatisfied. I liked being a social worker for a long time but finally I just got so tired of listening to people's problems. It just began to seem endless and there was a growing sense of hopelessness. If you helped one person, you found ten more waiting to be helped right behind. I started feeling what I did really didn't make any difference."

One night at the end of 1974 Carol arranged for two of

her charges, teenage prostitutes aged fifteen and seventeen, to accompany her to a local production of the George Bernard Shaw play about prostitution, *Mrs. Warren's Profession*. As things turned out, that was not a good idea. The girls were restless and bored.

Afterward they countered with a suggestion of their own. If she seriously wanted to understand their life, why not accompany them to First Avenue in the heart of Seattle's combat zone? Carol agreed. That was an even worse idea.

The police arrived at the café as the three women were spreading ketchup on their hamburgers. Two weeks later Carol was summoned by her boss. The police had filed a report about her visit to the café. She was accused of being a prostitute. Carol denied the charge but she admitted she had been naive.

The experience was not pleasant but for Carol the lesson was clear. Taking the girls to the play did not fall within her job description. She had done that on her own and it had not been successful. The aftermath crystallized a lot of things for her. She could play life by the book or she could toss out the book and forge out on her own. There was no in-between.

Despite her growing unhappiness, she never considered quitting her job.

"All this time it never occurred to me that I could change careers. One thing that I grew up with, that my mother taught me, was that if you are going into a profession, you stay with it."

At the same time, Carol, a woman alone, a single parent with a child, was seeking support. Seattle with its tradition of radical politics attracted active feminists. Carol drifted into the feminist movement. There she met lesbian women also. "I sometimes think that my becoming a lesbian was a fluke. A matter of being in the right place at the right time." Carol took a woman as a lover.

"I am quite certain that being gay had a lot to do with quitting my job. It was not just that I was hanging out with people more radical, who questioned why I was working in the criminal justice system anyway, but also that my whole life style was changing. It became easier to make other changes."

A colleague at the juvenile probation office, a man that Carol admired and had adopted as a mentor of sorts, quit to pick up a brush and become a house painter. Carol was stunned. How could he? His decision plunged her into an orgy of self-examination. Another question presented itself. If he could, why couldn't she? "This really helped me to leave. It was one more piece of information about what could and couldn't be done."

When her husband left, Carol realized that it wasn't necessary—indeed it wasn't always possible—to curl up within the cocoon of marriage and family. When her mentor quit, Carol began to see that she might not need the protection of her job.

All of this time Carol was collecting new facts about the world as it really is instead of the world as her parents had conceptualized it. Carol was shedding her old self-image. Out of those bits and pieces of the new facts and information she was gathering, she was weaving a new self-image that would encompass more of the adult Carol Anderson. Slowly, she was growing into it.

An essential part of her new image was: Carol is a person who is capable of taking risks.

Women are hobbled in their attempts to lead lives of their own choosings by a variety of factors. Their self-images and self-perceptions are among the most important. No one swings from a trapeze unless he believes he can hold on. No one changes careers unless he believes he can succeed. The people who instinctively believe they can tend to be "he's."

Among the women and men I studied, an important difference stood out. Men who switched careers evaluated the risks, weighed the pros and cons and decided. Despite their anxiety, which sometimes was considerable, they were able to externalize the inherent risks. They were comfortable with the notion of taking risks. The women were not. Before the women could even begin to contemplate changing careers, they had to conquer their fear of risks. The men's attitude was "This may fail." The women's attitude was "I may fail."

These different assumptions are acquired early in life and remain with us almost from the time we can walk until well into adulthood. Six-year-old boys and girls in a survey of children in the first through third grades already reacted in these characteristic ways.[4] Boys expected to succeed in their projects; girls anticipated failure. When the children did fail, the girls blamed themselves but the boys considered their failure to be the fault of circumstances beyond their control. Thus, young Ely Callaways learn to handle success well while young Carol Andersons learn to cope with failure. Boys move ahead. Girls stay where they are.

Twenty, thirty, even forty years later women still react as if they were still six years old. They learned the childhood lesson too well. Margaret Hennig and Anne Jardim, co-authors of the highly praised *The Managerial Woman*, re-searched the differences between men and women in man-agement. They asked more than 3,000 women and 1,000 men: what is risk and what does it mean? The answers were strikingly different. "Men," the authors wrote, "see risk as loss or gain; winning or losing; danger or opportunity. . . . Women see risk as entirely negative. It is loss, danger, injury, ruin, hurt. One avoids it as best one can. And there is yet another dimension: men see risk as affecting the future; it is risking one's potential, risking future gain, risking career advancement. A bad mistake and you may never move again. Women see risk as affecting the here and now, what they have so far managed to achieve, all that they have."[5]

Changing is a geometric process. With each step off the One Tried-and-True Path, the next becomes easier to take and the third easier still. Once we are assured we can successfully take a baby step forward, we feel confident to take a giant step. In Carol Anderson's case, as in the instance of others I talked to, she had to realize that change and catastrophe are not synonymous before she could move on.

But move on she did. One day in 1975 she handed in her resignation. She had no job to go to, not even any prospects of one, and furthermore she had not the slightest glimmer of what she would do. It was the second coming out of Carol Anderson.

She had managed to shake herself free of the life for which she had been programmed but that does not mean it was easy. "It was real hard for me. I didn't think I could quit a job without another job to go to. I had never not had a job so I was real worried. I muddled around for a long, long time, at least a year, maybe even longer before I quit. Once I did, I must say it seemed simple enough."

For years she had floated around cocktail parties, glass in hand, saying, "I am a social worker. Who are you?" Without that label to pin onto herself, she was . . . well, exactly who was she? "It's amazing how much of your status and identity is tied up with your job. I was terrified of announcing to people that I didn't want to be a social worker any more. I believed that once you embarked on a career you stayed with it. If I couldn't say that I was a social worker, my goodness, what would I say?"

Carol and Belize Brother became friends through the feminist movement. Like a lot of women in Seattle, Belize was working in the kind of blue-collar, manual-labor jobs that sociologists are apt to call "nontraditional occupations for women." She happened to read a newspaper article about a chimney sweep company in Connecticut and decided that was exactly what Seattle needed. Belize asked Carol if she would like to join such a venture. Carol said, "Why not?"

"I liked the idea that there was a beginning, a middle and an end in cleaning chimneys unlike social work where there was no end at all. I liked the independence of it, that I could work as little or as much as I wanted."

Belize went to Connecticut where she learned the trade and when she returned to Seattle, she taught Carol. The two used $4,000 of their savings to buy the equipment and a truck. Success was not guaranteed but the women were determined that the business would prosper. Carol had come a long way.

From being unwilling to risk anything, she was now willing to gamble all her time and a considerable amount of her savings.

"I was worried at first but once I decided to go ahead somehow I had a feeling that it would all work out."

Her ex-husband Don, a reporter for a wire service, had taught Carol the uses of the media and the values of free publicity. The women counted on attracting newspaper and television coverage to advertise and promote their business. "We were a novelty and real picturesque in our top hats. We hung around talking to the people who do weird stories until they agreed to do something on us." Their contacts got them a spot on the local nightly news program their first week. Through the publicity and word-of-mouth advertising, their business has continued to grow geometrically.

They charge $35 and last year the business grossed $13,000. Carol now earns significantly less than she did as a social worker but the changes in her life style have reduced her expenses. All in all, it works out evenly.

"I don't worry about money very much any more. It's funny because I used to worry about it all the time. All the changes in my life seem to have brought a renewed sense of self-confidence. I feel I can always make a living if I have to."

The last time I saw Carol we spent a few hours over cups of coffee and although I figured I already knew the answer, I asked her about her goals now. Did she want August West to become the McDonald's of the chimney-sweep world?

"I have this future fantasy that I'd like to get on with. I'd like to manage a wild old ladies' home. I'd like to gather all the eccentric old women in the country and we'd live together, maybe some place in the country and travel together and have a grand time."

Carol laughed uproariously and two elderly women, picking through their chicken salad lunches, bobbed their blue marcels in our direction and frowned their disapproval.

"Even them," Carol giggled. "Even them. I want them with me."

Of one thing I have no doubt. Carol has caught up with her times. She is where she belongs.

THE DIVERTED

They wanted a career in the arts but went to law school instead. They postponed a dream when they were dragged into the family business. They wanted to be doctors but lacked the money for medical school. One way or another the diverted ended up in careers which they never would have chosen for themselves. Once there they stayed. These people are not likely to rail against unjust fates or to rebel. They are the people who continue to do what is expected of them. They did their best and did not complain. For such people the mid-life crisis brings a liberation from the "ought to do's" and the "shoulds" of the twenties.

Some 10 percent of people who change careers may fit the diverted pattern. In a group of seventy men who started new careers the American Management Association found eight who could be so classified. All of these men were persuaded to join family-run businesses after they married the boss's daughter. They followed the tried and true, the safe and easy course. Their jobs were never really right for them but ensnared by emotional and family ties, they stayed year after unhappy year. They ignored the ulcers and head-aches and pushed on. It was not easy for them to escape although each man eventually did. For several it took psy-chotherapy before they could summon the courage to face their fathers-in-law and reclaim their lives. Their universal reaction afterward was: why did I wait so long?[6]

When I first embarked on this project, I expected to encounter a lot of men and women who represented the diverted pattern. That I didn't says a lot about the growing up we do after we are adults. To be sure, I often saw the child lurking in the adults I talked to. Ely Callaway, bouncing around his grape fields in his red BMW, conjured up images of a nine-year-old back in LaGrange, Georgia, tending his peach trees. But they were really not deflected from their present careers.

It was not until a mutual friend suggested I go see Iver Brook that I found a valid example of the diverted pattern.

The parking lot at the University of Miami marine lab on Key Biscayne was deserted when I arrived for our appointment but even if it hadn't been, I would have known Iver Brook at fifty paces. He wore the rare look of an unmistakably happy person. It was the Monday of a long Fourth of July weekend and most of the people who normally occupy the lab were spread out on both sides of Rickenbacker Causeway lapping up the sun. Brook already had a tan but that wasn't what produced his glow. It obviously went deeper just as the bounce that propelled his Adidas up the stairs two at a time came from more than large measures of Vitamin D.

Brook is a "speculative ecologist." He studies the "interaction of fish and organisms and other things in the environment"—the ecology part—and tries to devise "rational hypotheses for the things found"—the speculative part. To do this, Brook spends a lot of time out in Biscayne Bay collecting flora and fauna that enable him to write articles like his recent "Comparative macro-faunal abundance in turtlegrass (*Thalassia testudinum*) communities in South Florida characterized by high blade density" which are published in such periodicals as the *Bulletin of Marine Science*.

Out there in the midst of the Gulf Stream the world is Iver Brook's very own aquarium. The white sunlight, the hollow slaps of expiring waves, the deep plunges through the friendly bands of blue and green—he loves it all.

Brook didn't set out to be a marine biologist. Growing up in Brooklyn fifty-five years ago, he wanted to be a forest ranger. The choice is not as incongruous as it first appears. In the 1920s the Bay Ridge section where Brook was born was almost in the country.

His elementary school was in an old fort and at recess they played in its shadows and along the banks of the East

River. After school he chased birds through the Canarsie dump, not with a BB gun but with metal strips for banding and tracking birds. Four years of Boy Scout camp taught him what kind of moss grows on the north side of trees and how to tell directions from the stars. His merit badges bore pictures of leaves and animals. "I was very nature oriented," he says now. "Camping and hiking were the things I loved. We were pretty ocean oriented, too, most of us growing up there in those days."

The woods and the sea defined his boyhood.

When it came time for college, he settled on the woods. He applied and was accepted at the College of Forestry at Syracuse University. It was 1939 and the country, not yet caught up in World War II, was still recovering from the Depression. Iver Brook was among the fortunate few who could dream of college at all but it was college on the proverbial shoestring.

"My father was a lawyer but that didn't mean much in the Depression. Sometimes he went for six or seven months without collecting a fee. The good jobs then were cop, teacher, things like that. I was interested in getting the best and least expensive schooling I could. My attitude was: you went through school—you tried to go to school and if you were lucky, you did—and then you immediately translated that into a good job."

Brook hedged his bets. He took the exams for the Naval Academy and scored high. It was to be the ocean after all. Under his name in his high school yearbook was written "college: Annapolis." Before he could be formally admitted, he was required to take a physical. The verdict came back unexpected and implacable—rejected. Iver Brook couldn't cross his eyes and unless he could, the U.S. Navy didn't want him.

Brook scrambled and got into the College of William and Mary. Frustrated and bewildered, a sixteen-year-old college freshman, "not too aware of things," Iver Brook stored away his dreams of being a forest ranger and nights at sea on an open deck along with his merit badges and set about making the best of things.

A year later his father died. "Education became a means to an end then. There was no alternative but business and economics. I ended up an economics major." After Pearl Harbor was attacked, Brook, whose eyes weren't good enough for the Navy, enlisted in the Army Air Force.

Three years passed and a different person returned to a different world. The G.I.'s who were lucky enough to come home hustled to catch up. Too much time had been lost and ahead lives were waiting to be built. Iver Brook who started college at sixteen found himself at twenty-three still only a junior.

"Things changed so much between 1940 and 1945. My mother's income dropped by 50 percent with my father's death. I was fortunate to be able to go to school on the G.I. bill. I went back to William and Mary still not knowing what I wanted to do except to make a living. If someone were to have offered me $10,000 a year, hell, I would have thought that was a good living."

No time to dally now in the bayous of a delayed adolescent identity crisis. Brook sprinkled mothballs around the dreams of being a forest ranger or working near the ocean and put them away for good. He was a man now and men didn't chase birds and butterflies through sun-dappled fields. Brook was caught in the revolving door of society's shoulds.

He was lucky. Harold Bache, the founder of Bache and Company, was a family friend. He was more then willing to give a boost to his old friend's nephew. Iver Brook went to work for Harold Bache in 1947 as a brokerage trainee. In 1951 he bought a seat on the Chicago Board of Trade for $3,500.

Brook scrambled up the career ladder, never missing his footing, sometimes taking the rungs two at a time. Security, safety, a solid job, a nice income, something in the bank for retirement. These were the important things.

In 1962 Harold Bache who had given the eager young college graduate his first job made him a partner. Iver Brook was thirty-nine and he was responsible for the entire Midwest commodities exchange operations.

It was an exciting time. There was money to be made and Brook made it. Although the money was fine and paid the mortgage on a nice home in a leafy suburb of Chicago and the membership fees in country clubs, it wasn't the money alone that kept Brook going. It was the wheeling and dealing down there in the pit of the Chicago Board of Trade that made his corpuscles tingle. Like a high roller in a make-or-break craps game, he loved the feeling that fortunes could be won or lost with every slip of paper that exchanged hands.

"It's an exciting business and the people in it are honorable. You can do a million dollars worth of business in one day and just say sold. It's the last home of the verbal contract that sticks. You never have to worry about the fine points of a legal contract."

Unknown to him, the safe and sane world that Iver Brook had felt compelled to so carefully create was about to be shaken by a tremor that eventually hit ten on his personal Richter scale.

Harold Bache decided to incorporate. In 1965 Iver Brook became vice president of Bache and Company. He was still solely responsible for the Midwest commodities market but somehow the fun was gone.

"When Bache became a big corporation, my attitude changed. It was one thing to be a partner of Harold Bache and another to be vice president of Bache and Company. Financially the second was better than the first but it wasn't the same kind of feeling. I did exactly the same thing; I was still responsible for the Midwest commodities exchange. But suddenly everyone wanted tables of organization and more time was spent in day-to-day politics than in day-to-day operations."

Brook had never been a hanger for a gray flannel suit and at forty-three he had no desire to start.

"Harold Bache wanted me to work with people I didn't want to work with. There was no way to argue with him. There was no argument. I didn't choose to stay."

Brook paused.

"I have nothing but fond memories of Bache. I had a chance to trade. I worked from the floor and it gave me a chance to accumulate capital. They were good years."

A longer pause and he went on.

"I joined Gilderman and Company. They were people I had known for twenty years on the floor and I was one of only four partners. It was a small firm active only in commodities. I could trade to my heart's content and live in an atmosphere not scarred by office politics."

All of us continually write revisionist histories of our own lives and perhaps in retrospect Brook really believes that leaving Bache and Company was as easy as he insists it was. But consider. Brook had spent twenty years, his entire adult life, working in basically the same area for the same company, for the same man. Harold Bache was the family friend who gave Brook his first job and thought enough of him to eventually make Brook his partner. Bache and the company he founded were the depository of all of Brook's shoulds, all the things that he thought it was incumbent upon him as an adult in society to do. Bache was his mentor.

Daniel Levinson, professor of psychology at the School of Medicine at Yale University, first identified the importance of the mentor in men's careers.[7] The mentor relationship is enormously complex and difficult to define. Basically, the mentor is a guide on the treacherous and rocky path to adulthood for his protégé, holding the map of the way he will travel, offering a helping hand when he stumbles, scouting out the rough terrain ahead. The mentor helps his protégé to grow into his own personal vision of what an adult should be. The mentor helps the young man to become all that he is capable of being.

As valuable as the mentor is, the time comes when the protégé must leave. Just as the child must relinquish his mother's hand to take his first steps and just as the boy must unscrew the training wheels to ride his bike alone, the young man must break with his mentor to become a full-fledged adult. The mentor has served his purpose.

This is not easily accomplished although afterward it may seem so. "Mentoring," writes Levinson, "is best understood as a form of love relationship. It is difficult to terminate in a reasonable, civil manner." As a result of casting off his mentor, a man is freed to become his own person.

I ran into the mentor relationship time and again but in none of my cases was it as obvious or as crucial in terms of changing careers as it was with Iver Brook and Harold Bache.

Eleven years later Brook can look back and say evenly, "I think I first had to get away from Bache to be free to do what I wanted to do."

Brook was forty-four when he left Bache and Company. He had been married fifteen years. He had two children, a fourteen-year-old daughter and an eleven-year-old son. He also had a twenty-six-year-old time bomb tucked away, waiting to explode amidst the mothballs in the cedar chest of his mind.

One night in 1969 Iver Brook was thumbing through *Time* magazine when an article about a program at Columbia University which trained middle-aged men and women for second careers in education caught his eye.

"It really affected me. I felt that here I was, successful as a broker and a trader. I could foresee twenty additional years doing more of the same work. It wasn't as if it were not financially remunerative. I just started asking myself if I wanted to stay with the company for twenty more years. I guess, in retrospect, that's when I started to actively consider changing careers. I can't say, 'yes, it hit me in a flash of lightning.' But in the back of my mind I thought maybe I could try."

For two decades Iver Brook's eyes had been riveted on that next rung of the ladder. Now he took a look around.

"I knew men in their sixties, men who had given me good counsel in the brokerage business and I realized that they had little more in life except to go to the Chicago Board of Trade in the morning, to trade and after the market closed to play golf. I could see that they enjoyed what they were doing. They had a good life, a good family life and they were making a couple of hundred thousand dollars a year."

Iver Brook looked into the mirror and his future gazed back. Twenty years and there he would be—a gray-haired man playing a little golf, doing a little trading and waiting to die.

"When I looked at it from that perspective, I said: hell, I don't really want to do this for twenty more years."

Tick.

"The word growth didn't exist in their normal conversations."

Tick.

"The opportunities were unlimited, financially, but when I really looked at it, for me, in terms of my life, I said hell, I don't want to do it for twenty more years."

A time bomb exploded.

Brook shook the mothballs out of his childhood dreams and looked them over. He still loved the water. For years stolen moments away from the office had been spent on the shore of Lake Michigan with binoculars and a guide to birds. The environmental movement was beginning and the coming confrontation between public good and private right intrigued him. One thing was clear. If his interests were to become a profession, he would have to go back to school.

The next year was hectic. His science background was skimpy and woefully out of date. Iver enrolled in freshman chemistry and biology courses at the University of Illinois. His life's rhythms speeded up, became a polka batted out at triple time. After the market closed at 1:15 P.M., he hailed a cross-town taxi and sped to the Chicago Circle campus. His classes began at 1:30 P.M. While the friends he was starting to leave behind rehashed the morning's trading and laced up their golf shoes, Brook fiddled with test tubes and microscopes. His classes ended at 6:30 P.M. He came home at night smelling of formaldehyde. He had never been happier.

When the year ended, he applied to the University of Miami. His plan was to finish up the courses he would need for an undergraduate major in biology and to enter their Ph.D. program in marine biology.

He flew down to talk to the associate dean in person. The dean invited Brook into his office and listened carefully to his proposal. When Brook finished, the dean said, "That's ridiculous. You're too old to do that. So long." Brook persisted until the University of Miami agreed to admit him as a special undergraduate student. Beyond that they promised nothing.

"There was a lot of uncertainty. There was no guarantee that I would be able to get into graduate school if I managed to complete the undergraduate courses. Even if I did, I had no assurance that I would be able to use my Ph.D. once I got it. There was always the chance that I would put in all those years and not be able to find a job when I got out."

Iver had invested his money carefully and the investments had returned a handsome profit. Money was not a major worry. Time was. Six years is a big chunk out of the life of someone who is already forty-six. If he took those years and ended up without a Ph.D. or as one of the many unemployed Ph.D.'s, where would he be? The job market does not look favorable on fifty-two-year-old unemployed men. It looks even less favorably on fifty-two-year-olds who have spent the last few years pursuing will-o'-the-wisps in academia.

Peggy and the children stayed behind in Northfield and Iver shared an apartment with the son of a friend who was also a graduate student at the university.

"It was very touch and go the first few months down here. I didn't know if I would be able to make the grade academically. It took five months before I could draw a breath and say I think I am going to make it."

By the end of that first year Iver had completed his undergraduate work and been accepted into the Ph.D. program.

His family now moved to Coral Gables. For all he saw of them they might have stayed in Illinois. "I went to school, came home, worked out and hit the library. When I was doing the field research on my dissertation, I spent sixteen hours a day in the field, sacked out and went out the next day to do it again."

Iver thought that with his business background and his Ph.D. in marine biology he could approach environmental problems in a rational and organized way. He could bridge the two worlds and unite the best of both. Three years into his Ph.D. program Brook accepted a job as environmental advisor to Collier County on the West Coast of Florida. He discovered that the growth he sought entailed the shedding of a few illusions.

"It worked out quite differently than I expected. I discovered it was very difficult to be impartial, to look at things objectively. The people who hired me wanted to hear what I had to say as an environmentalist, period. I wasn't permitted to think as a businessman. I wanted to bring people together who would have all sorts of views to bear on a problem. They didn't want that."

Brook stuck it out for three years while he completed his dissertation. When the degree was granted, he moved his family back to Miami and took up his present position as a research associate at the University of Miami.

A research associate has the lowest position in academia. He frequently meets full professors who are ten years younger. But Brook measures his success differently. "I wouldn't mind a faculty position. I would like to be invited to lecture at other universities and to exchange ideas with others in my field. The important thing is that I have the credentials to call myself a professional. I am satisfied that one, I was able to graduate, that two, I've had some things published and that three, I have been able to get research funding. I like to think that I am growing as a scientist. I want to keep on doing things and I hope I am going to do something in science."

At last Iver Brook is marching to his own drum beat.

Part
TWO

Growing Up after 35   3

It begins with a murmur. The morning your son beats you at tennis for the first time. The day the zipper on the size eight skirt sticks before it reaches the top. "But I've always worn . . ." and the sales girl, fifteen years younger and ten pounds lighter, averts her eyes.

It erupts suddenly. One morning, the first true morning of spring, you awake and know with absolute finality that a spring will come that you will not share in. One night you go to your twentieth high-school reunion and glancing through the country club window, say too soon, "Oh, that's not our group. They're too *old*."

It is an unexpected jolt that shifts the mental furniture around and permanently rearranges it. A parent dies. The chairman of the political science department calls to say a colleague is in the intensive care unit following a massive heart attack. The husband of a friend runs away with a woman the age of his daughter. The wife of a friend departs to seek her fortune and leaves a "please remember Timmy's dental appointment next Wednesday" note. Your spouse sets up housekeeping with a member of the same sex. The daughter of the girl you passed notes to in Latin II graduates from high school.

Once a friend and I spent an evening exchanging the

latest tidings in the lives of our high-school friends. A divorce, a serious operation, unemployment, the death of a father. None of it was too terribly cheery. As the gloomy recital drew to a close, he mused, "You know we're now the people that adult things happen to." I spent a lot of time thinking about that remark and came to the reluctant conclusion that he was right. It was something of a shock. While we had been preoccupied with our families and our careers, we had grown into the theys and the thems of our childhood. We had become The Adults.

This turmoil goes by a lot of names now and none of them are very pleasant. The Deadline Decade. The Mid-Life Crisis. The Mid-Life Transition. Whatever the nomenclature, the message is the same. Life is not forever and youth is short. In her book *Passages* author Gail Sheehy described the disruptions of the late teens and the early twenties as a "flu of the personality." In that case the turmoil of the late thirties and early forties can be likened to a raging pneumonia of the psyche.

One word of caution. While generalizations are easy to make, they should not be accepted too readily. They are like the quizzes that appear in popular magazines—fun to take but not too seriously. If your answers to "Will Your Marriage Survive?" give a six-month life expectancy, some hasty re-examination may be in order but that is no reason to engage a divorce lawyer.

Obviously people vary tremendously. Some people speed through life as if they were on the inside lane of the Santa Monica Freeway. People who never stop to look at the landscape in their twenties and early thirties are not apt to do an abrupt reversal in their late thirties and forties. For them the mid-life transition may be a minor rumble. By the same measure the person who has always been introspective is likely to experience the same mid-life events more intensely and more painfully. For them the mid-life crisis can be a full-scale earthquake. The tumult of these years is produced by a volatile combination of our personalities and our environment.

Some researchers who have been studying stress propose that physical and mental breakdowns are caused not just by one major life catastrophe but by the cumulative effect of a series of strains. So it is with the mid-life crisis. A man who buries his father the same year that his oldest son leaves home is going to have a far rougher time of the mid-life passage. If his boss also announces that one of his subordinates is being promoted to the vice presidency, the mid-life crisis is going to be geometrically worse. A woman who starts experiencing hot flashes at the same time her husband moves in with his twenty-five-year-old mistress will find coping with the mid-life transition even more difficult.

Despite that fair warning, the evidence is pretty persuasive that most people go through a period when they feel as if they had opened a door to a familiar room and suddenly found themselves in the fun house of an amusement park. Unexpectedly we realize that the world and ourselves are different from what we imagined them to be. Some 80 percent of the men that psychiatrist Daniel Levinson studied endured a period of "tumultuous struggles within the self and with the external world" in the early forties. The mid-life crisis of women unfortunately has been neglected by serious researchers. Little is known about its pervasiveness or its severity in the lives of women. On one thing there is general agreement. Whatever its nature or duration, their mid-life crisis starts earlier, sometime around the age of thirty-four or thirty-five, when the biological boundaries imposed by women's ability to bear children, begin to loom. In any event there are few reasons to suppose that women sail serenely through these years while their mates flounder.

Life is never static and at no time is its dialectical nature so obvious as it is in the mid to late thirties. Those years are the mid-point of life. By that time we have built a structure for our maturity. If we have followed the usual pattern, we have married, had several children, established careers. We have acquired the appurtenances of adulthood. Depending on our economic situation, we have mortgages, life insurance premiums, business loans and tuition bills. The apprenticeship of the twenties is over. We are journeymen adults. We have come into our own.

We are confident. We are settled. We have a zest for life. And all of a sudden we skid to a halt.

We are halfway through. We can see to the end.

The physical destruction has already begun. Some of it looks back at us from the mirror each morning as we brush our teeth. There are gray hairs and wrinkles where before there were none. Chins, breasts, stomachs, penises all begin to sag. The second wind doesn't come as fast. Some of the changes are less obvious. We neither hear nor see as well as we once did. Our sense of taste dulls. Experts tell us that our mental abilities have already peaked and are now on the decline. Brain cells die daily and are not replaced.

At the center of the mid-life crisis is an awareness of death. We will not live forever. We are mortal after all. We are vulnerable. We, too, will die. Time before death becomes as important as time since birth. The years of our lives are now counted backward in time yet to live as well as forward in time already spent.

We mourn the end of youth. The ebbing of our physical vigor and youthful attractiveness is not all we have to grieve for. There is more, much more.

The myths and illusions which underlay our youth are dying. We mourn the loss of once-cherished beliefs. Life is not always fair. The best man does not always win. Neither does the best woman. People less deserving than we may get ahead while we languish among the also-rans. Hard work is not always rewarded. Promotions, fame and success may not follow in its wake. Loyalty and devotion are not necessarily respected. Fifteen years with a company may end with a pink slip and not a gold watch. There may not be justice. Truth, virtue and goodness do not always triumph.

Life is not as manageable as we once believed. It may not yield to our best efforts. No matter how hard we try, life has a way of propelling us into a revolving door going the wrong way.

These beliefs die hard. It is difficult to accept that life has a dark side that we can never completely comprehend. It is even harder to accept the truth about ourselves. We, too, have a dark side. We do not always play fair. We do not always give credit where credit is due. We do not always love our spouses, children or parents. We resent their demands. We should be generous, kind, loyal, trustworthy but we are often mean-spirited, petty, vindictive, demanding, back-stabbing. Inside of every adult lives a frustrated two-year-old who still demands to come first, to have everything his way. The truth is that as we do not always love, we are not always very lovable.

These confrontations are painful in the extreme and they all have in common one thing: loss.

Some of the best evidence that the awareness of death is responsible for the mid-life crisis comes from British psychoanalyst Elliott Jaques who coined the phrase in his study of the lives of artists of extraordinary achievement.[1]

Jaques first became aware of the upheavals of this period when he noticed an abrupt change in the work of these extraordinary men in their middle and late thirties. He pursued the notion that this is a critical stage of development by collecting at random the biographies of some 300 painters, composers, poets, writers and sculptors "of undoubted greatness or of genius." Michelangelo, Beethoven, Goethe, Verdi, Goya, Mozart and Keats were some of the men who were included. (No women were.) Once these were assembled Jaques found another striking phenomenon. The death rate among these men suddenly soared between the ages of thirty-five and thirty-nine, followed by an equally rapid drop to well below normal between the ages of forty and forty-four. "The closer one keeps to genius in the sample, the more striking and clear cut is this spiking of the death rate in mid-life," he wrote. Mozart, Raphael, Chopin, Rimbaud, Purcell, Baudelaire, Watteau all died during this period. Death was figurative rather than literal for some men and came in the form of an end to their artistic career. By forty-three Ben

Jonson, for instance, produced "all the plays worthy of his genius" although he lived another thirty-one years.

The creative ability may express itself in one of two ways.

It may surface for the first time as it did in the case of Bach. He was primarily an organist until he began his cantorship in Leipzig at the age of thirty-eight. He then devoted himself to composition. An even more familiar example is Paul Gauguin who left his wife, his banking career and his bourgeois life in his mid-thirties. By thirty-nine he had launched his painting career.

It may alter dramatically both in quality and content. Creativity in the twenties and thirties is spontaneous and intense. Thoughts and ideas are transformed immediately into words or music or set on canvas. Every sight, person, book, feeling is seized upon. Inspired, even driven, the artist yields only to the limits of his physical endurance. Thomas Wolfe comes instinctively to mind. Wolfe recorded the anecdotes, impressions and vignettes of his youth in Asheville, North Carolina, as fast as his large scrawl could write. Feverishly eager to write and rewrite the saga of one man's life, Wolfe threw the finished onionskin pages into ever-mounting piles in an old crate. At night he paced through the streets of New York, chanting, "I wrote 10,000 words today."*

Creativity in the late thirties and thereafter is a more-measured process. The difference is that of sculpting in stone instead of painting in water colors. The initial inspiration is no longer the final product. It is now the raw material of the work process and before the project is completed, it will be worked and reworked many times.

New creative themes emerge in his projects as the artist experiences the tragedy and hate and destructiveness of life. In his twenties and early thirties Shakespeare produced his lyrical comedies. *Two Gentlemen of Verona* and *A Midsummer Night's Dream* are the products of the blithe spirit of

---

* Wolfe is an example of the men who did not survive their mid-life crisis. He died at thirty-eight in 1938.

those years. When he was about thirty-one, Shakespeare paused in the midst of writing his comedies to produce *Romeo and Juliet*. He turned increasingly to tragic and historical themes. Between thirty-five and forty he is presumed to have written his greatest plays. *Julius Caesar, Hamlet, Othello, King Lear* and *Macbeth* are the triumphant works of his maturity.

In the lives and works of such genius is found the fullest expression of the mid-life crisis that all of us experience to a greater or lesser extent. Death is no longer out there. It is somewhere in the marrow of our bones. It becomes increasingly, frighteningly real. The symbolism that people use to describe their mid-life feelings are the metaphors of people who are struggling against total annihilation.

"I felt that I was plunging down and down into a pitch black pool and I didn't know if I would ever surface."

"I was traveling through a dark tunnel. There seemed to be no end to it."

"I was caught in a wave which was tossing me over and over at the bottom of the ocean. I was trying to fight my way to the surface but my lungs were bursting."

Mid-life tests our mettle. The most difficult aspect of these years may be that in order to cope with the challenge that lies ahead we must accept the turmoil they bring. The temptation is to fight or flee to avoid the pain but both of these responses have their price. The people who counterpunch, who lend their name to one more community drive, who challenge ever younger tennis partners, who have that change-of-life baby are denying their chance for authenticity. The people who flee into a bottle, a bed, a plastic surgeon's office are opting for superficiality. The only way to grow is to yield ourselves up to the darkness within and without.

This constructive resignation is more of an active mastery of our fate than a passive acquiescence to it. Dante Alighieri, the 14th century Italian poet, beautifully exemplifies the successful outcome of which Jaques wrote. Dante began writing *The Divine Comedy* at the age of thirty-seven after he had been banished from his native Florence. In the opening lines, he wrote, "In the middle of the journey of our life, I came to myself within a dark wood where the straight way was lost. Ah, how hard it is to tell of that wood, savage and harsh and dense, the thought of which renews my fear. So bitter is it that death is hardly more." Literary scholars have endlessly disputed the meaning of those words but whether the passage is an allegorical reference to the entrance to Hell in the poem or to his state of mind after his banishment from Florence is immaterial for our purposes. *The Divine Comedy* can also be interpreted as Everyman's and Everywoman's journey through the mid-life crisis. When Dante wrote those opening words, he was in the midst of a mid-life crisis which would have gripped his mind and soul whenever he lived and whatever the state of his external affairs. In *The Divine Comedy* Dante descends into hell, is guided through purgatory by his literary mentor Virgil and eventually finds his way into paradise with the help of his beloved Beatrice. Dante, meanwhile, was grappling with his own private demons throughout this period. He finally exorcised them and the final soaring lines express the resolution of his mid-life crisis as much as they describe his mystical and rapturous encounter with God. "But now my desire and will, like a wheel that spins with an even motion, were revolved by the Love that moves the sun and other stars," he writes. Dante had escaped from the dark and bitter wood at last.

"The successful outcome of mature creative work lies thus in constructive resignation both to the imperfections of men and to shortcomings in one's own work," wrote Jaques. "It is this constructive resignation that then imparts serenity to life and work."

In order to do the same, we, too, must knit together all of the disparate skeins of our lives and ourselves into a coherent whole.

This encounter with our own mortality and the finitude of life brings an inevitable sense of frustration. We realize that we will not accomplish everything we once hoped for.

We will not be the architect, professor, engineer of our dreams. Our aspirations will exceed our grasp. We may shoot for the stars but we are apt to land on a nearby palm tree. As galling as this is, there is an even greater frustration. We may not even accomplish those things that we are capable of. The greater our abilities, in fact, the more thwarted we feel.

That explains the intensity of the mid-life crisis in the men that Jaques studied. Capable of greatness, possessed of genius, they were constantly reminded of the limitations of time and doomed to the frustrations of visions that could never be realized.

Success or failure in an absolute sense has little to do with the mid-life crisis. If it did, the Bachs and Shakespeares would have marched double-time through their late thirties and the world would have been deprived of the greatest flowerings of their genius. In this regard I was particularly struck when I came across the story of biologist John Barnes.[2]

The youngest son of an upper-class family, Barnes was born into a world of summer estates and select New England boarding schools. By the age of twelve he had hit upon his life's ambition—to become a biochemist who would stretch the frontiers of science. After graduation from Harvard College, he earned a Ph. D. in biochemistry at Yale University and went on to do postdoctoral work there. A fellowship abroad and an assistant professorship at Columbia University which had graduated generations of his family followed.

He settled on a research problem and two years later at the age of thirty-two he made an important discovery in his field. The following year at an extraordinarily young age, he was awarded tenure. During his thirties he was made director of his own lab. He defined a new research problem and received funds to pursue it. He also became increasingly involved in the administration of his department. He spent three years as chairman and succeeded in strengthening its academic reputation.

Not long afterward he solved the research problem which had occupied his last twelve years. With a shock he learned

that a research team at another university had found the
solution two weeks earlier. Neither group of scientists was
nominated for the Nobel Prize. It was a bitter blow. He
accepted a prestigious and highly competitive Guggenheim
Fellowship and went abroad again.

At forty Barnes had achieved international recognition
as a pioneer in biochemistry. His advice was sought by
national and international policy-makers. The doors of the
scientific community stood open, ready to welcome him,
wherever he went.

A success? No question. A man that others, including
his colleagues, would envy? Without a doubt. And how did
John Barnes fare in his mid-life transition? He was crushed
by the realization that his life's work would never merit the
Nobel Prize. Surrounded by achievements, he believed he
had failed.

In his early forties Barnes drifted. He started new research
projects and accepted new administrative responsibilities but
he lacked the enthusiasm that had previously fired his work.
"The thing that's distressing to me at the moment," he said,
"is the absence of a goal that I consider worthwhile. I have
to couch it in the framework of science because that's the
only thing I'm really trained to do. But I think the problem
is perfectly general. I don't in all honesty see a goal that is
worth having at the moment."

Pessimism and despair took over. "But the [desire for a
legacy] is intimately related to the question of whether I think
it makes a damn whether anybody leaves anything behind or
not. That's a value judgment on society. If it really isn't worth
saving, then whether you leave something behind or not
really doesn't make any difference."

Gradually Barnes reconciled himself. His depression
began to lift. He surrendered his youthful illusions of immortality and saving the world. He gained new happiness in
his marriage and in his relationship with his nine-year-old
son. He also discovered pleasure in directing the work of his
graduate students and research fellows. He learned that he

was neither as good as he had hoped nor as bad as he had feared.

"He accepted himself," writes Levinson, "as a middle-aged man of considerable achievement, experience and integrity—and of serious shortcomings. He felt privileged to be able to do work he enjoys, and he was content to make a modest social contribution as parent, concerned citizen, scientist, teacher and mentor to the younger generation. He had a sense of well-being."

The mid-life crisis demands a lot of us. There is plenty of work to be done.

This word crisis has acquired a negative connotation which is at odds with its true meaning. The *American Heritage Dictionary of the English Language* says of crisis in its first definition: "a crucial point or situation in the course of anything; turning point;" and in its second definition: "a sudden change in the course of an acute disease, either toward improvement or deterioration." Both of these definitions provide needed information about the mid-life crisis. A crisis is not necessarily a disaster. It *is* a period of changes which determine for better or worse the future course of events.

From the early twenties through the mid-thirties we are busy constructing an adult world for ourselves. The mid-thirties to the early forties are a time when we can pause to catch our breath and to look around. It is a time for us to re-examine our world. Although this soul-searching is often painful, it is necessary. It is an opportunity for us to ask: Have I done the right thing? It is a chance for us to correct our life course before it is too late. It is a period when we can rework our dreams, when we can explore the uncharted geography of our internal terrain.

The assumption that we go through mid-life crises rests on developmental theories that see our lives as a series of starts and stops. Our lives unfold through various stages of development which occur at specific ages and which are integrated in the form of a hierarchy. The only way to get

from A to C is to go through B. At each stage we are forced
to master a particular task. If we succeed, we can go forward.
If we fail, our development is arrested. Just as our personalities
are shaped by a series of opposites which are as delicately
balanced as a seesaw, so are our lives composed by a system
of polarities.

Erik Erikson, a psychoanalyst trained in the classical
Freudian tradition in Vienna, was one of the first to write
about the life cycle in this sense and remains among the most
influential developmental theorists. In *Childhood and Society*,[3] a popular rendering of his theoretical work, Erikson
postulated eight life stages from infancy through old age.
Each stage consists of a developmental problem and the
resolution of that primary issue determines, for better or
worse, future psychological growth. The first stage which
occurs in early infancy offers the alternatives of a basic feeling
of trust or distrust in the world. The last stage occupying old
age juxtaposes integrity which requires an acceptance of the
life as lived and despair which brings fear of death.

At mid-life which is the stage that is of most concern to
us, Erikson framed the central developmental issue as a
choice between generativity and stagnation. People who
traverse this stage successfully, according to Erikson, shift
their focus from their own life interests and concerns to the
development and achievements of the next generation. They
willingly, gladly accept their responsibility for caring for
the generation to come. The people who fail find that life is
increasingly bereft of meaning. They stand pat and in the
end they become their own only child.

The fact that Erikson published his book in 1950 suggests
some of the flaws in his theories. Life has opened up
considerably in the last few decades. The concept of generativity is best understood now as the process of becoming
more creative and productive in the broadest sense. Men
have many more choices today. Mentoring is only one form
of generativity. Staying home with the children while the wife
works to support the family is another that was unavailable

in 1950. Women, as it often happens, are missing from Erikson's scheme of things. Women who have spent the last twenty years or so of their lives bearing and raising children have already done their bit for the next generation. For them generativity must have a different meaning which may take the form of a serious commitment to civic and charitable activities. For both men and women, starting a second career is an option which Erikson, who wrote at a time when people looked forward to gold watches upon retirement, would never have considered. As the twenty-first century looms, generativity is best understood as self-renewal and regeneration.

Erikson only sketched his theories of adult development and called on others to fill them in. Among the most respected of those who responded is Daniel Levinson, a professor of psychology at Yale University School of Medicine. Levinson and his team of psychologists, psychiatrists and sociologists spent twelve years studying the life course of forty men who were equally divided among business executives, factory workers, novelists and biologists on the faculties of leading universities. Drawing on the previous writings of Erikson, and psychoanalysts Carl Jung and Sigmund Freud, Levinson recast their theories into a broader social context. He identified nine distinct periods between the ages of seventeen and sixty-five. In describing the phases of middle adulthood, he adopted the symbolism of a ladder. At thirty a man is an apprentice adult who stands on the lowest rung of the ladder. His task during the Settling Down period which begins around thirty-two and ends around forty is to establish an orderly life structure and to advance within it. He forms commitments to a family, an occupation, a community. Stability is the key word. Throughout his thirties he struggles for recognition in his pursuits and confirmation of his choices. Toward the end of this period he is consumed by a need to become his own man, to push ahead of his cohorts, to break with the past, to be finally and truly independent. Individuality is the watch word. He has scaled the ladder. At last he can assume his rightful place in the world as a full-fledged adult. A period of reappraisal, lasting approximately five years and comprising the Mid-Life Transition, follows. The view from the top rung is clearer. He can see backward and forward. He reviews his accomplishments and decides if his life structure is satisfactory. He begins to grapple with his internal conflicts and selects specific aspects of his life which he will modify in the years to come. At the end of this life review, if he has been successful, he enters Middle Adulthood at age forty-five knowing who he is and where he is going.

Mid-life is a time when the hobgoblins that we thought had been exorcised return to haunt us. Raising children and getting ahead in the working world permits of little introspection. As our children leave home and our occupational legacy emerges, we have time to think. The inevitable tensions that arise in living together can no longer be conveniently deflected elsewhere. Across the breakfast table sits a not-so-perfect stranger and the problems that we thought were resolved years before have not been solved, only postponed. Neurotic conflicts return. The death of a parent frequently provokes a resurgence of unresolved dilemmas in our relationship with our father or mother. We are overwhelmed by free-floating anxiety. Even the "healthiest" and "most well adjusted" of us suffer from these reawakenings.

In many ways we experience these years as a tug at our sleeve as bits and pieces of our suppressed personalities demand to be recognized. So much emphasis has been placed on the losses of mid-life that the gains by which life adjusts the balance sheet are overlooked. One of the most important of these is the growing androgyny of men and women.

Biology plays a role here. All of us start life as females. That is, the fertilized embryo is initially a female. The genetic instructions which will determine our biological destiny are present at conception but it takes the activation of the male hormones in the fifth week of life to begin the sexual differentiation which will produce a male. Without this stimulation the fetus will grow into a female. Both the male sex hormone, testosterone, and the female sex hormone, estrogen, are continually produced in both men and women throughout life but in middle age the balance which heretofore has been carefully held in check begins to shift. The production of testosterone begins to fall off in men while the estrogen level in females begins to decline once her reproductive functions cease. These changing hormone levels are responsible for the tendency of men and women to take on the physical characteristics of the opposite sex. Men's bodies soften and acquire more female contours. Women's features sharpen and they develop facial hair. These changes are usually completed by the age of fifty. Backward we go, bending toward each other, merging again into one human being that is both male and female.

From our kick-off in that one egg how do we grow up "masculine" and "feminine"? Through the help of parents and teachers, television shows and *Boys' Life* and *Seventeen*. The cultural patterning which begins at birth and continues throughout life persistently rewards boys and girls for different behavior. While testosterone appears to be linked with aggression at least in animals, no biological evidence exists that competitiveness, assertiveness, independence, passivity, nurturance, emotional responsiveness are any more the exclusive property of one sex than the other. Yet, from infancy, boys are reinforced when they initiate activities while girls are applauded when they respond. Boys go on overnight camping trips; girls help make chocolate pudding for Daddy's dinner. It doesn't take too many years of this before the message gets through. He goes out in the world. She stays home. Men do. Women are. Boys repress their soft side and their tears. Girls learn to wait until they are asked.

No wonder researcher Matina Horner found that college women feared success. Women who want top grades must compete against men to do so and in taking on the very men who are potential dates and marriage partners they risk disapproval, even loss of popularity and love. A stereotype of the lonely lady who has clawed her way to the top and goes home every night to an empty apartment lingers on. The implication is a successful woman is an unhappy woman. (To see the difference in the cultural imperatives for men and women try to substitute "man" in the previous sentence.) Competition demands assertiveness. No one is called on who doesn't raise her hand. And that kind of assertive behavior is exactly what women have been taught from childhood to avoid. Women are caught in a bind. Horner found, in fact, that the more competent a woman the greater her conflict about success. When achievement is a real likelihood rather than a theoretical possibility, the ambivalence intensifies. The either-or dilemma is not solely self-imposed. Reinforcements are all around and easy to find. During my college days at Duke University the men complained loudly when they felt too many women were enrolled in a course. The women were assumed to keep the class curve high and to lower the men's grades. This compliment to our intellectual prowess went unappreciated at the time.

Birth order can mitigate some of these influences. Repeated studies have shown that first-born and only children are more achievement oriented than children who follow later.[4] This is true, of course, for boys as well as girls. Of the first twenty-three astronauts twenty-one were only children or the oldest in their family. Family position, however, has more impact on the subsequent development of women than it does for men. First and only children are highly motivated to succeed. They receive the full brunt of their parents' love, standards, attitudes and values. They become the family standard-bearers. Their progress is closely monitored and they learn that failure is not tolerated. First and only children develop a strong sense of self-esteem and high self-confidence. Because of their close relationship with their parents they acquire highly developed verbal abilities. They usually excel scholastically and are likely to continue their education. In the case of women, and especially only girls, this lavishing of parental attention and the focusing of unfulfilled hopes and dreams on them creates a strong need for continued accomplishment. They are granted permission to compete and achieve. Many have fathers who rear them as if they were boys, who take them into their confidence and introduce them to the work world early on. A distinctly different message is beamed at them. Not you mustn't compete but you must achieve.

Until recently men's lives have been defined by their careers; women have defined their lives by their relationships. Gail Sheehy noted in her interviews for *Passages* that men talked about their twenties and thirties in terms of career advancement. When they got tenure. When they were made a partner. After they got their M.B.A. Their wives and children were seen as help mates or hindrances in their career progress. Either way they were largely irrelevant to their main project in those years. Women unfolded their lives through their parents, husbands and children. After they left home. Before they met Peter. When the baby was born. As we squeeze into these culturally prescribed roles of The Man Who Goes to Work and The Woman Who Stays Home, we deposit those personality characteristics which no longer seem compatible in our spouses. Men express their nurturing impulses through their wives. They become their lares and penates, the keeper of the family flame, the guardian of the household hearth. Women find an outlet for their aggressive impulses in their husbands. More than one man at his wife's promptings has risen further in the business world than he would have gone otherwise and has the ulcers to prove it. Washington, D.C. is noted for the political wives who terrorize their husbands' aides and proudly tell reporters, "My husband is my career."

Mid-life is a time when we can reclaim those lost parts of ourselves. We can withdraw those aspects of ourselves which have been placed in the safety deposit boxes of our spouses. Men become more openly sensual and tender, responsive and accepting. Their feminine side emerges. They are freed to cultivate their rose gardens in peace. Women become more overtly assertive, achievement oriented and relatively tough minded. They begin forays out into the world. They land jobs and start careers. Their masculine side appears.

Before the age of forty the fusion of these two sides of

the personality is nearly impossible to achieve. It is an either-
or choice. We opt for one or the other and whichever was
neglected suddenly erupts in the mid-life crisis.

In the early 1970s Margaret Hennig and Anne Jardim,
both of whom hold doctorates from the Harvard Business
School, embarked on a study of women who, against all the
odds of their time and place, had risen to the top.[5] They were
women who held substantial positions in public utility companies in the Northeast and high-ranking positions in banking
around the country. Their life course is instructive. They
conceptualized their lives, as most women do, in mutually
exclusive terms. They could be successful in business or they
could marry and raise families. They chose to concentrate
their energies on business.

By and large, they were first-born children who enjoyed
exceptionally close relationships with their fathers. Their
mothers were vague figures and in adolescence they perceived
that their mothers turned against them. That cemented their
relationship with their fathers who continually urged them to
be special, to do what other girls did not, to get ahead. They
went to college where they rejected the pin curls and talcum
powder of sorority houses and chose instead to live among
the independents in the dormitories. Even then they were
defining their own lives.

After college they worked as secretaries in business and
finance companies, as administrative assistants and in one
case as an assistant buyer. They faced up to the either-or
conundrum and committed themselves to a career. They
devoted themselves to their company, developing few other
interests and almost no outside relationships. Their allegiance
was total. They became "rather extremely knowledgeable,
superbly efficient and unusually rational automatons."

At age thirty-five or so they suddenly called a halt. Some
sense of urgency was lost. They went on shopping sprees for
higher heeled shoes and frilly blouses, experimented with
new hair styles and make-up. For the first time they refused
extra responsibilities at work. Instead, they focused their

energies on their personal lives. They renewed old acquaintances and made new friends. Their social lives bloomed. Half
of them married during this period and became stepmothers.
After about two years they recommitted themselves to their
careers but their self-images had expanded. They now accepted their sexual identity and the traditional characteristics
that go with it. They were no longer waging an internal war.
The two sides of their personalities had negotiated a lasting
bilateral truce.

Interestingly enough, despite their career moratorium,
all of these women moved into top positions in their companies. A control group of women, who did not take time out
in their mid-thirties, were frozen in middle management.
None of them permitted themselves the luxury of a mid-life
crisis. Their acceptance of the either-or dilemma remained
total and, ironically, they lost as women and as executives.
They did not marry and they were not promoted.

David and Barbara Goldstein* are a couple in anguish.
He is forty; she is thirty-seven. Together, and separately, their
lives illustrate many common mid-life themes.

Boxes and crates were scattered around the living room
of their brownstone apartment in the West Village of New
York City when I visited. Books and plates sat on the floor
waiting to be packed. The Goldsteins were in the process of
moving into a co-op several blocks down the street.

The confusion in their apartment matches the jumble in
their lives. Barbara and David are in the throes of a full-blown
mid-life crisis. And if there is anything worse than having a
mid-life crisis, it is to be married to someone who is also
having one. Chaos swirls through the air like wood smoke.

"Every night we sit at the kitchen table after dinner and
dissect our latest crisis," said Barbara.

Ecstasy tempers the anguish. Barbara and David are too

* The names and some of the characteristics of the people have been
changed.

impetuous to do things halfway. They have rushed to embrace their mid-life crisis. For most people one change at a time is enough. Not for them. They have centered themselves in the whirlwind. In the midst of changing exteriors and shifting interiors, they are embarking on new careers.

For the last sixteen years David has been a film writer, director and producer. He has survived in an industry that is noted for chewing up and spewing out talented people. David got into the film industry by chance.

His father was a successful businessman who dreamed that his son would grow up to be a doctor. And like many such fathers he found that his son had a mind of his own. David balked. Under parental pressure he signed up for the pre-med course at Haverford College in suburban Philadelphia but a summer job in a hospital for emotionally disturbed children stoked his rebellion and showed him a way out. The hospital had a grant from a pharmaceutical company to prepare a film on autistic children. David spent the summer in a dark room, snipping loops of celluloid, editing the movie.

"I was in seventh heaven because I was combining my knowledge from the pre-med classes and my interest in film. I always had a dark room at home. When I was growing up, television held great promise. There was a lot of talk about bringing Greek tragedy to the masses. I had an early interest in educational television."

The film was widely successful. The hospital picked up a big federal grant as a result. "The film was a big step for me, too." David tucked the film canister under his arm and headed for New York City where it was aired by a local television station and won a slew of media awards. Medicine was abandoned for film-making. David enrolled in the film institute at City College.

If his father had been crass and materialistic, he would be sensitive and creative. If his father padded around a four bedroom Colonial, he would live in a cold water walk-up that lacked a shower and other amenities.

His pre-med background was useful. He had substantive knowledge as well as technical skills to offer and usually he worked. David, however, couldn't shake off enough of his middle-class background to be comfortable in the pick-up-stick world of the free-lance documentary film-maker. "Too nerve wracking." His need for security was too deeply embedded. But his old dream of bringing Greek drama to the masses was too rooted to permit the making of commercial films. He struck a compromise. He hired out to film companies and specialized in science and health subjects. He thought he was straddling the commercial and artistic worlds.

Barbara meanwhile proceeded in fits and starts. After graduation from Bryn Mawr, she taught school "off and on" for twelve years. Along the way she picked up a master's in teaching emotionally disturbed children and eventually was hired by a mental health center.

"I majored in liberal arts. That was the thing for women. My college put no emphasis on careers. There was no sense that we would have to work for a living. I fell into the typical career pattern of women. I sloughed off math and science courses. I never thought about earning money. Naturally I ended up as a teacher."

David and Barbara, who were college sweethearts, married soon after she was graduated. Barbara adopted his dream as hers. They would live in New York City. Film-makers, writers, photographers would flock to their living room. They would read the *New York Review of Books* and attend film festivals in the city. Orange crates were dandy for furniture and who needed a shower. It would be terribly intellectual and oh so much fun.

"We were wild-eyed kids," said Barbara. "We didn't care if we had a sofa or not. I'm not a stereotypical wife who demands a fur coat. We could get by on modest salaries."

They were never big earners but there was always enough in the checking account to pay the bills. They required little. One day in 1964 David landed an assignment to work with internationally known photographer Irving Penn on a Noxema skin cream commercial. Penn's fee for a couple of days' work equaled Goldstein's salary for an entire year. There was a lesson in that but David didn't learn it.

"I was stupid. I wanted to follow my artistic conscience and resisted commercial stuff. I couldn't see that Penn was well respected in his field and making big bucks, too. It took a long time for me to realize that if Penn didn't feel ashamed to take the money, there was no reason that I should."

Barbara broke in, "You would have hated yourself if you had done it differently. You always said if you left, you would be copping out. I remember we talked about selling out a lot. That's a phrase we used often in the sixties."

In their twenties and thirties David and Barbara each diverged in certain crucial respects from the traditional male and female roles. David was foot loose and fancy free. For him there would be no sales quotas to meet, no clients to line up. His emphasis on creativity, emotional expression and generation was more typical of a young woman than a young man. And Barbara was working to support David's dream and their life style. She was the provider, the responsible one with the weekly paycheck who made it all possible.

This barefoot in the park phase lasted fifteen years.

David felt the rumblings first. Slowly his attitude toward his work changed.

"I don't want to say that film-makers look down their noses at business but they are quite content to work for mostly rotten salaries and to not really plan their lives. Young people don't have a sense of moving up the occupational ladder. No one really thinks in terms of a career. There's not that kind of structure. There's no hierarchy. The film industry was going nowhere and I was bound for the same place."

At this point David had successfully pursued his dream for over a decade but when he began his mid-life reappraisal, he could point to little. His achievements were a string of credit lines in scores of film canisters. He was unsure of the response to the nagging question of these years: what have I done with my life? He toted up the professional accomplishments and the price he had paid for them and doubt set in. The inner walls crumbled. Depression tunneled under his defenses.

"I got lazy. I'd work intensely and then slack off. I wasn't enterprising. I was so tired of not being the one great thing I was meant to be."

David was discovering that he was not so very different from his father after all. Chasing up and down the streets of New York after a camera, scrounging for the rent money, standing in line in unemployment offices in between jobs— these David reluctantly concluded were not manly endeavors. He was approaching forty. The time had come to do "serious" things. He returned to the roots he had rejected twenty years before. He cared more about money and financial security than he would have liked to admit even to himself. In fact, he was most bothered now by the realization that the film industry was not very business-like which, of course, was the very reason he had been attracted to it. "I felt I should be both a creative genius and a sound businessman." But although David Rockefellers and Robert Motherwells exist, they are rarely combined in the same individual. Few people can command high incomes for pursuing their artistic visions and David was not among the fortunates.

David had always thought that life would somehow take care of him. He was learning that only David could take care of David.

"There was a time in life when even if we were not making money, we could visit our families on weekends and eat porterhouse steaks. When you're young, no one cares if you come for a weekend and stay a week. By the time you're forty, you're supposed to have made it on your own. You're not supposed to come around any more. You're supposed to be buying your own porterhouses."

Barbara watched his tension build. "We had the attitude that we were different from the crass and material people around us. It really did us in."

As the authenticity crisis arrived, a downstairs neighbor departed for California and asked if David would be interested in selling his co-op. David negotiated a lucrative deal and as word of his success spread, friends of friends began calling with the same question. David spent more time selling real estate and less time making films. "I was prime for something and real estate was right there." It was a fortunate coincidence.

By the time we talked David had passed his real estate exams and was selling commercial office space for a small real estate firm. Still, he was far from satisfied.

> When I started out, I was like everybody else. I wanted to sell brownstones in Brooklyn Heights. But since I couldn't find a position in residential real estate, I said, okay, commercial real estate it is. That's where the money is but the people you meet leave a lot to be desired. The actual activity is not that much fun. Mostly it consists of dragging in and out of pretty grubby places. There's no romance, no sweeping vistas of Central Park. All that matters is the bottom line. If I am going to stay in commercial real estate, however, I should be in a large company. That's what I am doing now—interviewing.

David teeters between one life and the next. Yesterday's exhilaration becomes tomorrow's dread.

"When I started out, I felt a total high. I still feel that high at times but I also feel that the new venture has to work out because if it doesn't, I'd have to go back to what I was doing before. We would have lost a lot of time and money. It would be a bitter, bitter pill. I would lose the fantasy I had before of doing something else. It would take an awful lot of courage to leave film-making again. I don't think I have it."

What is Barbara's reaction?

When David exchanged his dream, so did Barbara. Now that David wants financial security, Barbara has visions of certificates of deposit and General Electric stock. "I've always tried to believe in David and back him." She is still cheerleading for her hometown team.

Barbara is floundering, too. Eight months ago the funding for her position at the mental health center ran out. Since then she has been searching, not too successfully, for an escape from teaching. A friend dragged her to an all-day conference on women and business. She was shocked, then thrilled.

"I was locked into a female view of things. When I was a little girl, my mother made a nurse's uniform for me. That's the way I was taught to picture myself. Women provided support to men. Women were the nurses. Men were the doctors. The seminar changed that. I saw professional businesswomen differently. They weren't ball breakers after all! I would like to go into business myself. I don't know if I can. My upbringing still won't let go. I'm trying to decide now how much of my given make up I can change and how much I must accept. I'm just afraid that the die is already cast."

Barbara took a fling at sales. "It was a wonderful counterphobic leap but it was too foreign from what I had been doing. It called on too many skills that I hadn't developed. It was a case of too much, too soon. I'm not the little engine that could." She left after six months.

Now when David hustles off to his real estate office in the morning, Barbara curls up in the window seat and slowly turns the pages of the classified ad section of *The New York Times*, wondering where she should go with the rest of her life.

And what is David's response?

"I really want her to feel the sky's the limit. I felt it was high time that Barbara left teaching. Her skills and knowledge go way beyond one on one work with children." In the living room a BUT hovers over us. "I see with great alarm that she is dragging her feet. I'm very afraid that my own conflicts and anxieties have spilled over to her."

David and Barbara resume their discussion of their mid-life crisis. It is their favorite topic of conversation. The pain exerts a morbid fascination. Although it hurts to explore, they feel compelled to probe.

"There's a feeling of mid-life pressure," said Barbara. "We feel we've got to get the money fast because other people of our age have a twenty-year jump on us. Many, many people have a jump on us. We're not going to be bright young things much longer."

David agreed. "In these mid-life career changes the stakes

are much too high. We don't have the flexibility that we did when we were twenty years old."

"And yet," added Barbara, "we have to make the break now."

David made a weak joke. "If you're in this situation and you're not worried, you don't understand the situation."

Barbara tried to place their lives in perspective. "We have always been, and still are, babes in the woods."

"Why," cried forty-year-old David, "does it take so long to grow up?"

The uncertainty and anxiety that accompany the enthusiasm and excitement of their mid-life changes have extracted a toll. When people are in the midst of a mid-life crisis, they need more support than ever and find it even more difficult to give. David's and Barbara's marriage has suffered.

"We have less time to have fun together now," says David. "We can't afford to relax and be frivolous. We're just not open to enjoyment. Too many things are happening all at once."

Barbara, who has been in charge of building the home-coming bonfire, feels the weakening of ties more acutely.

"A while ago we had only joy. We have always had an exceptionally strong marriage. I see a breaking down of the whole system. At this point we just keep cranking along. I think that most other marriages would have collapsed. I really have to congratulate us. We have survived."

David ventured a final, telling comment. "I feel that I am moving into a whole new generation."

And so he is.

For most of the people that I studied, career changes were the culmination of the mid-life crisis. In the case of Barbara and David the career changes were just a mid-point that left both of them still grasping.

Artists and poets often get there before the rest of us. So it is with the mid-life crisis. For all the words that have waltzed, or more commonly plodded, across pages of books since, no one has described the turmoil of that period better than F. Scott Fitzgerald. He was forty when the first of his articles known as "The Crack-Up" series appeared in *Esquire* magazine and in 1936 the phrase mid-life crisis had yet to be coined. Nevertheless, Fitzgerald brilliantly and evocatively depicted its impact.[6]

By the time the installments appeared sixteen years had lapsed since Fitzgerald published his first novel, *This Side of Paradise*. It was a runaway best-seller that shaped, as it described, the post-World War I generation. In his obituary of Fitzgerald for *The New Republic*, Glenway Wescott wrote, "*This Side of Paradise* haunted the decade [of the 1920s] like a song, popular but perfect." With its publication Fitzgerald became an instant celebrity and his yearly income leaped from $800 in 1919 to $18,000 in 1920. Five years later he published *The Great Gatsby* to rave reviews. T.S. Eliot said the novel was the first step forward that American fiction had taken since Henry James.

By the age of twenty-nine Fitzgerald had it all. He was an enormous popular success and a critically acclaimed major American writer. Like one of his fictional characters, he had "shot across the firmament like a rocket." Plentifully endowed with talent, he found that success and money came easily. He believed, "Life was something that you dominated if you were any good. Life yielded easily to intelligence and effect, or to what proportion could be mustered of both." He believed he had "fair years to waste . . . in seeking the eternal Carnival by the Sea." He dreamed "of being an entire man in the Goethe-Byron-Shaw tradition, with an opulent American touch, a sort of combination of J.P. Morgan, Topham Beauclerk and St. Francis of Assisi."

One night in his mid-twenties as he drove along the High Corniche Road on the French Riviera, he stopped his car and gazed at the lights of Monte Carlo reflected in the Mediterranean Sea so far below. He seemed to hold all of life in his hand " . . . the fulfilled future and the wistful past were mingled in a single gorgeous moment. . . . "

Behind the glittering facade things were not well. The light that slanted down through the louvered windows on mornings after exposed cracks in the corners. He made a lot of money and spent it as fast as he earned it. He was chronically in debt to his publishers and his agent. *The Great Gatsby* on which he lavished his hopes as if it were his first-born son was not a commercial success. His wife Zelda suffered a psychotic breakdown and spent the rest of her life in and out of sanitariums. The flappers and the shieks of the Roaring Twenties became the prematurely gray women and men of the Depression. His decade ended in a crash. *Tender Is the Night* published in 1934 was a disappointing popular and artistic failure. In the new decade F. Scott Fitzgerald was, to the few people who still possessed the leisure to contemplate such things, a has been.

Toward the end of the 1930s Fitzgerald spent some time at a small hotel in Asheville, North Carolina, where Zelda was confined to a sanitarium. There he wrote "The Crack-Up."

His own crash came, he wrote, almost unawares "ten years this side of forty-nine." It came with the sharp realization that he had been living on emotional and intellectual capital which no longer existed. He had mortgaged himself physically and spiritually up to the hilt. The people and things he had once loved no longer elicited any feelings. The values and convictions of his youth—"a passionate belief in order," "a feeling that craft and industry would have a place in any world"—no longer held. The aspirations of his twenties were no match for the reality of his thirties. The old dream of being the Renaissance man was "relegated to the junk heap of the shoulder pads worn for one day on the Princeton freshman football field and the overseas hat never worn overseas."

Stripped of his loves, his illusions and his success, Fitzgerald believed he was a failure as a man and as a writer. In the midst of this turmoil he described its feeling: " . . . I was standing at twilight on a deserted range, with an empty rifle in my hands and the targets down. No problem set—simply a silence with only the sound of my own breathing."

A coda. There is a happy ending of sorts to his story. Fitzgerald survived the "real dark night of the soul [when] it is always three o'clock in the morning, day after day." His easy facility with words, his earlier ability to juggle story lines and characters, the swift sure coining of a phrase that is exactly right was never completely recaptured. Writing was more difficult; creation was more labored. But after a lengthy hiatus, Fitzgerald began to write again. When he died in 1940, he was working on the first chapters of *The Last Tycoon* which was published posthumously. Even in its unfinished state many critics praised *The Last Tycoon*, seeing in it the final maturing of Fitzgerald's considerable talents.

No one ever claimed that the mid-life passage is easy but then neither is most growth. If we chose wrongly before, we can correct our errors. If we flounder, we also have one last chance to reorient ourselves. The people who dare to experience the mid-life crisis in all of its dimensions are those who move most serenely into middle age. Picking up the pieces and putting them back together in a new order, we experience a burst of energy that can recharge our personalities, our marriages and our careers, that can propel us in directions which were undreamed, unimagined at thirty-five.

We can, as the poet once wrote, arrive at the place we started from and know it for the first time.

The Mid-Career Blues 4

And yet some go and others remain.

For every Carol Anderson who says, "I want to be me" and for every Iver Brook who says, "There must be more to life," there are others who endure the mid-life crisis with a stiff upper lip and stay put.

How can that be?

In the beginning I thought the answer might lie in the personalities and character of those who change careers and those individuals who continue in their courses. Certainly I found some distinctions which were borne out by the observations of career counselors. One such counselor mused that the career changers seemed to have a more finely honed, competitive edge to their personalities, that they were sort of the marathon men and women among us. Indeed, a Mainstream Associates client said, "I even enjoy beating my son at Ping-Pong." Will Clopton, a newspaper reporter who switched careers and became a clinical psychologist, found in his research that men who changed careers were distinguished by a marked sense of self-esteem, "a keen awareness of their personal mortality," and were emotionally stable.[1] Certainly the people on these pages possessed a rare zest and vitality and a spontaneous welling up of enthusiasm for life. They shared a wide-ranging curiosity and multi-faceted interests.

All of these essentially unmeasurable traits matter because in the end the difference between the people who
change careers and those who don't often comes down not
to the problems faced but the solutions chosen. We all have
our individual styles of coping. Some turn the other cheek
when they are hit and some punch back. Our personalities
clearly influence our response to the mid-life crisis.

But that proved to be only half the story. What of the
people like Ely Callaway who claim that they have never
wallowed in the throes of a post-adolescence identity diffusion?
They, too, switch careers. Just as not everyone who has a
mid-life crisis changes careers, not all the people who switch
occupations are thrust into a full-scale authenticity crisis at
this juncture. The other half of the explanation turned out
to be the mid-career crisis.

These two conditions often look alike. The symptoms
are bafflingly similar: a questioning of one's legacy, a wondering if the price was too high, a tendency to resign oneself,
depending on temperament, to God or the fates. The two
crises may exist side by side. But they are not the same. A
person in the grip of a mid-life crisis is thrown into doubt
about his entire life. A person experiencing the turmoil of a
mid-career crisis is pondering the ultimate value and meaning
of his achievements. A mid-life crisis is a full-fledged confla-
gration. A mid-career crisis is more of a brush fire. Which
doesn't mean the burns are any less painful.

The very concept of a career, of a sequence of jobs which
lead toward ever greater responsibility and compensation,
implies a timetable. People who are pursuing the same career
expect to arrive and depart on the same train. Along the way
little signposts point to the direction in which we are headed,
signal whether we are going forward or backward. The
partnership in the law firm. The vice presidency before forty.
Tenure. The published book. Off the assembly line and into
the front office. The million dollar sales club. But after thirty-
five—or sometimes even before—the track narrows. For every
individual who makes it to the end of the line, many more

are left standing on the station platform, watching the caboose clatter away into the far distance. Only an estimated 5 percent ever rise into middle management and an even smaller 1 percent reach the executive suite. It is not surprising then that few escape the mid-career crisis. Studies in California revealed that five out of six men heading into their thirties underwent some form of a mid-career crisis. The crunch comes when the train begins to pull out. From that point on, it becomes increasingly difficult to believe that our career ambitions will find future fulfillment.

The mid-career crisis is a confrontation between myth and reality. Our childhood fantasies turn into our adult dreams and visions. The particular illusions that we tuck into our knapsack for the journey into maturity vary but we all carry them along. A random sampling: "I will alleviate the sufferings of mankind through my scientific discoveries." "My paintings will hang in the Museum of Modern Art in New York City." "I will make a million dollars."

As reality gnaws away, we are able to accept diminished versions of those myths—up to a point. We may not write the Great American Novel. We may not find the cure for cancer. We may not become a captain of industry. At mid-career we are forced into a further reconciliation of our aspirations and achievements which is a lot harder to accomplish. We may not become chairperson of the chemistry department. We may not reach the vice presidency. We may not become head nurse.

Numerous theories have been advanced to explain the mid-career crisis but they gradually sift down to: the need to achieve in a shortened time span, the constant worry about competition from younger colleagues who may be better educated and more knowledgeable, the threat of defeat in the corporate hierarchy, the estrangement from subordinates and the envy of those who were not promoted, the continual pressure to perform and to accept responsibility for mistakes when one lacked the power to prevent them. Any—or all—of these may be true depending on the individual. The outcome, however, is not disputed. It shows up in frequent absenteeism, alcoholism, ulcers, heart attacks and a chronic malaise that lowers productivity and efficiency. All take their toll on the individual and the company.

The mid-career crisis occurs at all career levels and among all occupational groups. On the one end of the scale Ely Callaway seeks the mountain peak and quits when he only makes it to the timberline of the largest textile company in the Western world. On the other end of the scale the assembly-line worker dreams of the day when he will run his own business and suffers when he realizes that he will never escape the factory.

Industrial psychologist Harold L. Sheppard has written poignantly about the frustrations and despair of blue-collar workers who must face up to a life on the line.[2] But although the factory worker and his boss in quality control may experience the same feelings, there is an important difference. The middle manager expected so much more.

We begin with great expectations. Work will be challenging and rewarding. It will provide a sense of constant accomplishment and achievement. It will tickle our curiosity and challenge our capacities. Our parents and teachers encourage this line of thinking. (Go to college; make something of yourself. Go to the city where the good jobs are.) If their work has been less than rewarding, they maintain a conspiracy of silence or cultivate a similar belief about a different endeavor. The result is the same. And perhaps they believe they are right to do so. Surely, for their children and for their students, things will be different. The reality for once will live up to the myth.

We go to work and *bump*. Our great expectations and our jobs collide. Examples of the ensuing conflict are all around. But consider just one case—the doctor. Until recently the physician still retained some of the aura of the shaman. Only the doctor healed with a wave of the stethoscope and a "take two after meals and one before bedtime" prescription. For a long time the doctor was the new American hero, the latter-day counterpart of the cowboy who rode the plains in charge of his destiny. Think of the fathers who dreamed of "my son, the doctor." Think of the mothers who prodded their daughters to aspire to marry physicians. Medicine was intrinsically rewarding and the doctor was in control.

That was the public image. That was the expectation of every pre-med and doctor-to-be. But are they right?

In his book *One Man's Medicine* Dr. Charles Harris writes about his discovery that his vision of medicine as the healing arts and the practice of it crashed head on.[3] He anticipated sweeping fulfillment and he encountered bureaucracy. He thought he would be autonomous. He found himself at the center of a circle with the wagons drawn up and facing in. Because the gist of his experience is universal and only the details vary among professions, Harris is worth quoting at some length.

> . . . the physician becomes increasingly subordinate to organizations, governments, institutions, and men of neither license nor tradition in medicine, who have vaulted into positions of power in the newly created health syndicate: businessmen, lawyers, accountants, car salesmen, bankers and the new breed, the hospital administrator; paper doctors who treat paper. They see to the health of the by-laws, procedure manuals, bills, accounts, debits and insurance forms, beguiled by the delusion that if the records are neat and orderly, institutional care of the patient is neat and orderly.
>
> The doctor, as their hireling, is forced to use the tools and services they provide, which may not be the best available; urged to consider the community as a whole when treating his patient; coerced into violating the confidentiality of the doctor-patient relationship by monitoring the utilization of hospital beds by his colleagues.
>
> Clearly the precious bond that exists between a patient and his doctor is being riven by unqualified intruders with unlimited power. The physician, in his spiritual and serving role, may be the commodity that is squandered in this struggle. . . .

Change the specifics, alter the villains and Harris' cry becomes the plaint of angry men and women everywhere.

The nub of his complaint is this: He was unable to practice
medicine as he thought it ought to be. He thought that
medicine was special and found it was a job. There was no
magic and there were constraints. This is a discovery we all
make. We check out the myth and take home the reality.
The journalism student dreams of the next Watergate, not
realizing The Big Story comes once in a generation, and is
assigned obituaries. The young lawyer spends his days in the
law library and never sees the inside of a courtroom. The
whiz bang copywriter is reduced to girdle ads.

The truth is that most work is not very rewarding and we
are unprepared for this. Education heightens our expectations
about work. The better educated we are, the more we tend
to assume that our work will be fulfilling and gratifying,
enriching and productive. If it isn't, why spend all those years
in school? Unfortunately, reality is grating. Challenge is the
aspect of job satisfaction that has declined the most over the
years.[4] The decade of the 1970s saw a raft of newspaper
articles about Ph.D.'s in English who were driving taxis
because college English departments had no openings. That
all those graduate students were never alerted to the dearth
of jobs is indicative of the unreality of the college campus.
But even people who are lucky enough to work in their field
are likely to experience boredom and eventually apathy. The
bureaucracy has so divided and subdivided work that the
small piece of the whole which is ours to tackle is not likely
to be very interesting. Even the most prestigious and glamorous jobs can be monotonous. The surgeon may feel like a
plumber. The White House correspondent spends most of
the day sitting and waiting for the daily press briefing. The
political aide digests voluminous research material and spews
out short, pithy memos for the boss.

Another truth is that very few of us have the luxury of
performing our jobs as we would like. Sooner or later most
of us feel that rub. Carol Anderson, the social worker turned
chimney sweep, encountered it when she took two of her
clients to the play that night. She discovered that doing her

job meant doing it the way her boss said. Iver Brook, the commodities stockbroker who became a marine biologist, felt it when he was swept up in office politics. Doing his job required going along to get along.

This feeling of being hamstrung and circumscribed, of doing work that is neither very relevant nor very meaningful has come about in large measure because of the bureaucracy that has engulfed our working lives. A vast library of studies on the increasing bureaucratization of work has been assembled but there is no need to trudge through the regression analyses and the statistical data to see the results. The signposts are there in office manuals, requisition slips, manuals of style, rules of procedure, triplicate copies housed in three filing systems, and the endless paperwork that flows across our desks. Once I served a stint on the national staff of a presidential campaign where the campaign managers were so busy writing memos that they forgot to organize the country. My favorite memos from those days were the detailed procedures for taking telephone messages and the order in which the staff could read the morning newspapers. Needless to say, the candidate never survived the first primary.

Bureaucracies no doubt function very well for some purposes but they function poorly or not at all for those who are caught up in them. By their very nature bureaucracies demand a sacrifice of individual freedom for the good of the whole. The effects are as crippling for *The Washington Post* reporter and the Catholic priest as for the middle manager at General Motors and the GS-13 at the Department of Health, Education and Welfare. In researching the relationship between age and achievement, sociologist Harvey C. Lehman discovered the age of peak achievement formerly occurred *later* in life. Of the possible explanations the growth of bureaucracy is among the most likely. The bureaucracy tends to dampen our drive and curdle our creativity.

The end result is that we become removed from the product of our efforts. Enmeshed in flow charts and sales quotas, in reports to the boss and directives to employees, we find that it is difficult to recall our original goals. I remember an engineer who dreamed in school of designing sleek aircraft that would streak through the skies. At Pratt-Whitney he drafted specifications for airline coat closets and hangers. The first demanded the second but it was not the same. Work is increasingly abstract.

Sociologists call the psychological consequences of this alienation and the literature on that subject is as extensive as it is on the bureaucratization of work. C. Wright Mills first described the emotional ramifications of the bureaucracy in his classic *White Collar*.[5] He aptly summarizes what happens when things go wrong at work:

> *Alienation in work means that the most alert hours of one's life are sacrificed to the making of money with which to "live." Alienation means boredom and the frustration of potentially creative effort, of the productive sides of the personality. It means that while men must seek all values that matter to them outside of work, they must follow the rules and not violate the fetish of the "enterprise." In short, they must be serious and steady about something that does not mean anything to them, and moreover during the best hours of their day, the best hours of their life.*

All of this comes together in the mid-career crisis. Just as we demand that our mates gratify all of our emotional needs, so we ask that our work satisfy all of our intellectual requirements.

At mid-life we can choose among three courses.

The first is to give up, to succumb to what "they" want us to do, to become a paper pusher in the bureaucracy, to be one of those people who burn out at forty and retire at sixty-five. This requires that we surrender our original dreams. And many do. A man in his forties, supporting the children of his first marriage and his second wife, a computer programmer at the Department of Labor, said, "I wish they would just put me in a little corner until I can retire. I would do the programming there and I would be left alone."

Some of these people redirect their energies into their

hobbies. They become avid weekend sailors or growers of prize-winning roses. They may find new gratifications in watching their children grow or in quiet evenings rediscovering their spouses. Others involve themselves in local and national causes. They head the United Fund drive or write letters to save the snail darter. But in all these instances the people have been inspired by the blunting of their career aspirations. They have recharged their private lives with drives that once went into their work.

The second is to go the route described by Daniel Levinson and Erik Erikson and to become the mentor. For many people this is the easiest way. They foist their dreams off onto another generation and hold fast to their original scheme. Mentoring offers compensations. It helps to insure the continuity of the company or the profession. It reaffirms our choices. It is an inherently generative act. For some it is enough.

The third is to escape to a new career which offers autonomy in work and direct contact with the results. This is never an easy decision although it may be a necessary one and at mid-life the stakes often loom dizzyingly high. The risks seem near and real while the rewards appear remote and abstract. Unfortunately, we have no guarantees that ease and necessity will stroll into our lives hand in hand. What we must do does not always conveniently coincide with what is easiest to do. People who are bound and determined to say yes to life, however, generally choose second careers.

All of the people I talked with mentioned the pull of these two lures even if their decision to change careers was impelled by other reasons. Carol Anderson wanted a life that wouldn't fit neatly into an appointment book. David Goldstein wanted to be his own employer. And all chose careers where the relationship between their efforts and the results were readily apparent. Ely Callaway watches the grapes ripening in the sun beneath his office window. Iver Brook studies and writes about the aquatic organisms he has collected in Biscayne Bay.

An editor at a major publishing house who was in the process of starting his own company, mused, "This whole phenomenon of career changes grows out of a lust for control over one's life, for freedom, independence and autonomy." His Quaker grandfather once told him: never be afraid to leave a job which you like 60 percent of the time for one you will be happy in 65 percent of the time. Bob believed that. He also figured out for himself something which the experts are beginning to report. People who are self-employed rejoice in their work. Despite the uncertainties and insecurities of their lives, they rarely encounter one problem. Very few have trouble turning off the alarm clock in the morning. "The pastures," Bob summed up, "may not be greener but at least they will be of my own choosing." His comment might very well be emblazoned on the banners of all people who set out on new career paths after thirty-five.

Autonomy and freedom, meaning and independence—Jack Davies captured them all. He escaped the bureaucracy of big business and founded his own.

The grape vines of Schramsberg Vineyard cling tenaciously to the rugged hillsides facing Mount Saint Helena which guards the northern end of the Napa Valley. The vines have to be hardy to survive here. The terraces are almost perpendicular and the top soil is poor and scant. With luck the vines will last twenty to twenty-five years. They could also die at any time.

The fifty-five-year-old owner, Jack Davies, is inspecting his vines. He is wearing the standard uniform of the valley, the vineyard chic of rumpled burgundy corduroys, a Bordeaux checked long-sleeved shirt rolled up to his elbows and work boots for tramping through the fields. Right now he is pinching suckers, the little secondary shoots that appear between the branches, from the emerging vines.

"I never used to like to work with my hands. There was none of this home workshop stuff. I am the worst person in the world for fixing a screen door. But I like to work with the vines, cutting suckers, grafting. I planted a lot of the first roots myself."

Davies is a lot like his vines—sturdy, stubborn and resolute. He has had to be.

Schramsberg Vineyards is among the oldest in the Napa Valley. Its past is a snarl of romance and tragedy. Jacob Schram, a German immigrant, planted the vineyards in 1862. Chinese laborers hollowed the cellars out of the granite hills with picks. Their pick marks are still visible. They also helped to build the Eastlake Gothic frame house. In the 1880s Robert Louis Stevenson passed through in pursuit of a woman whom he later married. Stevenson stopped off to visit Schram and later described their wine-tasting session in *The Silverado Squatters*. The wine was "a pleasant music for the mind" and tasted of "the tang of the earth in this green valley." Schram died in 1905 and the giant redwoods and firs crept down the hills and reclaimed the vineyards.

In the 1940s a San Francisco physician tried to revive the winery but his unsuccessful attempt ended in tragedy. He managed to produce a few cases of champagne but they bore the mottled amber hue that betrays oxidation. He was able to sell the lot to Sally Stanford, the legendary madam of San Francisco who by then owned a restaurant across the bay in Sausalito. With a brilliant stroke of ingenuity she relabeled and sold it as "Forever Amber." Afterward, stunned by his failure, he took his life. The caves and house fell into disrepair and the vineyards again retreated into the forest.

When the Davies first visited Calistoga a little over thirteen years ago, the winery and vineyard were in ruins. The tunnels were blocked by rotted timbers. The roof on the two-story house leaked and the verandas sagged. They bought it anyway.

A lot of people in the Napa Valley thought the Davies were crazy. They said the Schramsberg Vineyards had only a past. There was no future in those overgrown, untended grape fields. An early visitor said, "You can never do it. If you do, it won't be good champagne. Even if it is, you will never sell it." Schramsberg Vineyards now bottles four varieties of champagne which many wine experts consider to be the finest of the sparkling wines produced domestically. So much for the people who said it couldn't be done.

Jack responded as he had to challenges all his life. "Just put your head down and bulldoze your way through all the people who'll tell you you're not going to make it." By then he had had plenty of practice.

Jack Davies was born in the Chicago area where his father was a salesman until the Depression wiped out his company and his job. The Davies migrated to Los Angeles and his father started again. Jack learned from his father's fortitude. Business, he discovered early, was exciting and creative. If the risks were great, so were the rewards. After graduation from Stanford, he earned a master's in business administration from the Harvard Business School.

His first job was in his father's furniture manufacturing factory but he soon set out on his own. He moved to the staff-planning group at Kaiser Aluminum when the company was mapping their future in that field. When he was asked to relocate to West Virginia, he refused and joined McKinsey and Company as a marketing consultant. "It was an outstanding experience—I must have worked in about thirty different industries and many, many companies." Fibreboard Corporation which was one of the companies he had advised eventually persuaded him to head their marketing division. He rose rapidly until he controlled an operating division that did about $15 million in folding cartons and corrugated boxes a year. "It was a big problem division, but I enjoyed it. The people were very good there and we turned it around very nicely."

He shifted to Docummun, Incorporated, which is one of the largest steel warehousing businesses in the country. As vice president he was in charge of an effort to diversify some of the company's assets into manufacturing. Docummun took over three small companies and Jack Davies was named president of each.

From a staff job to a line position to division head—Jack Davies was following the career track of the successful young corporate executive. His goal? "I very much wanted to become president of the biggest thing I could find."

He was well on his way when the mid-career crisis struck. He was forty years old and he had been in business for fifteen years. Other people's businesses. Jack still believed that business was exciting and creative but that belief was sometimes difficult to recall in the swamp of conferences, meetings, committees and studies which consumed his days.

"I really do believe that this method of management is almost as destructive as trying to do something wrong."

His routine at Docummun was more and more of a grind.

"I was becoming a little disenchanted with the commodity business, always beating on the plant manager to get the costs down. At the end of the year, if you made one half of one percent, everybody thought you were a hero. Most people in that business were losing money. It wasn't an encouraging way to spend one's life."

His frustration continued to build. He was near the top but not at the top so he was responsible but never really in control. He felt the lack of power keenly. He was forced to accept the blame when things went wrong but he was not in a position to prevent those blunders. In short, Jack Davies was caught in the bureaucracy.

"When you have the kind of job that I did at Docummun, you become identified with the way that Docummun does things. People could assume I had something to do with the decisions. I shared in the credit and the blame. That is fine if you feel 100 percent enthusiastic but it is not too good if you are not completely sold. I didn't have enough control to really do things the way I wanted. I didn't feel as if I were doing as much as I would have liked. I couldn't make that kind of impact."

Jack was not prepared to forfeit his business experience or surrender his faith in the free enterprise system. He set out to rechannel them. There were two requirements. He wanted independence and he needed a direct relationship with a quality product. He was too old—or so he felt—to adopt a completely different life style. He sought a different framework for the life he was convinced was right for him.

"Most people evolve in a direction that suits them. I have always thought that business was a very creative field and I still do. Unfortunately, the public image is quite different but I am here to tell you that in the broadest sense business is very creative.

"Some people find that it is best to work in a large corporation. The power appeals to them. They like the big payrolls and the big impact on society. Other people feel frustrated in big enterprises. They don't find themselves at home in the committee system and the checks and balances that are the epitome of big business.

"I found that I wanted to have my own company where I could try to do some things that I found interesting and exert immediate influence. I wanted to be in control of a business where quality was important."

Jack had become convinced that American businesses were more interested in growing bigger than they were in getting better. He thought things could be run differently. He was determined to find that better way.

"I felt that the overall quality of performance in American business had fallen to a level that it need not have. There was a lot of talk about quality but the actual delivery of quality had fallen below where it ought to be. I was anxious to prove that I could build a business where quality was essential."

Jack settled on a small, family-owned winery and vineyard. "Wine is a very individualistic business. It seemed to satisfy all of the criteria I was looking for."*

To a certain extent his experience at McKinsey and Company helped.

* For another side of his decision-making process and the part that his wife Jamie played in it, see chapter eight, Family Snapshots.

"I did collect a lot of data on the size of the wine business in general, the champagne business in particular and the rate at which both were growing. Then I assembled quite a few costs such as what packaging and grapes cost, what the yields were, et cetera. But you couldn't grace this information with the name of a marketing study. We were just looking at what the situation was, who the people were who were making champagne, and what the market was like."

In the end it was a decision of the heart and not the head.

"I never gave a second thought to the money I would lose or to the impact on my career. I never thought I would fail because I didn't try hard enough or because I made bad judgments. I always thought I could get a job someplace. So I didn't really carefully weigh all those odds. I don't think people really do if you are going to do something like this. You just do it."

It took a year for Jack and Jamie Davies to locate Schramsberg Vineyards which met their criteria and was for sale. When they discovered it, it was by chance. They were on an outing sponsored by the Wine and Food Society of San Francisco up in the Napa Valley. They decided to look at Schramsberg and when they did, they were immediately captivated despite the drawbacks. "We thought it was unique and we were quite impressed with the potential." They decided to buy the vineyard that day. "I've always believed if you are going to do something there is no time like the present moment. There is no reason to put it off." It took nine months to work out the financial arrangements. In August, 1965, they moved in.

Jack decided to limit his production and specialize in premium champagne. "I've always believed in picking out a niche in an area and trying to develop it." There is a mystique about champagne, an aura of exclusivity. Their smallness would be an asset rather than a handicap.

Small they were. The first year Jack borrowed a foreman from Mondavi Vineyards several miles back down the road toward San Francisco and the two of them oversaw the planting of five acres. He produced 500 gallons of wine which equals about 200 cases. The second year he planted fifteen acres and made 1,000 gallons of wine which is some 500 cases. Today they produce well over 14,000 cases which still represents only a small fraction of the production of a Gallo or Paul Masson.

"The only way to begin is to just go ahead and get started. You read everything you can read, talk to everybody you can talk to, hire somebody as a technical consultant to teach you and then you start small, taking tiny little steps at a time."

Jack was determined to do it right. "You can't just take any old white wine and put bubbles in it." Doing it right meant taking time. The quality of a fine bottle of wine is directly related to the patience of the vintner. That is even truer of champagne. First the wine must be made and then the champagne from that.

At Schramsberg it begins with the grapes. The vineyard produces all of Pinot Blanc, Chardonnay and Pinot Noir and Gamay grapes which are crushed into wine. Cognac for blending with the wine is imported from France. Specifications for bottle caps were sent to France and a machine for capping the bottles specially was designed in Italy. When he encountered problems with the corks, Jack went to Spain to consult a champagne cork specialist.

"I have patience when I need it. If it takes two years to be done right, I can wait. If it is supposed to take two months and it takes four, then I am not very patient."

Once the champagne is bottled, it is bedded down in those cool old tunnels and cellars to ferment and age. The riddling begins. Riddling is the unending task of shaking the sediment from the fermentation into the bottle necks. Jack does it by hand. The first bottles were aged for almost three years and that aging period is constantly increased.

While the inventory was building up, Davies was paying property taxes on the bottles, in addition to the labor and processing costs already incurred and not receiving any financial returns. It took ten years to show a profit.

"I've made more the five years before I started Schramsberg than I've made in the last twelve years here. If you consider inflation, I'll probably never catch up. Fortunately, I've never been attracted to owning big things. I never wanted to own a luxury car; I never had a desire for my own airplane. If I had taken the same amount of money that I personally put into Schramsberg Vineyards and put it into a couple of Holiday Inns or Tico Taco stands, I'm sure that today I'd have no worries in the world financially. But I don't want to run a Tico Taco stand or have a chain of laundromats. That's not my style."

When the first champagne was ready to be marketed in 1967, Jack drew up a list of 600 people in the wine business in California. He packed a few bottles in his briefcase and started to visit each of them personally. He also set out to call on the leading restaurateurs in the country. The Plaza and The Four Seasons in New York, the Ritz Carlton in Boston, the Madison and Sans Souci in Washington, D.C., and Brennan's in New Orleans. Jack Davies was proud of his wine and he was resolved to be in control of every aspect of the vineyard and winery from the planting of the grapes to the marketing of the finished product.

Selling the champagne was remarkably easy. No one Davies approached ever said no. "We had something that was really different and new. We told people that this product is the only thing we make; it's made in the traditional method and from the finest grapes that can be selected for this purpose; that it is well aged and that there isn't a similar product available today. Our standards from the beginning were high."

Five years later the telephone rang in the office where Jacob Schram and Robert Louis Stevenson once shared a bottle of the original Schramsberg wine. A protocol officer at the State Department in Washington, D.C., said he was in charge of a special dinner in New York City. He wanted to serve Schramsberg champagne. Could Jack Davies deliver the cases to Travis Air Force base? He could and did and went back to turning the bottles in his cellar.

A month or so later the telephone rang again. Maxine Cheshire of *The Washington Post* was asking how Schramsberg champagne was selected to represent the United States at President Richard Nixon's state dinner in Peking, China. Jack Davies didn't know what she was talking about.

Two days later Barbara Walters was reporting President Richard Nixon's historic trip to mainland China. When the president toasts Mao Tse-tung tonight, she said, it will be with an obscure California wine—Schramsberg. And so Jack Davies learned that the wine destined for New York City had ended up in Peking.

Schramsberg was no longer obscure. The "toast to peace" made the champagne, already well received in the wine trade, famous.

Jack was determined to achieve at his own enterprise and in his own fashion. By his standards he has been remarkably successful but his standards changed over the years. He stopped running for president. Once he commanded 400 people. Now his full-time staff numbers ten and basically Schramsberg Vineyards bears the imprint of Jack and Jamie Davies.

"As I mentioned earlier, I could be earning much more money if I weren't here. My sons ask me once in a while how come we don't have this or somebody else has that. I wouldn't have to answer that question if I were somewhere else."

Too often people who seek greener pastures forget that the field must be sowed from time to time and retreat before the Bermuda grass can reach maturity. Jack always accepted the fact that he could not have everything and settled on his priorities.

As we grow older and up, our expectations about work are forced to change and that causes a re-evaluation of what we want out of our work. Else Frenkel-Brunswik, a Vienna psychologist who studied adult development in the 1930s, was probably the first to note this change. Working from the biographies of 400 people who spanned all social classes and occupational groups, she discovered that maturity brought a new attitude toward life and work. Results were what counted and productivity was paramount. "If one asks a person in this phase to relate his abilities," she wrote, "he names very few of them and mostly those which are connected with his profession."[6]

This brings us almost full circle because our heightened interest in these qualities is in direct conflict with the bureaucracy in which the majority of us spend our working hours.

Some forty years after Frenkel-Brunswik uncovered this change, sociologists Paula I. Robbins and David W. Harvey talked to a random sampling of men in the New England area who had engineered some sort of career change after the age of thirty-three. (Not all of the career changes were of the radical nature that we are concerned with here.) The men were presented with a list of fourteen possible motivations for changing careers and asked to single out the ones that had been of primary importance to them. The top ranking choices turned out to be "more meaningful work" and "better fit of values and work." Far down on the scale was a "better salary." In fact, sixty-nine men said it was not a factor at all.[7] Their findings substantiate two things: the importance of work in mid-life and the inimical effect that the bureaucracy has on our growth.

The men in this study like the men and women in this book largely come from the middle and upper-middle income classes. Some are drawn from what a friend once termed the nouveau poor. They are the people who cast aside their middle-class origins to pursue the precarious existence of free-lance artists and writers and film-makers. Either way these individuals had choices about their lives. They are the kind of people that Abraham Maslow, a psychologist who wrote about motivation and personalities, would characterize as self-actualizers. Maslow posited a whole hierarchy of psychological needs beginning with the basic need to survive and ending with the need for self-actualization. As we satisfy one need, we progress to the next. Once we are assured that our physiological needs are met, we seek out security and structure and afterward we crave love and respect. Whereupon we search for self-fulfillment, to become truly ourselves, to be, in short, what we were meant to be. A few lucky souls, such as artists, are born knowing but for many of us it takes nearly half a lifetime or more of struggle to reach that spot. The people who change careers at mid-life arrived in time to do something about it.

I began this chapter by talking about the distinctions between mid-life and mid-career crises. On this point I am inclined to let Jack Davies have the next-to-last word. When I first broached the topic of our passages he disagreed violently. Later, after reflecting, he concurred—up to a point.

> *I don't think it is possible to slip in and out of life styles as if they are coats that we outgrow. I think as we grow up we learn more about ourselves and the world. I have read the motivational research of the Harvard Business School and I think there is some truth in it but I believe that basically we remain the same people and what happens to us is a combination of our abilities and the opportunities we encounter.*
>
> *It is very easy to say that the executive of sixty-five who has a million dollars in assets has a different life perspective than the management trainee who is twenty-two and is earning $18,000 a year. But to say that the executive wants to be a statesman and the trainee is concerned with getting ahead because of their ages is grossly underestimating the realities of their lives.*
>
> *You mature, you get more experience with time and the world itself changes. I think there is a continuum.*
>
> *There are no end of things to be done. If you run out of steam, basically you are at fault. The challenges are always there. You can get into Europe; you can invest in Africa. You can try to solve the problems of the inner city. I knew individuals all along the way who always did what management told them and never tried to embellish their jobs. It's easy to say that you are at a dead end. It's like saying that you have no control over how you use your time and your energy.*
>
> *I find the world a very interesting place. I can't imagine ever running out of things to do.*

And so we return to the starting point.

The original question of why some people respond to the mid-life crisis by changing careers while others stay put now can be rephrased to ask why some individuals react to the mid-career crisis by switching occupations when others go on enduring boring jobs and derailed careers. Each of these dilemmas demands an individual resolution and some are obviously more successful than others. Of one thing I am sure—the people who undertook to change careers made the right decision for them.

Two Strands, One Chord 5

Twenty-four hours aren't nearly long enough now. They haven't been since Nurse Johnson enrolled in nursing school at the University of Portland in Portland, Oregon, three years ago. The activities that must be crammed into each day spill over the boundaries. Sometimes it seems as if it is impossible to ever hope to catch up.

The mornings are notes hastily scribbled in spiral-bound theme books in university lecture halls. The afternoons are a blur of trays whizzing through corridors, of thermometers popped in and out of patients' mouths, of charts waiting to be updated. The nights are a few moments squeezed out of the evening to read bedtime stories to five-year-old Johanna and hours of textbooks opened to underlined passages that are likely to appear as questions on tomorrow's test.

Nurse Johnson is bright, attractive, competent and loves the work despite the pressure. But no patient will ever covertly admire Nurse Johnson's legs.

Nurse Johnson's first name is Gary.

Gary Johnson is forty-one. Until he was plunged into a depression that rippled through his life in ever-widening circles, Gary, born and educated in the United States, taught math and computer science at the University of British Columbia in Vancouver, Canada. In the depths of that crisis, he concluded that the life structure he had built would no

longer suffice. Too many neglected aspects of his self demanded attention. The career commitments of the twenties
were not the goals of his forties. As a result of this self-
examination, Gary Johnson was persuaded to pack away his
slide rule, uproot his wife and three children and move
hundreds of miles south to start a new career and a new life.

So far we have considered the developmental crises of
middle life and their influence on the decision to change
careers separately. But as the mid-life and mid-career crises
unfold in the lives of people the distinctions tend to blur. The
mid-life crisis may impel a decision to embark on a second
career. Likewise, the mid-career crisis may lead to a career
switch. More often, it is a one, two punch. When the two
crises coincide or, as it usually happens, follow sequentially,
the jolts have a force that neither could by themselves. In
order to change careers, we must be able to see ourselves in
new ways. The process of changing our perception of who
and what we are is facilitated by this double impact.
Let's look at the intertwining of these crises and the
decision to change careers as they evolve.
Gary was a self-contained, introspective child. He ex-
celled scholastically but his social world was circumscribed
by a severe stutter which went uncorrected until late in high
school. Isolated from the rough and tumble play of childhood
and the first tentative sexual gropings of adolescence, he
delved even further into his books. His parents, who never
had the advantage of a college education and believed he
would outgrow his speech impediment, encouraged his academic achievements and overlooked his stunted social development.
"I think I picked up from them the idea that I wouldn't
be good with people. Science and math were fields without
a lot of interaction with other people and that's where I
gravitated."
Gary concentrated his attention on those fields. He
collected his A's and his science awards and spent his Friday

and Saturday nights when his classmates were sipping their first clandestine beers building models for his laboratory science classes.

"I knew in the back of my mind that I had a penchant, a flair for figures. Math was the path of least resistance."

Gary was graduated with a B.A. in math from the University of Hawaii when the space race was beginning. The Russians had shot the first satellite into orbit and the country was gripped by Sputnik fever. The adequacy of science curriculums in the public schools and a worrisome, presumed technology gap were a matter of national debate.

"With all the emphasis on science I thought there would be a lot of opportunities there."

But a smidgen of doubt was surfacing. The lock which universities snap on most potential Ph.D.'s did not fasten so tightly on Gary Johnson. He worked for a year before earning his master's at Stanford University and for another year before enrolling in the Ph.D. program at the University of California at Los Angeles. Each break in his training ended in the same conclusion. "I thought I had so many eggs in one basket that I might as well go on with it."

This minuet of advance and retreat toward an occupational goal is more common, even among people in careers which require highly specialized and advanced training, than popular wisdom holds. The decision making goes on over a longer time period than is generally supposed and is not as straightforward as is imagined. It can forestall a too-early foreclosure of occupational identity or reaffirm a chosen career.

But Gary Johnson's minuet was trying to tell him something that he persistently refused to hear. No alternative presented itself and so he drifted on.

With his Ph.D. in his hip pocket he and a U.C.L.A. professor teamed up to get federal funding to construct mathematical models of electroencephalograms. While they waited for funding, Gary accepted a position as assistant professor of math at the University of British Columbia.

Swept up in the academic world, Gary somehow never got around to building the mathematical models, so clean and beautiful in their exactitude, he had once envisioned.

The competitive life of a junior faculty member at an outstanding university, struggling to publish in order not to perish and to prepare for several hours of teaching a week, permits of little contemplation. Gary was married by now and he and his wife Betty already had a son. As his two daughters arrived, Gary funneled his energies into simply surviving.

Gary loved the teaching and the students but the writing and publishing which the academic world demanded for advancement did not come easily. Six years passed while Gary awaited the make-or-break tenure decision. In December, 1974, the computer science department voted on Gary's tenure and shortly before Christmas the chairman of the department called Gary into his office and announced the result. Tenure was denied. Merry Christmas, Gary Johnson.

"I had the feelings that I would be denied tenure. I thought I was a good teacher and I had published a bit. I had people behind me who believed I would publish more. I felt I could go either way but I suppose I would have been more surprised if I had gotten it."

The decision hit hard. Gary had been pushed along a course he probably would not have chosen on his own and his efforts had failed. The denial of tenure sparked a career crisis but it quickly became the catalyst for a general life review. Gary discovered that doing the right thing guaranteed no pay off. No magic existed after all. What now? His ensuing depression lingered like the snow on the UBC campus well into the spring. Getting out of bed in the morning and going to work required such momentous effort that little energy was left for teaching. The enormity of his loss struck anew every time he drove into the faculty parking lot.

"That spring semester it was really very hard to teach. I was so frankly depressed. I really didn't know what to do with my life."

Gary had a year and a half to find a new job. His contract

extended through the spring of 1975 and the tenure decision included the gruesomely named terminal appointment for the 1976 academic year. When the last exam was graded in mid April, Gary faced an empty summer.

The summer was a pretty active time of seeking. I didn't want to go back to the industry kind of jobs I had had in between graduate school. Money was not that important to me. I learned that the hard way and it stuck in my brain a long time. Once I had two job offers—one for $475 a month and one for $490 a month. The $475 a month job had a lot of variations and the $490 a month job was a starting kind of program but because it was $15 a month more I took it. In 10 months I was so unhappy I was ready to go back to school. I knew the money was not worth the chasing after for the rest of my life. I talked to some people about another teaching job but somehow I couldn't work up much enthusiasm for it.

The Chinese symbol for crisis is also the symbol for opportunity and for Gary Johnson the two arrived together. The tenure decision was the result of external circumstances which were beyond his control but Gary Johnson could control his response. He could undertake the kind of self-examination which he had resisted earlier. He could reflect on the choices he had made in the past and decide if the commitments of his youth were right for his middle age. His credentials were such that a university appointment would not be difficult to find. He could drift into another teaching job as he had wandered through graduate school. That would have been easy enough. But Gary Johnson who in the past had accepted the way of least resistance chose differently this time. He paused long enough to explore those neglected aspects of his self that had been submerged for so long. For thirty-six years he had accepted unquestioningly the judgments of his parents and to a lesser degree academic advisors about what he could and could not do. Now he was ready to become his own person. He would make decisions on the basis of his own adult perceptions about his capabilities and what he wanted out of life.

Most of us leave the parental home sometime between the ages eighteen to twenty-one, depending on whether or not we attend college. That, however, is only the physical leave-taking. The emotional hammerlock with which parents grip their children extends well into their thirties. Once I heard a woman say angrily, "I wish my mother would stop controlling my life!" and then found out that the woman had not even seen her mother in two years. Still, I knew exactly what she meant and so did every other woman to whom I repeated the quote. Of course, some children renounce their parents early on and strike out on their own while other children lead crippled lives under the direct influence of their parents throughout their lives. Any relationship that is as emotionally charged as the relationship between parent and child has endless permutations. In my research, however, I became convinced that most people are pinioned by the simultaneous desire to honor their mother and father and to live lives of their own choosing. Most of the people I studied returned again and again to these themes. Reconciling the two requires several decades. Often they had chosen a career specifically to please their parents. If they hadn't actually joined the family business or lived out their parents' thwarted desire to be a doctor, they had at least chosen an occupation that would not clash with parental expectations and desires as in the case of Carol Anderson. The cliché that the hand that rocks the cradle rules the world holds more than a grain of truth. In most of my cases people could not escape their parental shoulds before the late thirties or early forties. By then the authority of parents who are now in their late fifties or sixties, who may be in ill health, who have begun to wrestle with the problem of retirement and old age has begun to lessen. Only at that point can most people cultivate their own distinctiveness.

To Gary Johnson's parents education was important because they had so little of it themselves. His father was a career Naval officer who received his high school diploma, not in a mortar board and gown, but through the mail. His mother, a high school graduate, went back to school when Gary was a teenager and became a licensed practical nurse. When Gary breezed through college and graduate school, their belief that education was the means to the Great American Dream was affirmed. When he went further on to become a college professor himself, they were thrilled. Lunching with their son at the Faculty Club, they beamed.

"My academic success was so important to my mother. Neither of my parents had an opportunity to go as far in school as they would have liked. They had education as a very high value. My mother felt that even if she hadn't gone on, her son had."

There was only one thing wrong with the scenario they had written for their son. Living it out, Gary Johnson was unhappy. He spent that summer following the tenure decision becoming acquainted with a Gary Johnson he had never had time to know.

"I started thinking what it was about teaching that I liked. It was not the computer math. That sort of shocked me. I thought more about teaching and the students. When they came in with a math problem, we would discuss it but after a while the talk would drift on to other things. What I liked was not helping them with the math but talking about the things that were going on in their lives and sharing similar things that had happened to me."

Gary Johnson realized with a sudden jolt that he might not have to find another teaching position after all, that there were other things he might enjoy even more and were available to him. "It occurred to me that maybe I didn't have to find another place to teach. It was a liberating thought." Instead of duplicating his résumé and collecting letters of recommendation from the tenured faculty, Gary Johnson began exploring different fields. Social work, physical therapy and nursing attracted him.

In this Gary Johnson was following a pattern that has been noted by several researchers. In a study of seventy men and women who returned to college in mid-life the men gravitated toward the "feminine professions" in the humanities and liberal arts, in social work and teaching.[1] In an American Management Association survey men who veered off their chosen track in mid-career often were drawn to teaching and to the same helping professions which Gary considered that spring and summer.

All these fields reward succoring and nurturing. They glorify the virtues culturally ascribed to women. They require empathy, receptivity, responsiveness, caring and sharing. Little wonder then that men who have spent their twenties and thirties repressing those aspects of themselves in a single-minded commitment to business success should find themselves erasing blackboards and climbing the steps into tenements in their forties. Some men are able to integrate their nurturing impulses in their personalities through community involvements or mentoring but for others a career change is necessary.

Different careers embody different meanings to different people. A doctor may wish to save humanity or to pay the dues at the country club and send his children to boarding school. A career Army officer may be motivated by patriotism or the security of the military life. A fledgling lawyer may visualize himself as a $100,000 a year partner in a Wall Street law firm or as a champion of the poor against those same corporate concerns.

Not all men who liberate their generative natures at mid-life do so as overtly as Gary Johnson did. I observed the same impulses more hidden but still there in men who had started their own companies. Their businesses became surrogate children to succor and to nurture into maturity. A man who founded a corporation said, "The company gives me a great deal of satisfaction. It's like seeing a baby grow. I really feel as if it is my child. And I have the feeling I will have an easier time with that child than with my own."

By July, 1975, Gary Johnson decided to try nursing. "I knew that Betty felt that nursing was unique because it dealt with the whole person, not just the physical side, not just the social world, but all of it together. When that hit me, it became obvious to me then that nursing was it." The clincher was a course he took that summer at UBC in microbiology.

His wife, coolly noncommital at first, not wanting to influence him one way or another, now pledged her whole-hearted support.

"I think she really wanted the decision to be all mine," he said. "At times she was even a little negative but once I decided, she helped me to write the applications."

Betty interrupted, "I knew he was serious then. No one would bother to go to the trouble of applying unless he really meant it. I realized it wasn't a lark."

"I felt," said Gary, "that you would have said something if you felt that I was heading in the wrong direction or if things didn't look too good. But I felt you were saying, in effect, 'You are not too happy here so it should be your decision because if I influence you and the decision is not right, it will be too easy to blame me.'"

His colleagues were appalled when they finally discovered his intentions. At one point Gary asked his chairman for a letter of recommendation. "Fine," he said. "Just tell me where I send it." Gary told him. "What kind of job is open there?" Gary said he wasn't applying for a job, he was going to nursing school.

"I had really been closemouthed about my plans and it was a definite shock for him. He kept shaking his head and asking me if I were sure. He asked if I had completely given up on landing a job in a computer science department. He couldn't conceive that I could be doing this except out of desperation."

The next year, the period of his terminal appointment, they slashed their living expenses drastically. Hamburger arrived on the dinner table in 101 disguises. They lived on her salary and banked his $20,000 a year salary toward the time he would be in nursing school. He taught during the day and took courses in anatomy and physiology at night. Juggling teaching and studying was easier than he had anticipated. Once he decided to change careers, he found tremendous energy was released.

Their plan was simple. The family would draw on their savings for a year while Gary went to nursing school and Betty looked for a job. Chance simplified things even further. Among the schools which Gary Johnson visited to discuss their nursing program was the University of Portland. The school needed a new nursing instructor and when Gary mentioned that his wife taught nursing at the University of British Columbia, they were more than casually interested. The school admitted Gary and hired Betty. Since Gary was now dependent on Betty for financial support, his tuition was waived.

Gary enrolled as a first-year nursing student at the University of Portland in September, 1975.

He had dared to dive into the darkness of the mid-life crisis, to discover the missing elements of his self, to restructure his life into a more satisfying shape and to surface at last on the other side. By facing up to his real self instead of struggling to be his parents' idealized self, Gary broke free to be his own person. He could give himself permission to lead his own life. This kind of self-approval is usually hard won but in the end comes, not exhaustion, but a tremendous spurt of enthusiasm.

The result in Gary's case?

"I'm more accepting of myself for whom I really am. Before I accepted parts of myself, the good and perfect so to speak. I liked the bright and logical parts of myself but I denied the illogical and the intuitive. Now it all fits together. I've found that the other parts of myself are also worthwhile. In fact, in some ways, like for what I'm studying now, they are even more valuable. They are enormously helpful in empathizing with patients."

I should be . . . yet I am. . . . Yes, we've heard it before. But Gary was beginning to fuse those separate parts of himself into one whole.

"He's happier," said Betty. "A jillion, jillion times happier than I've ever seen him since the first year we met. He just looks happy."

To be sure, it's hard to accept ourselves if our self-image stretches just so far and then snaps back before it encompasses the remaining personality parts. The search for those repressed parts and the desire to live out those aspects of ourselves manifest themselves in mid-life, mid-career changes. The changes are not always as radical as Gary's switch. More often they are a 15-degree correction of course rather than a 180-degree swing.

This is an important point: not all of these neglected aspects are linked to sexual stereotypes. There is evidence that men become more nurturing and women more assertive in mid-life but mid-career changes are not merely a matter of men enrolling in nursing school and women donning hard hats. Sometimes it is just that simple but most often it is a more subtle relationship. In our twenties we reach certain decisions about our lives and each subsequent choice tends to further solidify previous decisions. The decade of the twenties is spent walking down corridors and hearing doors bang shut. If we take a pre-med course in college we are likely to continue to medical school and a medical degree is a powerful incentive toward a lifetime of adherence to the Hippocratic Oath. If we spend our twenties in maternity wards, we are not likely to go to law school for the next fifteen years. Remember Iver Brook, for instance. Every decision of his twenties and thirties carried him further along the trajectory of the successful businessman and further away from the pattern of the naturalist. Only after twenty some years could Iver Brook call a halt and double back to start to claim the life he originally wanted. Sometimes it is not repressed personality traits or submerged interests that demand recognition at this point but a whole new life form. The stories of the Gauguins of the world, the middle-aged, middle-class men who shed their homes, family and business for the free-wheeling life of the artist or vagabond, have been told so often that they have become commonplace. Yet, they continue to happen and to fascinate. Carol Anderson, for example, is compelling because she was able to shuck her shell of security for a free-form life. In the early and middle 1970s articles on middle-aged dropouts, the second generation greening of America, became a staple in such publications as the *Wall Street Journal*. Less often reported are the stories of the free spirits who suddenly send down roots. Still I encountered them in my research. The need to envelop the other side of ourselves, whatever that may be, is universal now. Sometimes these transient people simply take longer than most to form commitments. They wander through the first part of their lives, unwilling to invest themselves emotionally, hopping from job to job, city to city, seeking experiences. At mid-life they abruptly find themselves rushing to marry, to have children, to own businesses and take on mortgages. One woman I talked to, Christi Finch, wandered foot loose and fancy free from the small town of Lincoln, Oregon, to Greenwich Village in New York City. In her thirties she abruptly settled down without ever making a conscious decision to do so. Today she is co-owner of a food store on New York City's chic Upper East Side.* Other people who experience this about-face are writers and artists. At age forty they find they care more about security and less about unbridled creativity. David Goldstein in chapter three was like that.

I tested this observation on William Pilder who, as president of Mainstream Associates, counsels a wide variety of clients. He confirmed it. "We have a number of clients who lived through the greening of America in the 1960s and now want back into the mainstream," he said. "Their attitude is: the sixties were great but they are over. We learned a good deal and had a lot of fun. Now how do we use all of this in the corporate world. They want structure and a sense of meaningfulness in society."

In short, there are a variety of recurrent themes in our lives which demand to be heard and finally played.

In Gary Johnson's case the authenticity crises of middle

* Christi's story is told in chapter six.

life detonated all at once. The same event precipitated both his mid-career and mid-life surveys and the decision to switch careers was reached swiftly in a matter of months.

Usually it takes longer. What then?

The slow evolution of Barbara Blaes from homemaker to successful businesswoman provides some illuminating answers. By following Barbara's twists and turns we can get a better idea of the challenges that confront people as they think through the decision to change careers.

A portrait of Barbara Blaes at forty-nine. Serenely self-confident, totally self-possessed, she moves through her days without a single misplaced strand to ruffle her upswept blonde hair. Not one chip spoils the brilliance of the lacquered finish of her lavender pink fingernails that coordinate perfectly with her lavender blouse. Her navy blue suit matches her navy blue high-heeled shoes. She wears the "woman's dress for success" look well which is understandable since, as the owner of Barbara Blaes and Associates in Washington, D.C., she advises her clients on achieving it.

A portrait of Barbara Blaes at thirty-one. She was a housewife in suburban Baltimore, Maryland. Married at the age of twenty-one, she was a mother for the first time at twenty-three and two other children followed in rapid succession. She had a hot-shot engineer husband, a family and a chronic case of housewife-itis.

The portraits of the two women are difficult to merge into one complete person. In between lie nearly two decades of painful personal growth and a rewoven social fabric. Women have come a long way and Barbara Blaes has kept pace with them.

When she read *The Feminine Mystique*, her discontent was distilled into a burning fever. One day she found herself stalking around a friend's kitchen, muttering, "There must be more. There just has to be more." The neighborhood coffee klatches, the bridge clubs, the community improvement association, all the trappings of suburban living which housewives use to fill up their days, were not the sort of things that could provide her with a sense of meaning or resolve. Years later she could look back and say, "I had a gnawing feeling of being unfulfilled. What I had was not enough."

Barbara Blaes didn't understand the import of the feelings that now engulfed her but she was embarking on her mid-life crisis. Her purpose in life, the three children she had borne and begun to raise, were now in school most of the day. They were slipping away from her and shepherding their comings and goings was not enough to provide the mainstay of an intelligent woman's time.

This is the typical sequence of the woman who is now over thirty-five. It is the way they are affected by the sexual transformations of mid-life. A woman who has channeled her energies into pursuit of a career is not so differently situated at this point than a man is. She is apt to discover to her surprise that her generative, nurturing impulses finally demand expression. The managerial women, remember, froze their careers at this point and bought dancing shoes. These women, however, are comparatively rare in the over-thirty-five age group. The woman who is now struggling through her mid-life transition tended to embrace the all-American dream of his and her towels and two children to match. As far back as 1964 the Department of Labor reported that nine out of ten women would work twenty-five years in their lifetimes but most women clung stubbornly, against all facts to the contrary, to the belief that they would be the tenth woman.

A woman who decides to be a wife and mother is by definition choosing to subordinate her needs and desires to the needs and desires of others. Strep throats and cross-country moves, Cub Scouts and dinners for potential clients sap energies and the shuttle that suburban women run from the commuter train to the elementary school to the dry cleaners to the piano lessons and home again eat so many holes into the day that it resembles a chunk of Swiss cheese.

When that last child is no longer underfoot, the woman who has chosen others over herself can say at last: and now for me. She not only can, she must. The fundamental problem as these women approach their forties is the necessity of forming new commitments to replace the ones they have lost. A woman who declared herself AWOL in her late thirties and signed up for a career development course said, "When I married my husband, I promised I would work to help him through college, but I didn't know how far he would go! After three degrees (his), fifteen moves (mine) and six children (ours), I am ready for new horizons." Another woman who in her early forties shed her husband and formed a business that has brought her national recognition said, "Most of my growth began after I turned thirty-five."

This kind of growth unfortunately has a price. All of the women who abandoned homemaking for better-paying jobs outside the house began their growing in the midst of a mid-life crisis. This is not to say that men don't sometimes arrive at the decision to change careers by experiencing a mid-life crisis. But for these women it was always the case.

Sociologist Bernice Neugarten writes, "Important differences exist between men and women as they age. Men seem to become more receptive to affiliative and nurturant promptings; women, more responsive toward and less guilty about, aggressive and egocentric impulses."[2]

For Barbara this surge of personal power was enough to carry her straight out her front door and into the business world. But her sense of adventure was tempered by fear of the source of her attraction. She started out slowly.

"At that point I wasn't really thinking seriously of a career, of something that progresses in stages toward some point and that climbs upward. I wanted to be something a little creative and a little challenging and put the kids in good private schools. That was about all."

The headmaster of a private school nearby advertised in the community newspaper for a secretary. When Barbara spotted the ad, she grabbed at it as if it were a parachute and hung on for her life. Driving up the long tree-lined path to the school, she was so frightened that her hands shook on the steering wheel.

"I really didn't know if any one would want to hire me. I hadn't worked in ten years and I only worked as a secretary for a short time before I got married and started to raise a family."

The headmaster hired her. "I could scarcely believe my good fortune."

When Barbara was a child, she had an older sister. The two girls got tagged as they do in many families. The sister was "the bright one" who made the honor roll. Barbara was "the fun one" who took her mascara on camping trips. While her sister collected A's, Barbara learned to use a lip brush and practiced curling her eyelashes. "I was considered a nice little girl but not very smart about things." And, in fact, a lot of school work did not come easily. Her schoolteacher mother tried to tutor her in math: if 5 apples cost 10 cents, what is the cost of 10 apples? Barbara, a forlorn figure huddled at the kitchen table with her dog-eared math book, strained to figure the answer. After a while she stopped trying so hard. The subliminal message was: Barbara isn't expected to succeed. "I was one of those women who grew up believing they were not particularly competent at anything."

No wonder then that she dropped out of Western Maryland State after two years because she had no clear career goals and went to secretarial school instead. Her marriage was an instant replay of her relationship in the home of her parents. "My husband was always seen as the brilliant engineer." Barbara was just the wife who cleared away the dinner plates; just the mother who bandaged scraped knees.

Barbara's youngest child was nine when she went to work. "After eight years it came time for all of us to graduate." Barbara was ready for more.

"Getting a job and finding I could do things was very satisfying. That I could handle a difficult job and do it well was a heady experience. It was hard to put that knowledge aside, to not want to continue."

Doubts had begun to surface about her life. Barbara was no longer content to be just a wife and just a mother. Her last child was packing for college. One career was ended. She wanted a replacement. A taste of independence is a dangerous thing. Barbara craved bigger and tougher challenges. The restrictions of her life in suburbia chafed more than ever.

Unfortunately, Barbara's need to test herself in the outside world collided head on with her husband's need to have a helpmate inside the home.

"A way of life had been established and it was totally acceptable to my husband. It was difficult for him to realize that there could be another way."

Barbara was growing up. Her new-found independence was yeast to her life. She was developing a self-concept that was not dependent on her relationships. Her new self-image could not squeeze into the old roles. Barbara Blaes was coming into her own. She had been running around the same track for twenty some years. Now she was eager to try a new course.

Her husband balked. He was happy with the way they were.

"I started evaluating things. It got to the point where I began to question if I was in the correct role (as a wife). It is very difficult to begin a sincere and serious commitment to a project when everybody around thinks of you as a not terribly serious person. Sometimes you have to remove yourself from the situation."

The problem was easily defined. She could go forward without her husband or she could go backward with him. The solution was not so simple. In the end Barbara Blaes made a wrenching decision. She would move ahead. Alone.

She left her husband and moved to Washington, D.C. She was lucky in one respect. Her children, all of them by now in college, cheered her on.

"I looked upon the move as adventure and freedom. It was terribly exciting. At the same time I was scared to death. It was very frightening."

Barbara knew what she was leaving behind. She had no idea what she was heading toward. But she was absolutely, unequivocably committed to becoming her own person. She was forty-four years old. Her only previous jobs had been as a secretary. She had never earned very much money and now she was competing against women with longer résumés and fewer lines on their faces.

Her first job was as a newsletter writer and administrative assistant for a trade association. Such jobs are not too difficult to come by in Washington since the salaries are generally so low that the people move on as rapidly as possible.

"I got tired of typing the speeches. I wanted to be making them instead."

Barbara had taught modeling and make-up courses off and on. In Washington she encountered a woman who, like her, put on mascara to take out the garbage. The two of them teamed up to start Ms.Tique. (The partnership has since been dissolved and the name changed to Barbara Blaes and Associates.) The idea behind the business was simple. To get ahead a woman had to look as if she commanded a solid mahogany desk and a Bigelow on the floor. Too many women did not.

The business would help professional women, as the company literature puts it, wear "a handsome look of quality, authority and imagination." Women who looked their best, the partners believed, would have more confidence. Even more important, women who were attractive and dressed well were expected to succeed and as they did, they would acquire even more assurance. A positive, self-perpetuating cycle would be established.

To accomplish this, the program embraces clothes, make-up, hair styles, body language including gestures, facial expression, eye contact and handshaking, speech and job interviewing techniques.

"I've ended up taking a lot of peripheral interests and skills which in themselves would never be a career—make-up, writing and public speaking—and managed to combine them into a business."

The women opened Ms.Tique by ordering business cards and placing a small ad in a community newspaper. "I just hoped somebody would answer it." They did and told others. Barbara began to land consulting jobs from the federal government. The Y.W.C.A. hired her to teach a course. Local television shows invited her to be a guest. Her business grew geometrically. Now she divides her time between individual clients and seminars for private businesses, the federal government and department stores.

The before and after photographs of her clients are startling. Photo one: Hand on a hip thrust forward, she is a mass of angles and awkward planes. Her hair is scrunched into a wispy top knot. She wears a knitted sweater across which Scottie dogs march, a skirt above her knees, several bangle bracelets, two long necklaces, hoop earrings and no make-up. Photo two: Her hair is now frizzed into a soft Afro. Lipstick glistens. The hoop earrings remain but the rest of the jewelry has vanished. A dark jacket and softly tied light-colored blouse match the striped skirt that ends well below her knees. And she is smiling broadly, head thrown back jauntily, chin jutting forward, obviously pleased with herself and her world. A woman who looked as if she had just stepped out of the typing pool appears now to be a sleekly polished junior executive.

It sounds easy and in a way it was. "The timing was very important. Ten or fifteen years ago we would never have succeeded. We happened at the right time. The media coverage that we got was tremendously important. In this kind of business one thing leads to another. It's not the kind of business where $100,000 is needed to get started. We could begin small and grow."

As the business developed, she gradually reduced the time she spent at the trade association but she still goes in two days a week. Her job there provided a temporary financial cushion. "My most serious decision was to leave the job full time and to cut my salary in half." That lost income has since been recouped but not without effort.

The business which now has her traveling around the country and collecting $200 an hour while doing so did not come to her automatically. Barbara had to pick up the telephone and schedule the appointments that landed the work. She had to offer to appear on TV shows around the country. "One of the challenging things about this business is that you have to sell yourself as well as the business." That comes from a woman whose hands once shook when she applied for a typing job. The girl who had difficulty mastering simple arithmetic now keeps the books of her own business and sets her own consulting fees.

The troublesome part was accepting that challenge. "What I've learned is: I don't have to be perfect. I can make mistakes. If I've never done something before, why should I have to be perfect the first time?"

Too many people freeze in their lives through the sheer terror that they might make a mistake. The problem is that the result of that fear is stagnation. The important thing to remember is that few mistakes can't be corrected and even fewer are irrevocable. As for looking foolish. . . . Most people are too busy maintaining their own balance to notice when we fall. Only by accepting our imperfections and owning up to our fallibility can we seize our future. If we can allow ourselves the freedom to make mistakes, we can continue to grow and to learn. Mid-life can be the spring thaw that releases our fullest potential.

One day in 1977 Barbara Blaes received a notice in her apartment mail box. Her building was being converted into condominiums. Barbara applied for a mortgage to buy her unit. And she was turned down. The loan officer decided her financial future was too shaky to secure their investment. Barbara set up an appointment with a bank official. Then she gathered up the material she had prepared about Barbara Blaes and Associates and her portfolio of before-and-after photographs. With them under her arm she marched into the bank and gulped. Hard. The old insecurities reared up again.

"I was scared to death when I went in but I was absolutely determined I would convince him that I was a good credit risk. I've never felt such a *tremendous* determination."

The meeting was a triumph. Her enthusiasm was contagious. The loan officer was swept away by the business' potential. The bank reversed its previous decision and approved the mortgage.

"I told him what I knew I could do and when I walked out with that mortgage, it was the most glorious feeling of my lifetime."

The mortgage became a symbol. Somehow the loan and the future of her business merged together in her mind. She had convinced a bank official that her business would prosper and in the process strengthened her own resolve to succeed. The mortgage was not just a financial investment in a piece of real estate. It represented an emotional investment in her business. If her seriousness of purpose and commitment to success had wavered in the past, it did no longer.

"It is so tempting to hide in the kitchen or behind the typewriter. Sometimes I wake up in the middle of the night and say to myself: what have I done? The old urge for security and stability is still there. And I still feel the temptation to flee back to that kind of security, a nice job with a paid-for Blue Cross policy and a retirement plan."

The fact is that in most major life decisions something is lost and something is gained. Whatever happens in this case belongs to Barbara Blaes. If she fails, the blame rests squarely with her but if she succeeds, the credit is singularly hers. At forty-nine Barbara Blaes is totally and completely in command of her life. The urge for security and stability, for a protector and buffer against the world, for a job with group medical insurance and a retirement plan, dies hard and still occasionally gasps for life deep within her. These are the tangible things she has given up. The exhilaration of setting her own schedule, the thrill of planning her own life, the intoxicating experience of creating herself moment by moment are the intangible things she has gained. The trade-off is immediately apparent only to those who have chosen, as Barbara did, to forge out on their own. Barbara readily defines the rewards of her choice:

*In your own business nothing about it is deadening or
stultifying. In your own business there is no limit to what you
can accomplish. In most businesses routine after a while begins
to limit you. There is no routine in running your own business.
When I worked for other people, all my efforts went toward
enhancing someone else's career. Now I work only for myself.
To take charge, as I did, demands a certain audacity that is
almost trained out of women. I was lucky. I was able to reclaim
it.*

This high speed pursuit of the missing parts of ourselves
which sends us careening down the roads not taken earlier
is a way that the mid-life crisis propels people into mid-career
changes.

Another way that decision is reached is in a final sprint
toward career goals, toward that elusive dream before it is too
late. "A rats in the belly feeling that it is now or never," said
a man about his career drive in his late thirties. "Being forty,"
said another, "is like having New Year's Eve every day." At
forty, even at forty-five, there is still time to get ahead. After
that we start hearing, as Andrew Marvell wrote in importuning
his reluctant lady friend to tarry no longer, "time's winged
chariot hurrying near."

There are parallels between the mid-life and mid-career
crises that explain how a person can begin at both starting
points and arrive at the same place. At the center of the mid-
life crisis is the awareness of our own mortality, that first
glimpse of death ahead. At the heart of the mid-career crisis
is another kind of dying, the metaphorical death of our
youthful aspirations. Either way it happens the result is a
feeling of stagnation, of numbness, of despair best summed
up by the refrain, "Is this all there is or ever will be?"

Consider the slow dying of hope that lies behind these
bare statistics:[3]

- At age thirty-eight over 50 percent of men confidently *predict*
  that they will continue to be promoted.
- At age forty most still *aspire* to advance occupationally but
  doubts are beginning to flicker.

- At age forty-eight fewer than 20 percent *expect* that they will be promoted.
- And by age fifty less than 20 percent even *hope* that their careers are not permanently stalled.

As the men get older, they lower first their expectations about success and then their hopes for further achievement. When they reach fifty, they have divided into three roughly equal groups: slightly over one-third who achieved their early aspirations, a few more who expected to reach their career goals and a final third who either lowered their hopes or switched both their field of work and their aspirations.

Men—and women—who haven't yet grasped the brass ring and are determined to keep on reaching are caught in a muddle. Work is where we create our identity so that we are more next week than we were last. But the older a person is the less likely he is to have that opportunity. The chances for promotion diminish with age and most jobs do not offer unlimited possibilities for expansion. Sooner or later they become mundane, routine, tiresome. In the person who is still bent on achieving, a restless vitality sets in.

About this time he is likely to hoist himself out of the container he is in and to replant himself in a new career. A primary difference between the people who change careers and the people who stay put is the need to continue to achieve. Harold L. Sheppard confirmed my own observation in his interviews with 210 white collar workers.[4] He found that people who expressed an interest in second careers were set apart in two fundamental ways. They had a higher need to achieve and the distance between their aspirations and their actual accomplishments was greater.

Radical career changes are a contemporary phenomenon but such shifts have always been surprisingly common in the lives of super-achievers. Such people seem to crave new experiences in new arenas. They have never possessed a gold watch mentality. Driven by an irrepressible curiosity and a quicksilver intellect, they shed the carapaces of their careers in order to keep growing and achieving. Even if Henry

Kissinger had not been tapped to be Secretary of State, for instance, it is difficult to imagine that he would have been content to live out his life as professor of government at Harvard University. A sampling of several hundred super-achievers who were listed in *Who's Who* over the last twenty-one years turned up surprisingly consistent results.[5] In each of the periods which were studied, between 39 and 42 percent of the entrants had changed careers. Professors became deans. Reporters edited the newspapers for which they had once covered the police beat. Lawyers ran for public office. Not all of these changes are radical career changes in the sense I am talking about but even by this definition some 8 to 9 percent switched from one professional field to another. The hallmark of successful people may very well be the inability to stay put.

A second career postpones into the distant future and sometimes forever the confrontation between the dreamed-of self and the real self at mid-life. It offers protection, sort of a camouflage for the soul.

The bitch goddess success is the name that Norman Mailer appended to the most widely revered of all contemporary icons. Our belief in the efficacy of success is as total as our ancestors' conviction that the Kingdom of Heaven could be reached through prayer. Despite overwhelming evidence to the contrary, we believe that in success lies safety. The next rung of the ladder will transport us into that magical realm. If we realize standing there on the newly reached step that we are still the same old "me" and are disappointed, we conclude that we simply haven't climbed high enough. One more rung should surely do it. The children of the bitch goddess success—money, fame, power, position—will protect us like sentinels at the gate.

Psychiatrist Roger Gould who has studied the illusion which we cart around explains, "Many men see work success as the route to immunity from death. I am not talking about the products of their work or their children living after them as the symbolic route to survival after death. Rather, those of us who are most shocked by the awareness of our own mortality had a pact with the world: if we continued to be good boys and worked hard, if we sacrificed and succeeded, the fear that we would be annihilated, which terrorized us as little boys, was never to return again."[6]

Paradoxically, each victory, instead of confirming our faith in this belief, only succeeds in chipping away at it bit by bit.

"This disillusionment with work as a magical protection against death reaches a critical awareness level in the mid-life decade," continues Gould. "When it ceases to function, when we feel the cold breath of death on our neck, we experience the demonic dread that it protected us against; in this way, work and the fear of death are intimately related."

At the center of the mid-life crisis, as I have said, death is curled up and waiting. In the middle of many career changes is the desire to escape this confrontation. The outcome of stripping away the illusion of invincibility can be an acceptance of our own mortality and an opening up to the hidden recesses in us. Another course is also possible. The conclusion may be that the conviction was right but the work was wrong. When the world refuses to validate our convictions, our response is often to conclude that the belief was right but the particular application of it was wrong. So it is with many people who change careers. If the first career doesn't offer the magic protective cloak, then perhaps the second one will. Piecing the old illusion back together, the person who changes careers may drape it on a new enterprise.

The story of Semih Ustun, a naturalized American, the Turkish born son of a diplomat, illustrates a number of these points. His office is in Chevy Chase, Maryland, but that is the last place he is apt to be. He may be testing the almond croissants at the Vie de France bakeries in Rockville, Maryland. Ustun is president of the bread company. He may be scouting out houses in Washington, D.C., which can be restored by Capitol Hill Management. Ustun is president of the realty company. But he may, just as likely, be sitting on the terrace of the Kenwood Country Club sipping a Bloody

Mary and listening to the shrieks of children in the swimming pool.

"I don't have to be in the office," he said. "The bakers are baking bread at Vie de France. The women at Capitol Hill Management are answering the telephones, renting apartments. The architects are working on a new project. Lots of things are happening but I don't have to be involved. It's all working to my benefit and I sit here in the sunlight."

It wasn't always like that, of course.

Ustun expected to follow his father and join the Turkish foreign service but World War II intervened. When the war started, the Ustuns were trapped in Washington, D.C., where Semih's father was the press attaché at the Turkish embassy. Semih enrolled at George Washington University there and eventually gravitated into the civil service in the United States.

As an undergraduate Ustun won a play-writing contest which was sponsored by the Voice of America. When the agency discovered that he was fluent in Turkish as well as English, he was offered a job. He started as a GS-8, making $4,200 a year in 1951, in the foreign-language section. He went on to be a writer and a producer of documentaries. When he left twenty-one years later, he was a GS-14 and an editor in the central features service which disseminates feature stories and cultural news abroad.

"The Voice of America more than any other government agency gives room for development and satisfaction. I did the kind of things that were very challenging for me. When I was writing documentaries, I was totally free and I covered a lot of events that were of interest to me. I was quite happy. I could go only so far as a writer, however. A real limit was built into the system. In order to get promoted, I had to give up writing and become an editor. That was painful and it became somewhat boring."

Ustun was stymied. Within the bureaucracy his writing skills and past achievements were no basis for advancement in his craft. Move up and accept routine or stay put and be creative were his choices and neither was particularly appealing. In his case promotion meant that he actually achieved less by his standards.

Ustun began to seek new outlets for his creativity and to focus his career ambitions into new directions. At the tell-tale age of thirty-seven, he started dabbling in the volatile Washington, D.C. real estate market, buying empty shells and run-down houses, restoring and reselling them at a handsome profit. Over a period of seven years he renovated nine houses. Reaching out for new challenges, he still valued the old stability.

"It was very nice to have the security and the satisfaction of a job and after 5:30 P.M. and on Saturdays and Sundays I had plenty of time to take care of my real estate ventures."

The real push began when he was forty-three. Two friends asked if Ustun would like to embark on a joint venture to make authentic French bread in the United States. Ustun flashed back to Orly Airport in the summer of 1968 when he and his wife were returning from a vacation in Paris. As they boarded the airplane, two teenage American girls, carrying armloads of baguettes, darted aboard. He had thought then: how sad good bread isn't available back in the States. He told them he would love to help bake French bread. *Naturellement*.

Among Washingtonians and gourmets everywhere the tale of Vie de France has become legendary. It has all the elements of a sure-fire thriller. A Vietnamese national and a Defense Department employee whose position is so sensitive that he is referred to in print as Mr. X, daydreaming after a tennis set about that chewy, crusty, fragrant and utterly unobtainable French bread. The search for a French baker who would be willing to come to the United States to teach the art of baking bread. The zany drives across town in the middle of the night to pizza ovens where they could bake the bread that the Frenchman had just finished shaping.

The successful combination of the right flour mixture, water, salt and yeast was finally achieved only after the baker had returned to France. The baker telegraphed one word "*Voilà!*" The partners signed a one-year contract with the

Frenchman who would be an advisor and leased 2,600 square feet of space in Rockville for a bakery. They also bought a French oven which required six months of negotiations to import and then sat in a warehouse while dock workers struck. After the oven reached Rockville, it had to be assembled like a stone jigsaw puzzle.

On May 5, 1972, the first 353 crispy, golden brown loaves in the traditional baguette shape emerged from the ovens. The men had already arranged to market the bread first in liquor stores and wine and cheese shops. Sales to the city's leading French restaurants quickly followed. Three months later the only problem was to produce the bread fast enough to meet the demand. Other French bakeries, started by Frenchmen who were trained in the Vie de France tradition, have since opened in the Washington area but for years Ustun and friends enjoyed a virtual monopoly on the tables of lovers of good bread. The Vie de France loaves were so good that in those early days normally sedate suburban housewives came to blows in supermarket aisles over the last baguette and homesick French nationals were said to burst into tears at first bite.

Like many naturalized citizens, Ustun believed passionately that the United States was a land of opportunity. But that opportunity would not be there forever, not for a man of his age and Ustun realized it. Ustun signed up for one last race to the top. He invested everything he had in it. Younger men may have more energy but the adrenalin flows faster in middle-aged men who know the race is almost over.

Ustun was spending sixty hours a week on Vie de France while he continued to work at Voice of America and to juggle his real estate projects. On Saturdays he retreated into his den and wrote the checks to pay the bills so the business would survive. Ustun worked like a man possessed. He was a typical example of the now or never mentality. A dervish could not have been more seized.

Finally he quit Voice of America to concentrate almost all his time and more of his energies at Vie de France. Why did he rearrange his life at precisely that point in time?

*I had to. I suppose my age forty crisis hit at forty-four. I felt
I had to leave Voice of America because my position there had
begun to hold me back. My business interests required me to
move around and Voice of America required me to be in an
office eight hours a day. The two were no longer compatible.
It was an enormous struggle. I had two children and a wife and
a mortgage and a car with installment payments but I felt the
time had come. I felt that in a couple of years Vie de France
would be enough of a success to make the financial sacrifice
worthwhile. I had a cushion from my real estate investments
but it's not the same as drawing a pay check every week.*

The first year the company couldn't afford to pay him a
salary. The Ustuns lived on savings while Vie de France
borrowed money in order to expand. In 1973 a bakery was
opened in Boston followed rapidly by Philadelphia, Atlanta
and Denver. In two years they launched five bakeries in that
many states.

Semih Ustun went to Vie de France expecting that he
would be the creative force in the company. Instead he
suddenly found himself in charge of 50 people and that the
staff kept multiplying until there were 200 employees. "Everyone became my personal responsibility in one way or another."
Flow charts, computer programs and personnel manuals
swirled past his desk. "They were difficult years for me. I was
forced to learn. I had to be an entrepreneur and a manager."
Ustun moved nimbly from one part of the business to another,
coordinating the individual pieces into one whole like an
impresario.

Vie de France has continued to grow. Its annual business
volume is 5.5 million and its net worth is over $2.5 million.
A substantial chunk of the stock is owned by Ustun.

Still he dreams. His sustaining vision is of a bigger and
better Vie de France. More bakeries, new products, retail
outlets, cafés, new lines of wine, pâté and French ice cream.
In 1979 Ustun presided over the opening of the first restaurant.

"I envisioned a $100 million a year corporation. It may
take about five years but I think that is a good goal. The
conception of an idea and bringing it to reality and creating

profits in the process appeals to me. If I was offered a job at General Motors that paid $1 million a year, I wouldn't be interested. I always want to remain in spirit an entrepreneur."

The sixty-hour weeks have paid a handsome return. The driving force has relented a little and at fifty Semih Ustun can sit in the sun for a few hours in the middle of the week and do nothing without stabs of guilt. Capturing the brass ring wins one ride free.

Nothing is as contagious as enthusiasm on the one hand and boredom on the other. The more we do, the more we are interested in doing and the less we do, the less ambition we have to do anything at all. In recharging his professional life, Ustun revved up his personal life as well. The effect spills over. The day that Ustun and I talked he had been searching the record stores for new Mozart recordings to add to his collection. Admittedly, few fifty-year-old men can spend their days in record stores but the unfortunate truth is not very many would want to. People who walk the same route for years eventually discover they have lost interest in detours.

"I have developed some new interests lately which I am making time for. I think everybody seeks, I suppose, to be free to pursue happiness. The pursuit of happiness in my case is to understand a little more about the world and the people in it. I have a lot of books I intend to read and a lot of music I want to hear. You can afford to seek these things if you have time. Success offers these choices and time, well, only God gives you that."

Ustun has rediscovered writing lately. There's a mystery novel that he is plotting in his head as he pilots his brown Cadillac Seville around town. The setting, appropriately enough, is a French bakery.

The richness and diversity of Semih Ustun's life is typical of people who dare to listen to the subterranean voice that whispers now, now, now is all there is.

Part
THREE

First Moves 6

We work for quite different reasons in our twenties than we do in our forties and the thirties is the decade when this transformation usually takes place. In our twenties we lust after the applause of the world. We want fame, recognition, success, power, wealth. We try to fulfill a heroic conception of ourselves. In our forties we grow content to hear the sound of our own hands clapping. We seek opportunities to grow, to utilize our talents, to express ourselves. We look for new experiences and hope to leave an impact on the corner of the world that we inhabit.

Once when I worked for a newspaper, I shared a city room with a reporter who hungered for success. Both of us were in our twenties, still young and innocent enough that the sharing of our inmost yearnings caused no embarrassment. My fellow reporter, who shall remain nameless, wasn't particular about the wrapper that fame came in. It could be the Pulitzer Prize. It might be a best-seller. Either would do because what he sought was not so much recognition for his accomplishments but awareness of his existence.

His hero was Jimmy Breslin, the newspaper reporter turned novelist turned celebrity, and one morning after Breslin appeared on the "Tonight" show, two of us found our friend slumped in a chair in the cafeteria, staring morosely at a cup of coffee.

"Why can't I be like Jimmy Breslin?" he asked.

My cohort and I exchanged a glance and converged on our would-be Breslin.

Why, we demanded, was success so important to him?

Because he wanted to be famous.

Why did he want to be famous?

So he could go on the "Tonight" show and meet interesting people and make a lot of money.

Then what?

"I would be able to tell anybody I want to go to Hell."

My friend is in his late thirties now. He has just completed his third book and the first two, even if they didn't earn a million dollars in royalties, received respectable reviews. Between books he writes for some of the country's leading magazines. He is establishing a growing reputation as a serious and talented writer. He has a better than even chance of entering that select circle of writers who trade barbs with Johnny Carson and grace the best-seller lists.

The funny thing is he no longer cares so intensely. The tyranny of success has loosened its grip. He now takes pride in his writing ability and is happy to partake of the adventures that his book and magazine assignments offer. He grimaces when he recalls that long ago incident. "Well," he says sheepishly, "I was much younger then."

This new definition of work comes out of the mid-life and mid-career crises. Some people like my writer friend are able to infuse new meanings into their existing work. More often the revised purpose of work becomes the fulcrum around which career changes are made. People can and, of course, do change careers at any age. The ones that I talked to ranged in age from thirty-four to fifty-five. But the mid-point of life is the most favored time. Consider these statistics:

Forty is the age at which American Baptist ministers are most likely to leave the church.

Of United Church of Christ ministers who quit the parish, 49.9 percent did so between the ages of thirty-five and forty-nine.

Late thirties is the median age of clients at Mainstream Associates, a counseling service in New York City which advises people on changing careers.

When teachers were asked "What would you most like to be doing ten years from now?" women between the age of thirty-five and forty and men between the age of forty and forty-five most often picked the answer "To get a different job." These age variations are consistent with the differences in the onset of the mid-life crisis for women and men.[1]

Men changed careers more often at the age of forty than at any other single time between thirty-three and fifty-four, according to an American Management Association report. And more than 33 percent of the sample abandoned their original careers between forty and forty-four.[2]

Now, to fill in the details. . . .

That work should acquire a new place and purpose in our lives as a result of the developmental crises of mid-life is scarcely surprising. Work and identity are too closely fused for it to be otherwise. People find their identity through their work and use their occupation to express themselves. Careers are a personal statement which is the reason that the comment "I am *just* a housewife" is such a sad commentary on the women who make it. Occupations are handy identification tags. Social and cultural expectations exist about people who pursue various careers. These assumptions lie behind the inevitable first question of new acquaintances: what do you do? The answer reveals more about a person than where he hangs his coat in the morning.

Work is an extension of the self which enables us to put down roots and send out shoots to connect us and the outside world. This is true whether the work takes place in an office or a home, whether those connections are to the American Medical Association, the Junior Chamber of Commerce or the P.T.A., whether those connected with are professional colleagues or the mothers in Susie's play group. The impulse to expand and to associate is so strong that people whose work demands solitude tend to gravitate to writers' and artists' colonies where they can find sympathetic souls at day's end.

The paradox is this. Although work and identity are inextricably linked, we rarely choose our occupations. More often they are chosen for us or they result from pure happenstance. It occurs when our self-identity is still unformed, when we are too inexperienced to project our talents and interests into the world of work. We must choose before we have gained enough judgment or self-knowledge to know the right activity for us.

Father was a lawyer and since he wants a child in the family firm, we go to law school. Mother was a teacher and since she finds satisfaction in introducing high school sophomores to *Silas Marner*, we get a teaching certificate. The family construction business awaits and we join it. We have a liberal arts degree which qualifies us for almost everything in general and nothing in particular and when the local insurance company has an opening, we seize it. We are pressured, we drift and somehow we end up selling real estate, in the civil service, on the staff of the local newspaper.

We have little time to seek out and test the possibilities that might tempt us if we only knew of their existence. Society prescribes that a man must complete this search and settle into an occupation by the age of twenty-six at the latest.[3]

Choice in the dictionary sense of selecting the best of a range of alternatives is conspicuous by its absence from career decisions. In a *Psychology Today* survey 40 percent said they happened into their present occupations and another 16 percent said they settled for their occupations because they couldn't find a job in their preferred field. Only 23 percent deliberately and consciously chose their present employment.[4]

When our personalities finally coalesce into their adult outlines, our careers may have little to do with the grownup we have become. In the shock of this recognition the decision to change careers begins.

Changes in our attitudes toward work herald the switch to come. The survey that Louis Harris undertook documented a transformation in social values which has provided a cultivating medium for career changes. The whole phenomenon of career switches represents a questioning of the place of materialism in our lives.

Money alone has ceased to be the motivator that it once was. People today expect more from their work. The salary that accompanies work is necessary for paying the mortgage and the weekly grocery bill but fewer people are working now simply to collect a paycheck every two weeks or so. Almost two-thirds of the *Psychology Today* respondents said they would not accept a higher paying job if the work were less interesting. In a Louis Harris poll a similar question elicited even more dramatic results. People were asked to choose between two alternatives: 10 percent more income in an interesting job or 50 percent more income in a boring job. Seventy-five percent chose the interesting job and less money.[5] The idea that work is to keep body and soul together no longer holds. In fact, close to 70 percent of the people in the country say they would continue to work even if they were financially independent.[6]

If material satisfactions have lost some of their allure for the general population, they seem to have even less claim on people who have experienced full-blown authenticity crises. I found two pathways to this juncture depending on the age of the people I talked to. Somewhere around forty-five was a definite dividing line. The older people, being children of the Depression, grew up worshipping at the altar of financial security. They came slowly to the realization that 18-carat money clips and a pocket full of credit cards do not necessarily add up to happiness. The younger people, having come of age in the prosperous 1950s, never learned to genuflect there. They came more readily to the notion that fulfillment cannot be toted up on a profits and loss sheet.

The different emphasis which we give to work at mid-life is not terribly mysterious. We have learned that money is not necessarily a life-preserver. One of the favorite themes of the popular media is that riches cannot buy invincibility. Think of the characters in Jacqueline Susann novels; think of the attention accorded—still—the real-life stories of Marilyn Monroe and Judy Garland. By our thirties we are apt to have experienced this truth in our own lives. We are also not likely to be earning that much more money after forty. Promotions and salary increases slow down. Internal and external realities dovetail. If our earning power is peaking and money isn't that magical after all, why not try an occupation that promises different rewards?

Gary Cline, a big, beefy hulk of a man who looks like the college football tackle he once was, was selling life insurance in Martinsburg, West Virginia, when his mid-life crisis erupted. Shortly after his thirty-sixth birthday he came to the reluctant realization that he had been pouring all of his energies into pursuing money and it was not making him happy.

The beginnings of his transformation had their start in a chance meeting that had taken place years before. Cline was introduced to the man who would eventually change his life at a party in 1969. His name was Jim Lewis and he was the rector at the Episcopalian church.

"When we met, I was immediately attracted to him. I talked to him for a while and later at the party I looked for him so I could talk to him some more. When I couldn't find him, I asked his wife where he was. She said he had left to go to a NAACP (National Association for the Advancement of Colored People) meeting. That really piqued my interest because it wasn't the kind of thing that was done at Martinsburg at that time."

The tug that Cline felt toward Lewis drew him into the Episcopal church. There the two struck up a friendship and the relationship pulled Cline even further into the church. After a while he joined. The congregation was growing rapidly and the rector was increasingly overworked. Lewis sought his new friend's assistance in the Sunday services. Cline began by bearing the chalice during communion and gradually increased his responsibilities.

Lewis left Martinsburg in 1974 but before he did, he urged that Cline seriously consider the ministry. "We talked about my going to the seminary and he thought it would be a good thing for me." Cline steadfastly refused to contemplate any suggestion that his was not the right course. "I was working my tail off at the time. I was on the city council. I thought I had it made. I had a wife and three kids. My reaction was: this is the last thing I need. It wasn't something I really wanted to think about."

Cline had tentative commitments to social justice and community improvements. The civil rights movement started when he was an undergraduate at the University of North Carolina and the lack of response of the Southern Baptist Church had led to a break with the church of his childhood. He was active in the Jaycees and on the board of directors of the Boys' Club. "I was always socially conscious but my attitude was—let me get mine too." Material goals and financial rewards were his primary aim. At this point in his life Cline perfectly embodied the attitude and values of our twenties and early thirties.

"I was a *What Makes Sammy Run* type guy. I never thought much about goals. I just wanted to get there. I had monetary goals but I never thought: what am I going to be twenty years from now? It seemed like all my relationships were ones of competition. It seemed like life was one long attempt to get somewhere but not really knowing where. I think back and wonder why it was all so important."

Increasingly Cline seemed to spin his life around the Episcopal Church. He took on the duties of the morning prayer service. Socially, too, the church was the nub of his life. "Most of my friends were members. My wife and I spent a lot of time with them. The church seemed like a common bond in our lives beyond anything else."

As his involvement deepened, his values began to shift. "It became less and less important to me to make $30,000 a year which is the goal that I had set for myself. I began to see my obligations to my fellow man differently. I came to realize that I was not happy at any time in my life except when I was involved in the Episcopal church. Everything else seemed like a chore."

Other friends that Gary Cline loved and respected began echoing Jim Lewis. "A lot of people were saying that I should go to the seminary. It was in the back of my head for a long time."

Cline ran for the at-large seat on the city council and won. Election night the mayor hosted a victory party at his home. Cline looked at the crepe paper banners and jubilant party regulars and thought: this is not making me happy. "Here I had just won a citywide election and I was miserable. I thought this is not what I want for my life." It was 3 A.M. before Cline got to sleep that night.

"Things went from bad to worse."

Gary started waking up in the middle of the night. The questions which he could successfully defend against during the day roiled in his mind in the pre-dawn hours. Should he go to the seminary? Could he leave Martinsburg and the friends he loved? And if he did decide to go, how would he be able to afford the tuition and support his family for three years? "I guess I finally decided that I had to give it a try or I would go crazy."

The worst part Cline found afterward was the soul searching that preceded his decision. "Once the decision was made things fell in place beautifully." The Bishop of West Virginia arranged for the tuition to Virginia Theological Seminary in Alexandria, Virginia. The church in Martinsburg pledged $300 a month toward his expenses.

In the fall of 1978 Gary Cline enrolled at VTS.

Three years had passed when Gary and I met one month before his graduation from Virginia Theological Seminary. As soon as his degree was granted, he was heading back to West Virginia to be the rector at two tiny churches in White Sulphur Springs and Oakhurst. The total congregation—135 members. His marriage had survived the stresses and Gary bubbled over with enthusiasm for his new career. He had already written his first sermon and couldn't wait to deliver it.

Cline still has ambivalence about the explosive rearrangement of his life. One minute he says, "The last three years in all honesty have been the best of my life. I know I am in the right place doing the right thing. The affirmation I feel about myself and what I've done the last three years makes me believe this is what I was meant to be. I don't have trouble sleeping at night." The next moment he makes a U-turn and says, "Sometimes I think in my mind: what am I doing? A friend of mine said I had just gone from selling life insurance to selling God. I said there is nothing wrong with the product."

One thing he doesn't vacillate about, however, are the ideals he has chosen to embrace. As he enters his forties, spiritual values have become paramount. The material goods he once chased are now far down in his personal hierarchy.

"My values about money have changed considerably. I believe the old saying that money can't buy happiness. I get $8,000 a year starting out. The whole package—house, retirement, car allowance, etc.—is worth about $16,000. That's okay. I don't worry about it.

"Realistically speaking, I don't think I am going to become the dean of the National Cathedral. All churches theoretically want someone who is thirty-four years old and has ten years experience. I don't fit into that mold. But I do think I can find a comfortable place in the church where I can do the ministry I was meant to do."

Gary Cline's biography should not be read as the story of a person who experienced a religious conversion and marched off to enter the priesthood. He himself does not interpret his mid-life career change in those terms.

I guess you could say that I was called to the ministry. At one time I would have hesitated to use those words but I have become comfortable with them. I feel I was called in the sense that I was meant to do what I am doing. Some people are called to be writers. Some are called to be doctors or lawyers. I just happened to be called to be a priest.

I'm not a whole new person. I use to go out, live it up, drink beer and dance until 3 A.M. Now a part of me is reluctant to let go that completely because I might be needed. In that respect I am different to a degree. Basically, though, I am who I am and I'm certainly no saint.

In Gary Cline's case the spiritual awakening was the same transformation that all career changers experience in one way or another. The key word here, "spiritual," should be construed in its broadest terms. What it means, quite simply, is that the accumulation and making of money is no longer the most important thing in life. Somewhere within the general definition of that word the people who change careers come to rest.

This new attitude toward money is crucial for most career changers. The value of money in our society rests not just on its ability to purchase a high standard of living but also on its symbolic meaning. Money is a measure of success. Each raise is the grown-up equivalent of the merit badges we won as boy and girl scouts. If money has lost some of its importance to these people, it is because their need to perform and compete has also slackened.

The overwhelming majority of career changers reported that they were working longer and harder than ever. But they are now motivated by entirely different purposes. Being number one is no longer crucial. They are no longer running their lives so they can meet the career timetables in their fields. The external tokens of success whether it is the title on the company letterhead or the number of employees who will jump on command are not so seductive. They work to create something in their image that they can be proud of. Achievements and accomplishments still matter but the standards by which they are judged are personal and individual. People who change careers develop their own touchstones. The commitment is to self-approval.

The most dramatic and articulate representative of this transformation that I encountered is a man named Hal Lyon, Jr. Hal set out to be a career Army officer and commanded

a crack company of paratroopers in the 101st Airborne
Division in Vietnam. When I interviewed him, he was serving
as Abraham Maslow professor at Antioch College in Columbia, Maryland, and teaching humanistic psychology at
Georgetown University in Washington, D.C.

In high school and at West Point Hal Lyon ran cross-
country track. In high school he was co-captain of his team.
At West Point where the competition was keener he was
never a star. He was just close enough to the front of the
pack to earn his varsity letter and to keep the first- and second-
rated runners up to their potential. Some athletes find running
an almost spiritual experience which enables them to tap
their creative potential. Lyon was not one. Running for him
was grueling work but whether he was winning or losing he
kept on sprinting toward the finish line.

Later on Hal came to see this as a metaphor for his entire
life. He was always running toward the final goal and never
particularly enjoying the race. He didn't have to look hard to
see the connection that his subconscious had made. At West
Point he had once written a poem titled "The Race of Life"
and given it to his track coach.

Lyon locked in to this competitive ethos when he was
five years old. It has taken a decade of self-divining and three
years of therapy for him to trace the beginning so far back.

The start was a departure. His father, a career Army
officer, left his wife and young son behind in Cambridge,
Massachusetts, when he left in 1941 to fight in World War II.
In his father's absence he was told he would be in charge.
"I remember it all so well even though I was only five. We
were at the train station and my father's parting words as he
got on were 'You're the man of the house now.' I tried so
hard to live up to those words."

Hal took a few casual words and blazed them across his
life. "I tried so hard to be good. I literally leapfrogged over
the carefree times of childhood. I was driven to be an
overachiever, not to achieve for myself, for my own inner

approval, but to satisfy everybody else. It seemed to take bigger and bigger doses of winning."

Hal Lyon, Sr. didn't pressure his son to follow in his bootsteps but he was a powerful role model. "The military wasn't really what I wanted. What I really wanted was my father's approval." That realization, however, surfaced after he left the Army. He was a gung-ho cadet and an enterprising first lieutenant. Another, even more surprising discovery also came later. His father was never the macho figure of his teenage fantasies. When Hal, Jr., was a young officer, he encountered men who had served under Hal, Sr. All of them praised his father's understanding and compassion. Shock! It was Hal, Jr., the son, not the father who resented on behalf of Hal, Sr. such "demeaning" tasks as washing the supper dishes. "I realize now that as a teenager I was probably much more macho than he was."

Hal embarked on a marriage that was one more variation on this same theme. "I wanted a heroine and she wanted a hero."

Slogging through the rice paddies of Vietnam, dodging fire from an invisible enemy, Hal began to see the essential falseness of the position into which he had locked himself. Hal found that heroes have no special claim on invincibility and that many Congressional Medals of Honor are awarded posthumously. "My best friend in the military got killed in Vietnam. We felt we could do anything in the world. We were determined not to be denied. We were so sure we could do anything. When he got killed, I learned that he had limits, I had limits." Hal experienced the death at the center of the mid-life crisis in a particularly poignant and personal way. He started casting about for a new definition of hero.

After his return the emotions and energies so long suppressed erupted in one long flare.

I began to see that this track I had been racing down was not really getting me where I wanted to be going. All my life I had been achieving so I could be loved but I wasn't loved and I wasn't appreciated. I began to think that maybe people are not loved for those things after all. I started looking inward. I found incredible parts of myself that had been buried and I began to realize that if I could accept and love those parts of myself, then maybe someone else could, too.

Unsurprisingly, since he had never really belonged there anyway, these self-discoveries propelled Hal Lyon straight out of the military. If competing and achieving in conformity with his perception of other's requirements were not producing the desired payoff, nothing remained to hold him there. And since his marriage was based on the same kind of thinking which had led him into the army, it is not remarkable that his shift in motivations precipitated a divorce.

There is an important point which crops up in Hal Lyon's story that needs to be understood. The fact that so many people switch motivations in mid-life does not imply that something is intrinsically wrong with those incentives. *The drives to compete and achieve are not bad.* If we feel that we have a special contribution to make anywhere, then we should shoot for the top so that we can reach the biggest audience or influence the most number of people. If we love research and are determined to be the best scientist since Albert Einstein because we feel that is our potential, there is nothing wrong with striving toward that goal. If we think that we are best capable of managing the fortunes of our corporation which we take pride in, running for president is not to be criticized. The people who are driven to compete and achieve in response to a compulsion to do their best usually arrive at mid-life in fine shape. But often, as in the case of Hal Lyon, people simply seek the rewards of getting ahead. The difference is this. If we set out to build a better mousetrap and the world beats a path to our door, we will probably be all right. If we want the world to come to us and then we seize on creating a more efficient mousetrap, we probably will not be. The trouble begins when external rewards supplant internal gratifications. Newspaper reporters have an adage that applies here. They say: "it's only the next story that counts." If we work to fulfill our potential, we will not bask in the luxury of the by-lines or the Pulitzer Prizes that result from that effort. We will be out scrambling just as eagerly the day after because we will be working for our own self-approval.

This is a truth that Hal Lyon uncovered after he had chipped away at the veneer that covered up his real self. He was at George Washington University in Washington, D.C. studying for a master's degree when his authenticity crisis forced this self-examination. As he began the search for a new career, he learned that the president of Ohio University was looking for an assistant. Hal sent off a résumé and found himself hired. "I couldn't believe someone would actually give me an opportunity to do what I wanted to do." He spent two years, a period of transition, there. "This was an important step to me in establishing credibility in a new career."

His stint at Ohio University established contacts in the education field which he was now trying to conquer. His next move was to the Department of Health, Education and Welfare and a post as assistant deputy commissioner of education. After two more years he walked into the revolving door of high government posts and university teaching which is common in Washington and academia. Each of these steps led him further away from the rigidity of the military and into a more free-flowing, expressive work life.

"It is hard to be creative in the military because by the time you have reached a position where you can be innovative you have become a conditioned yes man. At the lower levels there are few outlets for creativity. Once I got into education it seemed that influential people created room for me to have creativity."

Hal's first adult decision was to leave the military. When he struck out on his own, breaking the unconscious bonds to his family and defining his own terms for his life, he entered therapy, seeking to strip away even more of the layers that covered up his core self. Now, deeply immersed in the human potential movement, he looks for ways to help others to become more fully themselves. As his work changed directions and helped him to grow, his work has increasingly become helping others to do the same. He serves on the board of directors of EST and has set up a foundation that he would like to see sponsor sort of an intellectual Olympics.

Recently he wrote a book that delves into some of the experiences we talked about. In *Tenderness Is Strength: From Machismo to Masculinity*, he said:

> *I no longer jump through everyone else's hoops. I take my vacations when I want to, because I care enough about myself. I refuse to take my work home or to work on weekends unless it is something I personally want to do, because that time belongs to me and my family. If I feel sick, instead of acting stoic, as I always did in the military, I am beginning to allow myself to have my sickness—to feel it rather than to deny it. This has been difficult for me, getting over my scornfulness toward those who were weak or couldn't discipline themselves enough to finish the race or the six A.M. five-mile runs on which I used to lead my paratrooper company; or the so-called deadbeats who invariably joined the sick-call ranks to escape military training, even among the elite airborne paratroopers. When others were feeling sick or tired or depressed, I had a problem not laying my scorn on them and not allowing them— or myself—to feel sick.*
>
> *The "you don't have to meet everyone else's expectations" part of my personal mantra is still difficult for me. I have discovered that many of these expectations are really my own projections. I expect me to be fair, witty, bright, clever, successful, entertaining, lovable, sexy, open-minded, fearless, and much more. . . .*
>
> *I'm finding that it is mostly my own assumptions of what I think others expect that I try to meet, and I am working on giving this up. . . .*
>
> *As I look back over my first thirty years of my life and the varied pursuits I've followed it is as though I felt I had to fill my life—fill each day, fill each week—with spectacular achievements. I did this even when I was thinking or fearing that there was nothing spectacular within me, or between me and others.*[7]

Once Hal abandoned the notion that he would achieve approval and started looking within himself for confirmation,

a remarkable thing happened. Hal and his father were reconciled. For the first time a real intimacy developed between
them.

"My father never really knew what was going on with
me. I always told him about my successes. I thought that was
what he wanted to hear. I always kept the burdens on my
own shoulders. I felt I had that responsibility to bear. I didn't
think it was appropriate to burden him. When he finally
found out what I was going through, he was so hurt that I
had never come to him, that I was so stoic."

The ultimate irony is this. By growing up, Hal Lyon
captured what he had sought as a child and looked for in all
the wrong ways.

Once we seek to work for external rewards and look to
work for self-gratification, a variety of other intangible forces
come into play. When values such as authenticity, autonomy,
self-expression dominate our lives, they change what we wish
to experience in our work. "They [career changers] want a
career that is a bold statement of their personal philosophy,"
reports Mainstream Associates.

Some of the best proof of this comes from the fact that
so many people who aren't required to work for a living are
rushing in mid-life to fill out W-2 forms. A number of
examples come readily to mind. Socialite Lee Radziwell
opened an interior design firm. Charlotte Ford, the daughter
of Henry Ford II, founded a dress manufacturing business
that bears her name. Jacqueline Kennedy Onassis is an editor
at a New York publishing house. None of these women
needed money or power or fame. All three already possessed
some of these things in abundance. Their compulsion to work
sprang out of other needs.

There is a reason why these examples are all women and
the biographies in this chapter have been of men. Women,
too, revise the meaning of work in their lives but in order to
do so, they must have a career and they must take their work
and themselves seriously. This is the starting point for both
sexes but for women who are over thirty-five it has been more
difficult for them to get to the departure gate.

The March, 1979, issue of *Ms.* magazine featured a photograph of Jacqueline Kennedy Onassis on its cover and attached the cover line "Why Does This Woman Work?" Inside Onassis provided an answer.

> *What has been sad for many women of my generation is that they weren't supposed to work if they had families. There they were, with the highest education, and what were they to do when the children were grown—watch the raindrops coming down the windowpane? Leave their fine minds unexercised? Of course women should work if they want to. You have to be doing something you enjoy. That is a definition of happiness: "complete use of one's faculties along lines leading to excellence in a life affording them scope." It applies to women as well as to men.*

Onassis went on to say that she encountered no resentment from others because of her salary or the fact that she worked.

"I think that people who work themselves have respect for the work of others," she wrote. "I remember a taxi driver who took me to the office. He said, 'Lady, you work, and you don't *have* to?' I said yes. He turned around and said, 'I think that's great.'"[8]

Women like Jacqueline Kennedy Onassis who came of age *before*, in the era that preceded *The Feminine Mystique*, the pill and the feminist movement comprise a special case of career changes. When they were growing up, little girls chanted the nursery rhyme, "rich man, poor man . . . doctor, lawyer, Indian chief," to see whom they might marry. They were never told that they might amass their own money, become a doctor or lawyer themselves. There were few role models then of successful working women and much ambiguity about the place of talented, not to mention ambitious, women in society. They might aspire to be superwomen but the number of telephone booths then accepting women was limited.

One has only to consider the case of the *Mademoiselle* magazine guest editors to comprehend the hurdles they were expected to leap. Each year *Mademoiselle* scours the country for the most promising of the next generation of writers, artists and fashion designers and awards them a month-long internship at the magazine. The college students who were the class of 1953, immortalized in Sylvia Plath's *The Bell Jar*, peered into their future and predicted "both a career and marriage with at least three children." Only nine of these nineteen already visibly accomplished young women even came close. (And are there many doubts about the course they would have embraced if they had been forced to settle on one?) The other ten elected to work inside the home, to boost their husband's careers instead of their own and to help their children achieve rather than fighting for their own promotions.[9]

Men have never had to battle these conflicted images. They have never been forced to choose between work and family, home and career. No one ever speaks of a working husband or a working father. In its zeal for breaking down the barriers that constrain women, the feminist movement has overlooked one untoward consequence of this prejudice and discrimination. Men's options are also limited although in a quite different way from the circumscribed choices of women. And women have the luxury of alternatives that men do not. Men are forced to take their work seriously. Women can retreat into dependency and the three-bedroom split level in the suburbs. "My husband won't let me" is an easily available, socially approved excuse. Few listeners will pause to question why permission was requested in the first place. It is always easier to grasp the cloak of the victim than to assume responsibility for one's life.

The redefinition of work for women starts with the decision to carve out an independent niche of their own. The pursuit of a career requires the acceptance of certain inevitables: competition, rejection, fighting for recognition, anxieties about failure and also success. None of these are very pleasant experiences for either sex but they are the exact opposites of the qualities that women over thirty-five were taught to embrace. No wonder it took so long for them to subdue their inner timidity.

Colette Dowling is a free-lance writer who slid into the traditional pattern. Growing up in the 1950s, the product of a working-class Baltimore family and Catholic schools, she followed the conventional course that was prescribed for a person of her generation and origin. Marriage. Three children. A fling at writing that was taken seriously neither by herself nor by the others in her family. And then came the break. In one year, 1971, she left her husband of nine years, published her first book and received her first magazine cover by-line. She thought she had come of age. She was only deluding herself.

Three years later, she met and fell in love with a man ten years younger, "a new-generation, under-thirty, educated-at-Sarah Lawrence" man. He wanted her to fly. She wanted to nest. Forgotten were the notions of self-sufficiency, out went the drive which sent her zooming around the country, all expenses paid, researching articles. Now she had a man.

Colette drifted back into domesticity. She and her lover and her children moved into an old farmhouse in upstate New York. Her lover was also a writer working on a novel. Their plan was to form an artists' colony of two. They would live together and write together. They would encourage and support each other. After all, they both believed only another writer could understand the perpetual glaze in the eyes of a person who has a book in progress. There was one thing wrong with the plan. Once they were ensconced in their farmhouse her lover wrote and Colette played house.

One night she woke in the bedroom they shared and thought seriously about killing herself. In 1977 she could find no room which she could comfortably call home. Brought up by a set of rules about men and women that no longer fit her life, she found she unexpectedly longed for the very thing she despised:

> *I want to be supported. It's not simply a question of having someone else pay the bills. What I want is full-time emotional protection, a buffer between me and the world. Over the past two years, events have conspired to bring home a peculiar truth: At base, I do not believe I should have to bear the full*

responsibility for my life. I want what I was born and bred to want, in Baltimore, in the fifties which is that someone else should do the hard stuff, not me. . . . But the problem is, being a modern woman, I loathe dependence, too. The price for security such as I yearn for is mute obeisance.

Dowling was thirty-nine when she lay there watching the wan moon and realized she had yet to reach maturity, that she had grown older but not necessarily up. She decided as a result of that night that for her next project she should tackle adulthood. An essential element of maturity, as she saw it, was the acceptance of the centrality of creative work in her life. Which didn't mean she liked it one bit:

Triumphs such as [baking pistachio pound cakes and refinishing the kitchen counters], I've come to conclude are the small creative droppings of a certain kind of frightened woman. Simply, it is not as scary to make do, to slip geraniums and pare the wardrobe and invent ways of feeding five people dinner for $3.32 a night as it is to be on the line, continually hustling assignments, approaching celebrities for interviews, fighting for every word of every sentence with a copy editor at The New York Times. *It is easier by far to reign in a small domestic kingdom . . . than it is to be so damnably exposed, so open to the possibility of rejection (to say nothing of the possibility of success). This give-and-take, this opening oneself to the potential ravages of human encounter, is what's involved in being an adult. And you know something, I resent hell out of it.*[10]

Dowling at least had a lover who admired her writing and encouraged, even urged, her to work. How much harder it is for women who don't have fans on the sidelines.

To be sure, it is difficult to take one's work seriously when no one else does. That requires a single-mindedness of intent and a self-possession that is rare in the twenties. Slim chance that the woman who is in her mid-life decade now received reinforcement when she was making the fateful decisions that would determine her next twenty years. For most it was easier to pick a partner and resume the traditional dance.

Lest there be any uncertainty about the regard in which women's careers are held, consider these passages which I came across in my research.

"Women . . . do perceive themselves as successful when they enjoy love (and power and status) from their husbands and children and when they give love and support. They conceive of this as their major function, and their success in affiliative relationships defines their personal success."[11]

Perhaps the most surprising aspect of this comment is that it was made by Judith Bardwick, a psychologist, the holder of a Ph.D., a professor at the University of Michigan, who obviously was not content simply to be a year-round fireplace. But then we are apt to exempt ourselves from the general rules of behavior which we prescribe for others.

That Harry Levinson, who is a management consultant, should embrace this opinion also is less startling. After listing seven reasons that men work ranging from "the need for money" to "the need to master," he turns to women. Why do they work, he asks and provides this answer:

Gratifications at work recharge the woman to return to her home responsibilities refreshed by her absence and diversion from them (providing the work situation does not increase her tensions). She can have a greater sense of partnership with her husband for, less burdened, she complains less. She is freer to be with him, to go places and do things which the extra paycheck makes it possible to afford. She has more time to devote to the partnership, more freedom to listen and to support him, and less anger in her discussion of family problems.[12]

In short, men work out of a complexity of motives because they must and want to; women work simply so they can be better wives. But while she is a receptive audience to his stories at day's end, who is going to listen to her? And who will change the sheets and blow the noses, clean the oven and polish the silver while the two gallivant? Totally missing in this scheme of the working world are the single women and the female heads of households who comprise 43 percent of employed women. Certainly they are not holding jobs in order to increase their marital compatibility quotients. Also absent here are the additional 21 percent of working women who are married to men who earn less than $10,000 a year and can't afford time-saving Cuisinarts and life-freeing house-keepers. When these blue-collar wives go off to work, they are acquiring double duties. They are accepting more burdens and less leisure. Little chance that they will feel refreshed by the time the dishes are put away and the children are in bed.

Like Dowling, women frequently are unable to come to grips with the givens of work until their late thirties. And that remains true of all women who are currently working, not just those who entered the work force in the 1950s and 1960s. Some 60 percent of women say that their job is just a job compared to some 40 percent of them who say their job is a career. The median age of the woman who considers her work a career is 36.1.[13]

This upswing of interest in a career at this time is not too difficult to fathom. Thirty-five is when the average mother sends her last child off to school. Thirty-five is also the age that the average married woman reenters the work force.

The outcome of this inner propensity to relinquish responsibility and the external roadblocks that are put before women is serial careers. For some women this means a sequence of red and green lights, time out for marriage and raising children. For other women this means spells in deadend jobs and plateaus while once-promising romances shrivel and die. Their conundrum may be even more difficult to bear because the pain that accompanies it is so intensely private. The single career woman in such a position often feels like a wanderer who has lost track of both major routes through life. The woman who refuses promotions that require a transfer or stays in place when she could leapfrog ahead because of a love relationship is doubly jinxed. She hasn't chosen career over family in accordance with the feminist movement and she has not slipped into the wife and mother role that society would mandate. One way or another most women vacillate for a long time. "Until I was thirty I really didn't care much what I did," said a single woman who changed careers. "After I reached that age I became much more concerned about responsibility and preoccupied by thoughts of the future." The career tracks of successful men resemble a straight line that shoots upward. The career pattern of achieving women, even the most successful, is apt to approximate a roller coaster curve. Late bloomers are rare among men. They are as common as chrysanthemums among women. Barbara Walters, one of the highest paid people in the country in her forties, was a copy writer at NBC in her early thirties. Katharine Graham, chairman of the board of The Washington Post Company which publishes *The Washington Post* and *Newsweek* and owns several television stations, did not come into her own until middle age and the death of her husband. Women, especially those now in their thirties and forties, simply take longer to get to the place that men start from.

The biography of businesswoman Christi Finch, whom I first introduced in chapter five, illustrates the shifting meanings that work and relationships hold for women.

Back in Lincoln City, Oregon, where she grew up Christi Finch dressed her Katy Keene paper dolls and thought she might be a fashion designer. Then again she might be a Bohemian artist.

When she was graduated from high school, she spurned college. Instead she went to work as a psychiatric aide in a mental hospital "baby sitting for twenty people." The sooner she went to work, she reasoned, the quicker she could earn the money to buy a one-way ticket to Europe. Florence where Dante was born and Michelangelo thrived under the Medicis beckoned. There in the Renaissance city she would devote herself to Art. "I was going to be arty and marry an Italian."

As the time approached for her to leave and undertake a serious commitment, Christi turned and fled. Dreams of the gypsy life were one thing. The reality was something else again. Fantasies are no threat as long as they remain in the realm of the imagination but acting on them risks exposure and failure. Christi was not ready. She retreated, classically, into marriage. One aspect of her dream she managed to salvage. Her husband was Italian.

Christi and Leonardo, as I'll call him, moved to New York City. "He was studying acting and he was going to become rich and famous." While Leonardo learned to open and close his tear ducts at will, Christi trudged to work at an insurance company in Wall Street. "I've never had a job before or since where I spent so much time watching the clock." Christi had expected glitter and glamour in New York but the women who filed the insurance forms with her were no more sophisticated than the people back in Lincoln City. "It was an interesting introduction to the big city, I must admit," she says wryly.

Moored in the safe harbor of her marriage, Christi gained strength and courage. She finally felt secure enough to risk a few quick sails.

She quit the insurance company and was hired by a dress shop in Greenwich Village. "A *very* cheesy operation." Through her work she was introduced to a woman who had also spent her girlhood playing with Katy Keene. The two opened a design studio on West 59th Street. Christi found she had to hustle to survive. "We were constantly sewing and doing things for other people. Looking back, I don't know how I had the energy." Along with other stores, Henri Bendel, the ultra-chic specialty shop, bought a few of their dresses. That was a promising beginning for such a business and other young designers might have exploited it for all of its considerable worth in the New York fashion world. Christi, however, still lacked a solid commitment to accomplishment. "It got to the point where it either had to grow or die. We didn't care enough to make it work so it died." Christi remained a transient. She took a leap back from permanence and a firm identity. Once again her momentum was lost. She chose to keep herself open to new experiences. The edges of her personality remained diffused. Unwilling to foreclose her options, she bolted in a different direction.

Christi set out to land a job as a photo stylist. She ended

up running the abortion counseling service at Flower and Fifth Avenue Hospital. The U.S. Supreme Court had just overturned state anti-abortion laws, declaring that up to the end of the first trimester the decision to terminate a pregnancy was between the woman and her doctor. A dozen women a day, struggling to come to grips with the ambivalence of conceiving an unwanted child, were coming in, seeking support for their decision. "I loved it. I thought it was a terrific job. There was lots of involvement with people and it incorporated all those Mumsy aspects of me. And as a woman I was very interested in the issues."

That same year Christi and Leonardo separated. If she lost her dockage, she gained time and energy for work. Without Leonardo she began investing more of herself in her job.

"I can't say I really considered my work at the hospital a career although it approached that. There was not quite enough respect, not quite enough seriousness, not quite enough money attached to it." And, perhaps in retrospect, most important of all: "There really wasn't enough maturity on my part. I wasn't ready."

But she was coming close.

After she was there for four years, Flower and Fifth Avenue Hospital began to change and not for the better from Christi's perspective. "The job I was doing became less and less secure." For the first time in years she began to contemplate the rest of her life. Again an acquaintance helped to define the switch that led to growth. Eileen Weinberg also worked at the hospital. Like Christi she was increasingly dissatisfied with where she was headed. By her terms it was precisely no place. And like Christi she loved to cook and entertain.

Eileen nudged Christi into agreeing to open a catering service in their off hours. They printed up business cards and stationery and announced their new enterprise to all their friends and acquaintances. "We were not very professional but we got a lot of jobs considering the little effort we put into it."

Although she scarcely suspected then, the catering was a first step toward a serious work commitment. It was also in a sense a step back into her past. In the family circle in which she grew up food was the fulcrum. When she was a child, her parents ran a grocery store "in which I hated to work." As a teenager she cooked the family dinner. The coffee hour was sacrosanct "sort of like English high tea with loads of vulgar pastries." In one way or another many career changers are drawn to symbols of their childhood security and privilege. So it was with Christi. Somewhere down in Christi's subconscious, freshly baked loaves of bread and bunches of spring asparagus had become equated with happiness. (As it also did for her oldest sister who became a home economics teacher.)

The catering business meandered along for a year while Christi and Eileen spent the hours from 9 A.M. to 5 P.M. fervently wishing they were elsewhere. Christi leafleted the city with résumés and Eileen lobbied for converting their catering service into a food store. "I had a lot of concern about going into business. I knew there was nothing glamorous about it. I knew I wasn't going to wear high heels to work every day. I understood how hard it was because I had seen my parents do it." Christi mulled the pros and cons for several weeks. "It was a very difficult decision. I got a lot of pimples that month." Then she quit her job. That was step number two.

"We went into business to satisfy our creative needs. We wanted to do something and knew exactly how to do it. I think that is one of the reasons behind our success. Many people go into business wanting to make money and looking for a way to make it and they fail."

Christi had a new live-in lover who shared her dream and urged her on. His solidity became the lightning rod for her anxieties as the two women sought financing and lists of things to do billowed into the corners of Christi's peach-and-green living room. "Robert has given me a lot of support in this. I have had other relationships which would not have survived." On the other hand, "Being married demands a commitment of time and energy to the relationship. Not being married, I am freer to say this is what I have to do. If I were married, I would have to think: is this going to be right for us?"

Christi had feasted on the transient life. And she had finally gained strength from her wanderings. "I think of myself as an adventurer really, more than a gambler. Gambling implies a certain risking of what you don't have and I don't see myself as that kind of person. I like security. I felt very capable of taking care of myself. My attitude was: if the business works, fine and if it doesn't, I'll find something else." Her spirit had been tested and passed.

A year went by before the women could locate financing and a shop for rent. They survived by dashing around town catering corporate lunches and baking up a storm. "Oh, we were terrible. We never even got cake boxes. We were carrying them around in baskets with plates on top."

The First Women's Bank finally approved their loan application. "They were new and inexperienced enough to consider us. The other banks we talked to and the Small Business Administration adopted the attitude: this is cute but where is the man?" The bank loan and personal loans "wrenched agonizingly out of friends' hands" totaled $25,000. They rented the store on East 72nd Street in May and after a summer of sanding and painting they opened in September, 1977.

Word of Mouth was a smash. Even before the painting was finished hungry neighbors were peering in the brownstone windows and watching the blackboard out front for the opening date. "I never doubted that we would be successful but I never visualized the teeming hordes who now come in." When Mimi Sheraton of *The New York Times* who had been munching anonymously on their lemon bars for some months wrote a rave review, Word of Mouth acquired instant cachet. "I know we are supposed to be chic which is funny because the shop itself could not be less chic."

And, in fact, it is a jumble of stock pots, kitchen

equipment, cardboard boxes, a garden of vegetables, staff and customers crammed into a room the size of a large walk-in closet. An unsuspecting visitor trips over a can of tomato paste stored on the floor. Some ten to twelve employees rotate in and out of the exposed kitchen. Christi now has trouble remembering their names. At 5:30 P.M. the pace is chaotic. Customers can't edge close enough to the chalkboard to see the daily specials. Chicken with prunes and almonds one day, Italian pasta the next and the salads of scallops in remoulade sauce and beets with fennel. A chocolate addict would overdose on the brownies.

"There is a sense of pride in what we've accomplished and that we've achieved a certain recognition. I've always liked that."

Not all the rewards are psychic. Despite enormous expenses—the butcher bill alone is $2,000 a week and going up—Christi is making three times her salary at the hospital.

Christi had worked for over a decade at a variety of jobs before she devoted herself to a single enterprise. She was ripe for commitment.

"I think I would have made some kind of commitment to some kind of work even if the shop hadn't evolved. I was not aimlessly searching for something to do but I felt the time suitable for it."

Some women in their twenties attempt marriage, motherhood and careers in a single sweeping embrace and most who try fail. The ability to integrate these diverse roles presupposes a sense of perspective and priorities that few people (of either sex) then possess. It also requires inexhaustible reservoirs of physical and psychic energy.

A woman I know whose juggling skills are much admired by her high school friends once spent a few dizzying years bouncing from her husband and two small daughters to a teaching job to graduate school classes and back home again.

"Louise," we marveled, "you do everything."

"And I do it all so poorly," she replied. Which, of course, was not true.

Much more likely, a woman will subtract one of those roles.

Marriage is a liability. Reaching for the next rung on the career ladder is harder when one hand is removing a roast from the oven. Women scientists and engineers are *six times* as likely to remain single as their male counterparts.[14] That sentence can bear rereading.

But children are the real time stealers and attention grabbers. If she has children, she will abandon her personal vision of herself. The brilliant young scientist will mix formula. The aspiring Pulitzer Prize winner will read Mother Goose. If she pursues a career, her dreams will be haunted by visions of unborn children that might have been. The lives of most women simply will not stretch enough to embrace both children and a career.

Two simple statistics tell the story. Only 7 percent of women between the ages of thirty and forty-four have worked at least half of every year since they left school. Of the compelling factors the single most important was whether or not they had children. Almost half of the single women have been continuously employed; only 3 percent of the mothers have.[15]

These women who choose children over career mothball their ambitions but those earlier stirrings are not so easily extinguished. Submerged in those layers of school lunches, carpool schedules and 2 A.M. feedings is a prematurely silenced "I" that will sooner or later demand to be heard. In her late thirties or early forties when her children are reaching maturity a woman will start listening again. A new friskiness, the result of those mid-life personality changes, is surfacing. And her creativity is flowing into different courses, seeking new outlets. The timing of these events will vary depending on her previous educational attainments. If she has a college degree, the magic age is thirty-six. (The average age, remember, of the self-defined career woman.) If she is a high school graduate, it will be somewhat later, after the age of forty.[16]

What is this woman like who resumes her career or sets off in pursuit of the one she never had?

She was an only child or the oldest in her family. She majored in the humanities or the social sciences and married not long after graduation from college. She was then 22.9 years old. She taught school or held a nonprofessional job in an office for almost five years before the first child arrived. She bore 2.7 children and her life swirled around their school activities, the covered-dish suppers at the church activities and volunteer work, the Red Cross perhaps or the Girl Scouts. Eleven years have lapsed since her last job and her youngest child is now nine. At forty she emerged from her cocoon and cautiously flexed her wings.[17]

The vitality and vigor of such women is startling. Their energies so long swaddled erupt in a thousand directions. Their sense of freedom and self-determination is electrifying. They literally take off. In researching the career patterns of women who entered a life development program at George Washington University, I was amazed at their achievements.

At thirty-six Grace had five sons and two years of woefully outdated college courses in math and chemistry. Two years later she had a B.A. in environmental health and was employed by the Environmental Health Service at Bethesda Naval Hospital in Bethesda, Maryland.

Kate was the mother of two teenage daughters and was a former high school music teacher in Tennessee. At forty-eight she summoned the courage to end her twenty-eight-year-old marriage and plunged back into the work world. She was accepted into the management trainee program at a major department store. Five years later she was in charge of 140 people. She later wrote the program director at George Washington, "My age has proved to be one of my biggest assets . . . I am a person who has found peace, accomplishment, confidence and new horizons in life."

Stephanie was a college dropout and her work résumé was short: one year teaching finger painting in kindergarten, two years at a bank teller's window. When the youngest of her three sons died of a drug overdose at the age of twenty, she was galvanized into action. She enrolled in a bachelor's degree program in child therapy and began work at a drug rehabilitation clinic.

The stories of women who march off to become Washington newspaper correspondents and radio producers, run planning and development programs at art museums, to earn Ph.D.'s go on and on.

Only one question lingers. What might they have done if they had not had to choose way back when?

There are two conditions that must be present before a person changes careers. The redefinition of work represents the first tentative groping toward that switch. But the same impetus that causes some people to search for new careers that will embody those meanings can lead other people to center their lives in private pursuits. If work ceases to offer challenges or the potential for growth and self-expression, a person may seek those things elsewhere. If we can't be revived through our jobs, we will search for renewal on weekends. This is the reason so many men and women in middle life become frenetic weekend tennis players or Sunday afternoon painters or suddenly decide to have the most perfectly clipped box hedges on their block.

Before this redefinition of work can be transmuted into a career change, a person must be comfortable with the notion of change itself. Change—an emotionally loaded word at best. Few of us are intrepid enough to face alterations in our lives with complete equanimity. Habits are compelling. Routine is as comforting as the fuzzy Shetland sweater we cuddle into on autumn nights alone. Even minor dislocations can be upsetting. The closing of the dry cleaner who knows without asking how we like our shirts done. A new bus route into town. The absence of a familiar face at the coffee shop where we habitually pick up a Danish on the way to the office. We search for familiarity and strangeness can set off momentary flares in our synapses.

If such minor reweavings in the textures in our lives can unsettle us, the prospect of even more fundamental reorderings can be awesome in its impact. The idea of moving to new cities (and in big cities even new neighborhoods), changing marriage partners, switching jobs and careers can produce neurological traumas. Unsurprisingly, psychiatrists rate life events such as these three that involve change as among the most stressful we will ever endure.

Change is always easier when we know what lies behind the unopened door. The fewer risks that we can foresee the easier it is to chance something new and different. Radical career shifts present the possibility of real loss. Financial setbacks and the time wasted in unsuccessful endeavors are two that come readily to mind. Spouses who decide a mate has suffered a mental burnout and choose to leave are occupational hazards of changing careers. More subtle losses also exist—a mutilated ego, a shrunken identity, the disapproval of friends and colleagues.

Career counselor John Landgraf says, "Radical career changes presuppose flexibility and the courage to take existential leaps into the dark." In order to do this, people must have a sense of personal security. A person must trust himself and life enough to have the confidence that he will land right side up. Few threads ran through all my interviews with people who changed careers but one was this. Despite the obvious differences among them, the variations in age, marital status, family backgrounds and career patterns, they all shared one thing in common. All of them saw themselves as individuals who were comfortable with the notion of change. This was not always readily apparent in their lives. Some of them seemed to me to be people who had chosen security over risk. But in each of my cases, to the people themselves, as they read the story of their lives, they saw at one time or another before they changed careers people who took risks. They perceived themselves as adventurers. Without this self-image the redefinition of work will not lead to career changes.

Once change has been established as a mode of life it has a synergetic effect. This phenomenon was so commonplace in the lives of those I studied that I came to label it "the one change leads to another" syndrome. (Ely Callaway was a notable exception but then as a friend once said, "Ely is sui generis.")

When Ernest Hemingway was asked how to write a novel, he replied with equal doses of wit and wisdom, "First clean out the refrigerator." He meant that the creative process works in a mysterious fashion and the best way to court that muse is to go quietly about one's business and let it ferment. So it is with career changers. Time and again the people in this book chose remarkably similar words to describe their decisions to switch careers. "There was no bolt out of the blue." "No lights flashed; no bells rang." "I was never struck by lightning." No one woke up one morning, glanced out a window and suddenly said, "Tomorrow I enlist in a new cause." Instead the decision evolved over such a lengthy period of time that when it happened it seemed to carry the certitude of inevitability.

But somewhere in the past, long before the turning point was reached, the decision to change began with a change of a far different sort. On the surface these shifts had nothing at all to do with changing careers but in fact they were the planting of the seed that sprouted into new growth. Each career change emerged from this kernel. Gary Cline joined the Episcopal church. Carol Anderson left her husband and adopted the gay life style. Iver Brook severed his relationship with his mentor Hal Bache. Jack Davies got married. None suspected at the time that these decisions would send ripples in ever-widening circles through their entire lives.

The two departures that most often precipitate career changes are the decision to get a divorce and to enter therapy. Some 20 percent of the women and 10 percent of the men who abandon their first careers are already divorced. Another 15 percent of men and women are in the process of obtaining divorces. About 10 percent of career changers are or have been in therapy.[18]

That this is so should not be too surprising. Both divorce and therapy bear witness to certain underlying truths in our lives. They represent an admission that the past structure is far from satisfying and that new walls and roofs are in order. They also signal a willingness to spend some time taking apart, studying and putting back together our personalities. The person who can't or won't probe his dangling nerve endings is an unlikely candidate for a second career.

Changing careers demands a willingness to concede that somewhere along the way the dream went awry and the confidence to abandon it for a new revised version. John Landgraf says, "People who are changing careers are admitting unfulfillment and seeking wholeness or health."

For many people change is upsetting, actually threatening. Betty Johnson whose husband entered nursing school said, "I think it is a very, very hard thing to give up a secure job, even if it is a job you don't like, I think it is very hard. A lot of things like moving, giving up friends are hard to inflict on oneself. The easiest thing is to stay put." People whose equilibrium is seriously disturbed by change will be loath to stretch. They will prefer to cling to the safe and familiar, even if the cost is stagnation, rather than accept the risks that come with letting go. Behind the fear of change stretches the terror of the unknown. Experience can help. The more change in our lives, the more comfortable we become with it. The skill to cope with change, like the ability to tread water or to create a perfect lemon soufflé, improves with practice.

However this expertise develops, wherever this flair comes from, it must happen. It is necessary for successful navigation of the mid-life passages. It is essential for mid-career changes. The redefinition of work will only lead to frustration and the sound of teeth gnashing in the night without the flexibility and courage to take an existential leap into the dark.

Joe Jordan could never be accused of lack of experience in change. As some people seek comfort in the routine, Joe gloried in the freedom and expansion of flux. For years Joe's hobby was jumping out of airplanes with a parachute on his back, falling, falling, falling and then, at the last possible moment, yanking the rip cord and drifting to earth. I always think of Joe like that—riding the winds of change and landing on his feet. Joe might be a product of the 1950s but he was an easy rider when Peter Fonda was still playing tag with Jane in the hills above Sunset Boulevard.

"It has often looked to me like my philosophy of life is to never own more than I can carry at a full run."

When we met at the *Palm Beach Post* in West Palm Beach, Florida, in 1970, Joe was on his second marriage and his umpteenth newspaper job. Even then he was no stranger to change.

Like many young people of talent and ambition before and since, Joe gravitated into reporting because it was a way out. Few professions reward merit more and care less about formal credentials. For him it was an escape hatch from his lower-middle-class family, from the provincialness of his home town of Charleston, South Carolina, in the 1950s.

Joe didn't start out as a reporter. His first newspaper job was in the advertising department of the *News and Courier* in Charleston. "It seemed creative enough and fun enough. But I was smart enough to see that I was never going anywhere in advertising unless I went to college or unless I was willing to wait for a long, long time. I had acquired the notion that a newspaper reporter had even more fun than an advertising salesman. (Fun obviously played a predominant part in all this.) I thought reporters did interesting things and got to meet interesting people."

Joe enrolled in the news sequence at the journalism school of the University of South Carolina. He was the first member of his family to go to college. As it turned out, he was not the first Jordan to graduate. The streak of independence and autonomy that helps to keep him afloat in the cauldron of change had already surfaced. Somehow Joe never got around to taking the required newspaper management and feature-writing courses. When he dropped out to marry his first wife, he had more credits than anybody else in the school and still couldn't pick up his B.A.

Joe became a husband, a father and a newspaper reporter in the space of a few months. He suspected that chasing the police cruisers and listening to the statehouse gossip at the *State Journal* in Columbia would be fun and it was. He thought marriage and fatherhood would not be and he was right about that, too. Some men would have been trapped. Joe escaped that lock. Soon his wife and baby left. "That was in the days before legalized abortions and I was determined to do the right thing which later turned out to be the wrong thing so we got married. Then I was at the *State Journal* sending her $25 a week and still trying to do the right thing."

Reporting is engrossing but too many newspapers traditionally have felt that their reporters should be satisfied with a by-line instead of a raise. The career pattern is: a newsman stays in one place and rises through the editor ranks or he hops from job to job, improving his salary and assignment with each move. Joe chose the latter course. He drifted through South and North Carolina and down into Florida. In the late 1960s he arrived in Melbourne to work for brand new *Today* which the Gannett newspaper chain was touting as their prize newspaper. In that setting Joe sparkled and his copy eventually attracted the attention of another new venture.

In 1969 the Cox newspaper chain bought two moribund newspapers, the *Palm Beach Post* and the *Palm Beach Times* and placed a team of aggressive newsmen in their early thirties, Greg Favre and David Lawrence, in charge of the *Post*. Favre and Lawrence set about recruiting a staff of young reporters who would share their idealism about what journalism could and should be.

Joe arrived for his interview that August in cut-off denims and sandals. "I had no intention of working for that rag." Greg and Dave double-teamed him. Together they possessed all the charm and persistence of journalists at their best. The *Post* was going to be the best newspaper in the state. It would be innovative and daring. Reporters would have freedom to pursue their stories. The *Post* would sweep the national newspaper award contests. A position on the staff was a not-to-be-missed opportunity. Joe's head swirled. As he walked out of the city room and down the stairs into the parking lot, he wondered how much time the editors at *Today* would demand when he handed in his resignation. "I could see that it was time to leave *Today* and actually I was glad to have a place to go. I've always liked new things."

Joe was named chief of the Boca Raton bureau and a halcyon period began.

Favre and Lawrence were serious about their intentions. The *Post* building faced Lake Worth and that bastion of wealth and privilege, Palm Beach, which lay on the other side but the *Post* deliberately turned its back on the social scene and looked in other directions for news. The paper informally adopted as its slogan Joseph Pulitzer's famous statement, "The purpose of a newspaper is to comfort the afflicted and afflict the comfortable." Reporters were soon fanning out around the county and state writing about people and exposing conditions that the residents of Palm Beach County had never known existed. The eager young staff began hanging out with drug addicts and writing about their world. They went to live in the state prisons. They knocked on the doors of the migrant shacks in the sugar cane fields and asked the migrants about the conditions in the camps. They exposed the peccadillos of the county sheriff. They drove miles into the Everglades to talk to the Seminole Indians. The *Palm Beach Post* couldn't compete with such newspapers as the *Miami Herald* or the *St. Petersburg Times* in terms of budget or size of staff but it became the Avis of the Florida newspaper world. It wasn't large but it left a big mark.

And the prizes followed one after the other: the Pulitzer, the Ernie Pyle, the Robert F. Kennedy, the National Head-liners Club, the Associated Press of Florida, the Florida Society of Newspaper Editors.

Like the other reporters at the *Post*, Joe couldn't wait to get to work in the morning. He took as his special beat the continuing story of the efforts of the migrants who worked the fields on the edge of the Everglades to live decently. The Florida Legal Services Corporation, funded by the federal war on poverty, was championing their cause and Joe was there night and day, reporting on the meetings that lasted well after midnight.

The *Post* became a reporters' newspaper.

Some staff writers thought it was too good to last and it didn't. Dave Lawrence left in 1971. Greg Favre quit a year later. Greg announced that he was resigning a few weeks before the 1972 election. For the first time the owners of the Cox newspaper chain had issued marching orders to its individual editors: endorse Richard Nixon for president. "Richard Nixon is the antithesis of everything this newspaper has tried to stand for," Greg told the staff. "I cannot in good conscience endorse Richard Nixon and continue as editor of this paper."

Joe walked into the city room, sat down at a typewriter and typed out his resignation. Then he handed it to Greg and promptly burst into tears.

"Please don't," Greg told Joe and all the other people who threatened to walk out that day. "I've invested so much here that if you go, it will all be lost. You have to stay."

Joe went back to Boca Raton.

"You know," he said years later, "we were all so emotionally wrought up that day that his argument seemed to make sense. Of course, it was totally illogical. So I sat around like everybody else and waited to see what would happen without Greg. Then we saw."

For the original staff who owed their loyalties to now-departed leaders, life at the *Post* could never be the same. The new editors sensed that and spared little sympathy for the reporters who clung to the notion of a restoration of sorts. People stopped speaking and drifted into cliques of old and new staff. The paper seemed to lose some of its focus.

Newspapers like people have distinct personalities. In 1973 the *Post* seemed to be suffering from an identity crisis. The coverage slipped. The editing was less sure.

"In the past we had never minced words and I had written a lot of pretty hard stories. Now there seemed to be a general softening."

Joe was also getting caught up in the classic journalistic conflict. Reporters are expected to expose and cover the news but they also like to see their work produce results and when the end product continues to be by-lines instead of improvements, the frustration sets in. Stories rarely create change. The *Post* won a Pulitzer Prize in 1970 for photography for a series on the conditions in the same migrant labor camps which Edward R. Murrow had originally dramatized back in the 1950s.

A rent strike in Harlem, a little speck on the Palm Beach County map in the Glades, clicked things into place. Joe had been writing about the conditions in the camps there. Nothing happened. A lawyer from Florida Legal Services wandered into town and organized a rent strike. Events began to unfold.

"I would write stories which would get a big yawn and a lawyer would come in and things would start happening. There was a great deal of restlessness because I could never seem to get things done but in journalism that is not the objective. I began to see there were lots of lawyers around who were really helping to make things work."

The idea that law might be more fulfilling and rewarding than journalism wedged itself into Joe's mind and refused to go away. When Joe mentioned this strange notion that had crept into his head to the lawyers he knew, they were uniformly enthusiastic. Nelson Bailey, then of the Palm Beach County state attorney's office and now Joe's law partner, urged him to apply to law school.

In 1973, the year after the *Post* began to unravel for Joe, he and his second wife, Betty, separated. "The marriage had been going to hell for a long time." The years of pursuing stories all over the South Florida landscape had taken their toll. Betty was a businesswoman and rising in her corporation. A lot of his stories had Big Business as the chief villain. "Journalism, if it is done right, takes all your time and energy. It became a big part of my life and she became a little part. After a while we had nothing left to say to each other."

The seeds of Joe's change were Greg's departure and the events that followed and his separation from his wife. "I had gone through a series of changes and the tendency was to keep spinning further and further away from the starting point. I was becoming a different person."

Joe was assigned to write a series of articles about the Florida Parole and Probation Commission. The commission had been embroiled in controversy for years and it appeared that the debate would begin all over again in the state legislature which would convene in a couple of months. The series, however, was doomed from the start.

Joe and the two editors with whom he would be working huddled one morning in the cafeteria. Editor One placed a legal pad on the table and started scribbling. "I see this as a five part series leading off with some real horror stories about the parole and probation commission that will guarantee readership for the next few days," he said. Editor Two shook his head. "Not at all," he said. "I see it as three parts starting with a description of how the parole and probation commission works." Neither of them asked for Joe's thoughts. He looked at them and knew his days at the *Post* were numbered.

"I could see a quitting coming up. I had quit so many newspapers that I could see the pattern re-emerging. There was a growing intractability and a declining respect on both sides."

Joe decided the time had come to think seriously about law school. He signed up to take the Law School Admissions Test.

"I've found out that if you go through enough changes, then you always know when a change is coming. You may not know exactly when but you can feel it coming, creeping up on you."

Beneath his utterly pragmatic blue oxford cloth shirt

armor, Joe still hid notions of changing the world. Only journalism now seemed like the least likely method. "I guess the idealistic motives I had led me to work on the newspapers I did. It is said that something like 85 percent of the people in the country read small dailies and I always figured if you were going to do good work those papers were the place to do it." But Joe had already worked at some of the better small dailies in the country and the experience had not been encouraging.

Joe applied to the law schools at Florida International University in Miami and Florida State University in Tallahassee.

The collision which Joe had foreseen between him and his editors occurred—head on. The three never agreed on the approach for the series. The pulling and tugging among them did not produce a compromise. It only locked each further into his original position. The arguments escalated to the point of no return and beyond. Joe felt he had no recourse but to quit the *Post*. It was March, 1974, and Joe was thirty-six years old. He focused on law school. "There really was no other choice at that point. I could have gone to another small daily which was interested in raising hell and which would be satisfying until the editors became pillars of the community. Or I could go to a big newspaper and become caught up in the factory syndrome which I had always avoided. Or I could try free-lancing which is fraught with peril. Or I could go to law school. Which is what I decided to do."

By then Joe had charmed the admissions officers at Florida State University into serious consideration of an application from a middle-aged journalist who never received a college diploma. "Much to my startled bewilderment the folks at Florida State actually let me in." He sold his sports car and boat, borrowed some money and earned a little more that summer free-lancing magazine articles and working as an aide to a state senator. He set off to Tallahassee that fall with enough money to pay for one year and hoped that it would all work out.

"Once I really decided to go to law school and figured it

was a good idea, I thought that somehow I could swing it. I just figured that hunker down and suffer time had come. If I had to go to law school one year and work the next for as long as it took, then that is what I would do."

Joe discovered he didn't have to take that course. Through part-time jobs and student loans and by living with a friend, he went straight through.

Joe survived law school as he had once landed alive from his parachute jumps. He leapt in and landed upright. Joe has always been a person who is comfortable daring the unknown.

"The way it happened was the best way. If I had stayed married and gone to law school, I would not have had to worry about the finances but in a funny way I would have been less secure. I would not have had the emotional freedom to take the risk. It would have been more difficult. I would have felt less free. And, of course, if things had gone differently at the *Post*, I might never have gone to law school at all and that would have been a mistake."

After Joe entered law school, four years passed before we got together again. He had passed his law boards and he and Bailey were now partners. We met in their law offices, a couple of blocks from the Palm Beach County courthouse. As we started to talk, he opened his briefcase and the current issue of *Head* fell out. The cover line was: "I Scored at the Big Top—San Francisco's Pot Supermarket." Joe grabbed it, stuffed it back into his briefcase and grinned sheepishly. "Well," he said, "I have to keep up with my clients." A lot of Joe's clients these days are people who don't pay their bills because the police have put liens on their property. That property tends to be marijuana. They are wheelers and dealers in the Palm Beach County drug subculture.

Joe is forty years old. He still hasn't changed the world. More important, perhaps, he has changed himself. We ended our conversations in a small, hole-in-the-wall restaurant which was less than half a mile from the *Post*. In the distance that Joe had traveled mentally and emotionally since those days, however, it could have been situated several light years away.

Joe started talking about change. The idea had captured his imagination, seized upon it as the notion of law school once had. He had spent a goodly amount of time thinking about the changing process.

Sometimes I think about life as a pinball game. You know how that works. If you shoot a ball up and it hits enough little bumpers, then you get a free game. I think life is like that too. If you go through enough, then you end up with some experiences that you don't have to pay the price for.

Somewhere along the way I realized as the I Ching says, change is eternal. Nothing is forever. If nothing is forever, then all is change. If you go through enough change, then you eventually start looking forward to the next change. At some point in life if you encounter enough change, you become accustomed to it. At that point people themselves change.

The next change becomes easier and the one after that easier still. In fact, it is sort of fun. We are all really living in one big soap opera. When you realize that, it becomes difficult to take yourself seriously. You realize if you screw up, you just try again.

By the time I got to law school, enough had happened to me that I was no longer afraid. I figured if I didn't make it through—and everything pointed to the fact that I wouldn't— I would just try again and there was no way it could hurt me if I went looking for another journalism job.

It is like the soap operas, you never know how it will turn out until it does. In my case I figure in some ways it was mainly luck. Hell, maybe in all ways it was luck.

Ordinarily I would conclude Joe's story here as he was just winding up the most recent of the changes in his life. But a sudden shift in Joe's attitude harkens back to something I said before and should be mentioned.

"For the first time in my life I am faced with the absolute whatever of being in a place for a while. Before I always faced the probability of moving on in a year or so. I'm actually looking at houses to buy."

Later still I heard that Joe had remarried and he and his

new wife had settled in West Palm Beach. Joe unexpectedly decided to root. The consummate changer decided to stay in place.

Like everyone else in this book, Joe is at his mid-life turning. And as we saw before, the transients send down roots and the rooted transplant themselves.

.

New Careers, New Lives 7

Despite the growing phenomenon of second careers, radical career shifts are enough of a novelty to be difficult to fathom. A hasty glance at the quicksand in their lives of mortgages, orthodontist bills, college tuition payments and the total on the supermarket's cash register and too many people conclude that career changes are a luxury they could ill afford. "Fine for them but it would never work for me" was a comment I often heard. This is mostly wrong.

A number of myths, which are usually incorrect, surround second careers. Here are some of the questions, embodying those myths, that are frequently asked.

Aren't people who change careers somehow different from you and me? Not really. As the case of Joe Jordan, the newspaper reporter turned lawyer, revealed in the last chapter, people who switch careers are not alarmed by change, even welcome it into their lives. To be sure, this can be a big difference but it is the only one. And even here people differed. Some wove safety nets and tied them fast before they proceeded. Others leaped off the high diving board before they plumbed the depth of the water below. The majority of career changers landed somewhere in between. Although they did not shrink from change, they were sometimes apprehensive about its effects.

The people in this book had no monopoly on good

fortune or luck. When I began my search, I deliberately excluded the very famous and concentrated on people whose success fell within the normal range. As a result they carried the same emotional luggage of strengths and weaknesses, or neuroses and mental health as the rest of us and in roughly the same proportions. The people who changed careers and lives after thirty-five were not set apart. In short, they were unusual in a single way. What others dreamed of, they dared to do.

If that is true, they must not have had any family responsibilities, right? Not so. Only three of my subjects were single and childless. The rest had spouses or children or both to support. In fact, they tended to form rather large families. By a strange coincidence the majority had three children. Two couples who were undertaking career changes together had only one child. Some were in second marriages and also had alimony and child-support payments to meet.

Were they wealthy then? Again no. They were largely and formidably middle class. For the most part their salaries paid their bills and they had little left over.

Does this mean anyone can change careers? Generally yes. If we are willing to take the risks and the commitment is there, almost all of us have a chance for satisfying and rewarding second careers.

Does that mean if I try, I will succeed? A good question that. Unfortunately there are no guarantees. A single lesson, however, emerges from all the stories of people who change careers that offers some guidance. If you can dream it, begin. If you can imagine it, proceed. Commitment and vision form a momentum of their own which can bring a successful conclusion. As Goethe wrote over a hundred years ago, "Boldness has genius, power and magic in it."

None of the people in this book, if they won a second chance, would change careers again in precisely the same way. They all made mistakes of judgment and sometimes those errors cost them money or time or both. In retrospect, looking back from the plaza of security that success can construct, they often shuddered and wondered that they had survived intact. But if they were forced to do it over and in the identical fashion, if the choice were between that and not changing at all, they would. Despite the hazards, not one was sorry. Mistakes, as Barbara Blaes pointed out, are not the worst things that can happen to a person. Much more damaging in the final analysis is the refusal to grow. Mistakes can be corrected; courses can be rectified. But the shriveling of the mind and spirit that accompanies the inability or unwillingness to make new starts leads to a psychological drought that is less easily remedied. Indeed it is often fatal to the personality.

In the end a more appropriate question might be: what if I never tried?

Tell me then, where do I begin? Wherever you are right now is, in fact, the correct place.

By the time the people here reached their decision to change careers, they had largely weathered their mid-life and mid-career crises. They realized that their careers, started with such high hopes and great expectations, were less than satisfying and that the lives they had constructed around those careers, more often than not, left plenty to be desired.

The people who embarked on second careers did not believe that they were trapped in their lives. They did not accept their unhappiness as a sturdy weed so firmly rooted in their lives that it could never be eradicated. They did not believe that the failings of their lives lay in them. They did not feel helpless. They did not stumble into the pitfall of assuming that their unhappiness was the result of a genetic defect. They felt their dissatisfaction was caused by external forces which could be brought under control and changed.

The people who determined to change careers knew there must be more to life. The question they grappled with was: where did that more lie?

"To work at something that affirms one's personal philosophy presupposes being able to define such a philosophy," concludes a Mainstream Associates report. "For many intelligent, capable people that is the first hurdle. . . . They can find inner direction only through a tremendous personal struggle."

To find the answer, they turned to the person they knew best—themselves.

They proceeded in one of two mutually exclusive and diametrically opposite ways. Some first reconnoitered the world around them. Others began by surveying their own interior landscapes.

Typical is a word rarely applied to Eleanor and George Pavloff, the inn owners we first encountered in chapter one. They chose the first and less-traveled route in switching careers. That is one way they are different but there is also a divergence of temperaments. Eleanor, whose friends call her Ellie, was the mover and shaker. George was the stodgier of the two who needed her prodding to relinquish the security he had always embraced. He needed Ellie to create for him the freedom she had established for herself a decade earlier. Their marriage was the perfect intersection of the irresistible force and immovable object.

In a sense Ellie's whole adult life has been an escape from the rigorous discipline of her childhood. "Growing up I was always the responsible child." On her eldest child shoulders devolved the obligation of caring for her brothers and sisters. She was the one who had to remember the dentist appointments and to get the report cards signed. For a long time "responsible" clung to her like a middle name. But wanderlust had always been in her genes. Her grandfather had been an explorer. When her father died, she reclaimed that inheritance. "After my father died, I quit my job and took off. That's what set me free."

She was only twenty-four then and the world was still in the offing. She shucked the shackles of responsibility and ran a free-form blitz at life. Germany was her original destination. There she ran student tours and in the process discovered Europe. After a couple of years, when she tired of touring the continent with a group of wide-eyed college students, she decided to return home. She worked for her passage on a cruise ship bound for the United States.

She ended up in Washington, D.C., where she taught in a Catholic high school. Her boss was George Pavloff. He was a priest. "I always thought if he weren't a priest, well, then. . . . I found out later on that he always had similar thoughts." The connection was never made. And Ellie eventually found that her wanderlust was reasserting itself with vengeance. She enlisted in the Peace Corps.

Her two years in the Peace Corps culminated in several years of teaching arts and crafts at Fisk University, a predominantly black school in Nashville, Tennessee. After a while she felt she was growing stale. "I felt I had done as much as I could and it was really time for a black to take over the program that I had begun." Ellie once again slung her knapsack over her shoulder and consulted her road maps. She ended up back in Washington, D.C.

There she rediscovered George Pavloff and this time they connected.

Back in 1968 he and other priests had joined in a public dissent to Pope John's encyclical on birth control. In their statement they said they did not believe that the church should necessarily forbid artificial means of contraception. For that they were suspended from their priestly duties for two years. George was a canon lawyer at the church court so the impact of the suspension on him was minimal but the tempest left him shaken and confused.

While he was suspended, he pursued a master's degree in psychology. By the time that the church was ready to reinstate him, George was prepared to leave the priesthood. His fortieth year was a hurricane of doubt and resolution. He bent and then snapped back. He made two hard-fought decisions that year. Early in 1970 he resigned from the priesthood and in December he married Ellie and irrevocably broke his priestly vows.

On their honeymoon George said, "I want roots, stability and no more change." Ellie laughed inside and was silent. She knew that both of them had a lot more growing to do.

They settled themselves into a house on Geranium Street

in Washington and an uneventful life. Ellie opened a pottery studio. George worked at the National Institute on Alcohol Abuse and Alcoholism which is in the Department of Health, Education and Welfare. They rarely saw each other.

George said, "The decision to leave came about gradually in this sense. I think that we are probably a little better than average in communicating our own feelings with each other. We began to be frustrated and depressed with our lives and we were able to communicate this with each other."

Ellie interrupted, "We began to feel: is this all there is to life?"

"We began to believe," said George, "that if we went on forever as dead people, then we would end up as dead people. We would be zombies. We came to share this conclusion because we were fairly well in touch."

George's nights became haunted by dreams of entrapment. He had a recurring nightmare. He was trapped. He tried to escape but this something that clawed at his ankles would not let go. The harder he struggled, the more the thing pulled him down. The thing was all enveloping. There was no escape in his night world. He woke up and found that rivulets of perspiration had drenched his armpits.

His training in psychology left him in little doubt about the meaning of his dreams. The something that made him feel as if he had spent the night rolled over and over on the ocean floor by a persistent wave which finally cast him spent and exhausted on a morning beach was his job and his life. The message of the nightmares was no secret. But despite their closeness George never shared these nighttime visions with Ellie. He believed that if he were to choose to leave Washington, then he would have to have a job and a house somewhere else to offer her.

"I casted about. I thought what else can I do. I wondered if I could be somebody other than what I had become."

One Monday morning after he had spent a restless night struggling up from that ocean bottom, George went off to work as usual but once he arrived at his office in Rockville,

Maryland, he did something which was not quite as ordinary. He called Ellie.

"I don't want to work," he said.

Her answer was quick and sure and totally unpredicted. "Why don't we sell the house?" she said. "We'll get the mortgage out of it and we'll find something else to do."

That day George accomplished very few things for the Department of Health, Education and Welfare. A different version of life tiptoed into his mind. Once it had a toe hold it refused to go away. "I never conceived of anything like this. I never really conceived of changing careers as a financial deal that could be arranged or of taking a year off to find what I wanted to do. But all of a sudden I thought, sure, why not take a year off and see where we want to go. This is where Ellie had brought me. I thought, well, I can get over the fear. I don't have to be so anxious and uptight. When she hit me with this, it suddenly seemed so right."

When George slid into the back seat of his car that evening, his mind was made up. "I remember I got into the carpool that night and looked at the people I worked with and thought, 'How simple it is, really.' "

He walked in the house and told Ellie, "Let's do this." George found as others who have changed careers before and since that the rest came relatively easily. "After all it was really evolutionary."

Years later Ellie looks back at that time and says, "I have wanderlust. I knew I wasn't destined to live on Geranium Street forever. I knew we weren't going to pay off the mortgage on that house. I also knew that it didn't really matter what kind of change it was as long as it was part of the process of growth."

"Ellie had always been free," says George. "She helped me to grow and put aside some of my anxieties and insecurities. When we married, I thought I had found the perfect house and what I thought was a marvelous job and I said, 'That's it.' But after a couple of years I became aware of a feeling of dissatisfaction and I realized how imperfect it really was.

"When we got married and I said I wanted no more change, she was confident that I would grow. She never told me that."

"I had jumped around a bit," she explains, "but I feel that I've always finished what I've started before I went on to something else. When I saw that he wasn't growing and that our time together was less satisfying because his work took up so much of the day, I felt that we needed a change. I guess I felt that we could do this together."

Not long after the Pavloffs agreed on the necessity of a new career and a new life, they put their house on the market and drove to Maine. They had circled no destination. They were resolutely determined to listen to their instincts. They wanted a town that offered the charm of a picture postcard. They eventually discovered Blue Hill as the shipbuilders of the nineteenth century had long before.

"We were looking for a town that we felt confident about and we found Blue Hill," says George.

Blue Hill offered all they had sought and more. Perched on a hill, overlooking the Atlantic Ocean, were a clutch of old New England houses whose white clapboards and mullioned windows belonged on that picture postcard.

Maine was the one compass point on their still-uncharted plan to switch careers. Both of them, and Ellie in particular, felt strong ties there. "I steered us to Maine," she says. They conceived their daughter in Maine and Ellie has always fantasied a life there. She was nineteen when she first visited the state but even then she knew that one day she would long to settle herself on its rocky outcroppings.

Not knowing what they wanted to do, they settled on where to do it. A first concrete step. They were determined to explore all the possibilities that Maine might offer. The transformation into inn owners started to evolve and take shape shortly after they had located in Blue Hill. They learned that the inn in their newly adopted hometown was for sale. An inn, they decided in their late-night give-and-take sessions, might provide the new life they were seeking. Ellie says, "I had this thing about being a marvelous hostess and a good cook and George in a tweedy jacket, smoking a pipe and greeting our guests."

In retrospect an inn seems a logical, perhaps even inevitable, choice. Her attorney father thought chopping vegetables was a fine way to escape from the pressures of the courtroom. "He always had a fantasy about being a chef." Perhaps his influence propelled Ellie's brother into the hotel management business. When the Pavloffs embarked for Maine, he was the general manager of a Holiday Inn in Bar Harbor. Yet they had not set out to buy an inn. Chance intervened there.

They made an offer on the Blue Hill Inn and found they had been eclipsed. The price tag on the winning bid was $110,000. "My reaction," says George, "was to faint."

Ellie and George, inn owners. The idea seemed to fit. At last they had a goal. A second positive step. In the highest of spirits they returned to Washington to pack a large rental truck with their household possessions. They wasted no time.

"It was important psychologically the way we did it. We had a sense of euphoria," says George. "I left my job on a Friday and Saturday we finished packing and on Sunday we drove an enormous U-Haul-It to Maine. On Monday we were there."

They were too naive to be intimidated. They skidded into Maine early in February, 1976. All they had to do was find an inn. A third and hardest step. They expected they would be in business that summer. "We had every intention of buying an inn and being ready to go by June 1," says George. "To say that we were overeager would be an understatement." They had no practical knowledge of innkeeping. The enormity of their undertaking totally escaped them.

"It was marvelous for a few months. It was sort of a game," says Ellie.

"It was really, really fun," echoes George.

In the beginning. Six months later they had shed their illusions. They had marched in and out of eighty different properties and not one fully met their requirements or, just as important, sparked a responsive twitch. "We had one rule: that either one of us could say no to a place," says Ellie. A lot of vetoes were issued between February and June.

The season in Maine stretches between Memorial Day and Labor Day. That is the time when the businesses which rely on tourists either make money or review chapter XI of the bankruptcy act. The Pavloffs sighed and began to dream of 1977. "When we saw this was not going to work out, we decided we might as well relax. It was a psychological relief. It really freed us up for another year," says George. "Some of the franticness left."

That extra year granted time for reflection. "We were completely uneducated about all the things that went into a wise decision," says George. Ellie adds, "The real estate agents quickly found out they had a couple of crazy people on their hands." The Maine winter would allow further refinement of their plan. They had talked to a lot of inn owners and in the process learned something about innkeeping. They had also learned about Maine and the routes the tourists traveled. All of this knowledge was caulking for the hundreds of punctures those first six months had put in their illusions. They were wiser but not necessarily happier.

Now they had to survive for a second year. Help arrived in the form of a consulting contract for George. The state of Maine could use his expertise in alcohol and drug-abuse programs. They desperately needed the money. George says, "Our bank roll was ridiculous." Ellie says, "We used to laugh about our capital."

They spotted the ad for the inn on Deer Isle in the *Maine Times*. It was a day when the bills in the morning mail outweighed the deposit slips in their checking account. Actually they had seen the inn months before and a single glance told them that it was picturesque and that charm sold high. "Only pure desperation drove us back," says Ellie. But this time they found the price had been slashed and, happily now, they fell in love. The final price was $90,000. "It is a ridiculously modest amount of money but it took everything we had or could possibly borrow," says George. And that was just the initial expense. They invested in a commercial stove and dishwasher, spent $1,500 on refurbishing the barn as a second dining room and are still untangling the snarls in the plumbing and electricity.

They moved into the red-shingled main house in February, 1977. Ninety days later they tacked their Pilgrim's Inn sign to the tree in the front yard and officially opened. Why the "Pilgrim's" Inn? "We're pilgrims and the people who come to our door are pilgrims. We were charmed by the idea of the old hostel type of inn where people come for respite on life's journey," says Ellie.

Before their Memorial Day opening they wondered if they would have any guests. They also wondered if they could manage if guests came. Ellie cried into the broccoli molds the first night. "I thought: I can't do it." By the middle of July she was serving thirty-six meals a night. A month later she, still struggling to do all the shopping and cooking herself, was near collapse.

"The biggest lesson of the first year was that we needed help," says George. "We thought we could do everything alone and we found we couldn't. We underestimated the amount of help we needed and were very fearful of the cost."

They claim they have committed so many mistakes they have already forgotten half. But they haven't retreated in the face of them any more than they double-timed back to Washington in the midst of their first ghastly winter. They willed themselves to survive and as a result they did. Now they are buoyant.

They were determined to create an inn where they would want to stay and so it is a perfect reflection of their personalities. They have surrounded themselves with the things they find comfortable which makes the inn itself comforting. Paintings of Deer Isle are grouped on the dining room walls. Antiques furnish the bedrooms and Oriental rugs cover the painted floors. In the common room where guests gather for pre-dinner cocktails cribbage boards and dog-eared books are piled on the coffee table in front of the fireplace.

The price of the room includes breakfast and dinner and most guests find lunch is an afterthought when the day begins with cereal and French toast and juice and bacon. Dinner numbs the hardiest palate, overpowers the shy appetite. Typically it opens with crackers and pâtés, crudities and dipping sauce to be nibbled with drinks as a fire licks the dampness from the air. In the dining room it builds—cream of cucumber soup, fresh whole salmon, mashed potatoes, broccoli with hollandaise sauce, salad—and for those who are still upright, walnut pudding anointed with vanilla ice cream.

"When I go back out and do consulting work I sometimes wonder if Pilgrim's Inn is really there," says George. "I feel it is sort of magical. Every time I get off the plane I am glad to be back. I feel this is the real world and the rest doesn't matter."

But that other world is still subsidizing that magic. George continues his consulting projects. At first he thought he would be able to close his contracts after a year or two. Now he doesn't even hazard a guess when that time will come. "We've got to grow every year so the question is how much we can grow and how fast," he says. "It seems to be going okay with the consulting money but there is a lot to do with it."

Old houses make greedy demands and the Pilgrim's Inn which was built as a private home in 1793 is no exception. Around the turn of the century decay settled in until the previous owner launched a rescue mission in the 1960s. The Pavloffs have funneled all their money back into the house. They have yet to pay themselves a salary.

But when the Pavloffs are listing the pluses and minuses of their career change, the assets always outweigh the debits. They have a life of variety and challenge and they have their daughter and each other. They brim with pride. "I feel," says George quite simply, "that we know how to do something well here."

Very few career changers can or will proceed as the Pavloffs did. To surrender the security of a monthly paycheck and depart for unknown destinations requires more psychological reserves than most of us can muster. Their random approach demanded courage and even a reckless disregard of reality. In a way Ellie had been in training her entire life for their career switch. Her anchor had always been dropped in the present. The past had never held much allure. Most of us have more binding ties to the lives we have fashioned and the people we have become than she did.

Most of the people I talked to who changed careers were more judicious. Once they reached a juncture where they knew they needed and wanted a second career, they assayed their strengths and weaknesses. They looked at their lives and asked themselves: what do I have that I can build on? By dredging the foundations of their existing selves, they discovered they could find the material to reconstruct their lives. They did not have to create themselves anew. They could assemble their future on their past. From that center core their career changes sprung.

At the same time serendipity was as important for them as it was for the Pavloffs. Thomas Edison once wrote that success is 90 percent perspiration and 10 percent inspiration and he had a point. But luck is a factor that can never be totally discounted. The biggest and most important decisions in life are always something of a gamble and fate can intervene to determine the outcome. However, the meaning of the experiences of the people who successfully changed careers is that they were prepared to seize and capitalize on the opportunities that presented themselves. They were ready to open the door before fate ever knocked.

In different ways Barbara Wennerstein and Bill Andrews illustrate this sequence. Both of them started at the same point. They held administrative positions in the academic community. Their goals came to be similar. Both ended up in the restaurant business. Barbara and Bill also demonstrate some of the different twistings and turnings that women and men take in switching careers.

A year ago everyone told Barbara Wennerstein she was a success. And so by conventional standards she was. As a librarian at William Paterson State College in Paterson, New Jersey, she made $18,000 a year which put her into the top 5 percent bracket for working women. There was only one problem. Barbara wasn't happy with her life.

In fact, she felt she had come to a dead end there amidst the Dewey Decimal system. She was languishing and knew it. She had grown up in Glen Rock only a cloverleaf intersection or so away from Paterson. She had attended undergraduate school at William Paterson as a math major and when student teaching failed to excite her, she enrolled in the library school at Columbia University. Several jobs later she was back at Paterson. Another eight years and she decided she had reached the end of that particular life corridor.

"I felt I had gotten enough out of being a librarian after twelve years. I felt I wouldn't progress much further. The only place for me to go really was to be the director of the library and that would have meant going back to school and getting a doctorate. I found that the responsibility was fine but I didn't really think I wanted to run the whole business."

When Barbara started to cast about for another career on which to hinge her life, she was brought right back to her origins. She had grown up in a family that traced their not-so-distant beginnings back to the Middle East and Scandinavia. Food was always the family fulcrum. "Growing up I was always surrounded by food and I was taught that it was important to prepare food well." At one point her parents had owned a luncheonette. Her uncle had been the manager of a grocery store. "I can remember at the age of nine or ten when other kids were playing nurse and doctor, I played restaurant."

To a large extent Barbara had carried that element of her childhood into her adult life. Cooking for and entertaining her friends were where she flourished. "I started to cook once I moved out of the family home. I really liked to entertain and cook. I'd rather read a cookbook than a novel. Cooking never seemed like work to me."

Barbara dimly realized that it was more fun cooking for friends on the weekends than it was cataloguing books Mondays to Fridays. Almost as a postscript to her life, Barbara announced to her family and friends that she was now in the catering business.

"I just decided at some point to make cooking a business instead of a hobby. I had always enjoyed cooking for friends and after a while I ended up cooking for friends of friends. I decided to see if I could expand by word of mouth. I didn't know if it would work out or if I could handle the volume in my apartment kitchen if it did."

She had a number of cards imprinted which bore the legend "The Swede Tooth" to give to friends. Much to her surprise she received as many calls as she could handle. One weekend she found herself adrift in flour, baking the desserts for a wedding party of 150. She didn't leave the kitchen for two days.

Here was the clearest of opportunities but for Barbara Wennerstein they were murky at best. Bored with her job, she had drawn on her strengths to create the catering business. "I really didn't know anything else besides food." When it prospered no one was more surprised than she. Barbara knew what she could do. She had no idea where her talent could take her. A familiar refrain begins to be heard here. Barbara did not begin to build systematically on the contacts she was accumulating in the catering business. It was a sideline, nothing more. She had gone just so far and saw no way to go further. She waited for fate to show her the way.

Events conspired in her favor. The year 1977 was all around a difficult time but it could not have been more propitious for her future development. Her dependency needs had loomed larger than she had suspected. The year she turned thirty-four, she ended a long-term relationship and said goodbye to her psychiatrist. A few months before her father had died. Like Ellie Pavloff she found that her father's death helped to sever an umbilical cord that now threatened to strangle her.

She resigned her job at William Paterson State College the same month that she culminated years of psychotherapy. "I had felt demoralized by everything. Now I felt that I was ready to do anything." What she did was escape. She had always dreamed of a respite in which she would turn her skills to the well-being of the disadvantaged. This she now did. After a summer of teaching in a school for Native Americans in New Mexico, she was ready to return to New York City. Her sabbatical replenished her. As did the autumn in New York.

She enrolled in the restaurant management school in a New York community college. One day, seized by a momentary whim, she picked up the phone and called Restaurant Associates which operates some of the best-known restaurants in the city. Barbara offered herself to them as a management trainee. Restaurant Associates accepted her in the class of 1977. "I feel I was kind of lucky. I've always been lucky and I've often gotten the best jobs by simply calling and walking in off the street."

A recurring refrain in Barbara's recital is: if it weren't for luck. This harkens back to women's unwillingness to accept risks and explains the reason I encountered difficulty in locating women who changed careers.* A number of studies, including the interviews that Margaret Hennig and Anne Jardim conducted for their book *The Managerial Woman*, have attested to the fact that women habitually place themselves in a psychological trap. Women characteristically credit "good fortune," "luck" and "being in the right place at the right time" for their success. When they fail, women rarely ascribe blame to these same kinds of random happenings. Instead, they accept failure as life's judgment on their indi-

---

* Another reason for that, of course, was the nature of the group itself and the way I defined career change. Relatively few women who are over 35 today have worked continuously outside their homes.

vidual self-worth. Success is something that "happens." Failure is "my" fault. The result is a feeling of entrapment. A lifetime is whiled away in the anteroom waiting to be called.

The number of women who say they are highly satisfied with their jobs has declined since 1967.[1] The women who read *Psychology Today* report more often than the men do that they would be willing to change jobs in the next five years. But as they confront the actual decision to switch careers, women, according to my interviews and sampling, tend to shrink back. Women may think about changing careers but men are more likely to go ahead.

A successful career switch does not "just happen." It requires thought and planning, decisions and action. Yet, the women were curiously oblivious of the role they had played in ordering the events that led to their new careers. Carol Anderson thought she became a chimney sweep because she had been swept up in the feminist movement and the gay rights' cause. Barbara Blaes and Christi Finch talked about their meeting the women who eventually became their business partners. By contrast the men perceived themselves as the initiators and managers of their career changes.

Barbara Wennerstein would not be nearly as interesting if fate alone had reordered her life. She chose to undertake a new challenge and rose to it. If her steps were halting, her triumph is that much more breathtaking. If she groped, so do most career changers.

"Whatever I now am," said Barbara, "had always been there. The difference is this. I always waited for someone else to lead the way. Now I don't."

When Barbara said that, she was halfway to her new career destination. She had recently decided that she wanted a restaurant of her own to nurture. The next stumbling point will come when she has to leave the safety of Restaurant Associates and strike out for herself.

And yet even the feistiness of that final statement is so very different from the calm assurance that Bill Andrews brought to his career change. Here is how he describes his decision. "It was a very thought out, conscious thing."

Bill also was raised in an ethnic family where the kitchen and evening meal were the center of life but it wasn't until he was out of college and on his own that he started cooking himself. "It was cook or starve." He began "classically" by ripping out the recipes beyond the center folds in *Playboy* magazine. From there he progressed through the *Better Homes and Garden* cookbook to *Joy of Cooking* and eventually graduated to Julia Child's *The Art of French Cooking*. Along the way he discovered what had begun as a necessity was also a lot of fun.

By the time he met and married his wife Kathleen, he was an accomplished chef and gourmet dinner parties quickly became the mainstay of their married life in Urbana, Illinois. "Cooking was my hobby but it was really a major hobby. It took up a great deal of my time and there were more and more dinners." The act of cooking, he found, was sustenance itself.

It was Illinois State that bought the butter and cream for all those French dinners. There he was head of student services. In the late 1960s when flames of student discontent were burning on college campuses across the country, Andrews loved his job. He worked twelve, sometimes fourteen hours a day putting out the brush fires on the Urbana campus, rushing home some mornings only to shower and change his clothes and head back to school. "In 1969 we were the only major college campus in Illinois that stayed open the whole year."

The feeling of accomplishment was exhilarating and then abruptly it was all over. The students stopped marching and a new college president decided to disband the student services program. Bill landed a job as assistant dean of students at the University of Wisconsin at Oshkosh. Bill quickly discovered the program there was an embryo of the one he had left. Two years of budget wars convinced him the victories weren't worth the battles.

He didn't have to look beyond his kitchen to discover something that would be worthwhile. The idea of opening a restaurant had floated through his mind before but always as a someday fantasy. Bill and friends of his from the Urbana days, Jerry and Mary Johnson, had even toyed with the idea of going into the restaurant business together. At thirty-five he knew the time had come. "I decided I was going to do it myself regardless."

Bill methodically set about drafting a plan. "I felt I knew how to cook. What I needed was to learn the business side. Most people in the restaurant business I knew had worked their way up. The problem as I defined it was: how do you learn how to run a restaurant without that?" He decided he would devote six months to his initial research and promptly discovered an even more basic problem. "Not knowing anybody in the business it was hard to even find people to talk to. I didn't know where to go to look for the answer."

The first help he got came from his boss who steered his young assistant to the dean of another branch of the University of Wisconsin which was more vocationally oriented. The dean offered some names and addresses. Bill began to collect the catalogues of hotel schools, cooking schools, hotel management schools—whatever he could find—as if they were flip-top bottle caps. They were also about as useful. "I read as much as I could. I quickly found out that no place really taught you how to run a restaurant."

In the process of looking and talking, Bill created the conditions in which serendipity could flourish. One day a note from his sister arrived in the mail. "I think this might interest you," she wrote and attached a small ad for the Restaurant School in Philadelphia that had appeared in *New York* magazine.

Bill read through their catalogue with mounting excitement. "It sounded like the answer to my prayer." The Restaurant School offered a curriculum that combined cooking and management. It also ran a restaurant where students could gain practical experience.

During Easter vacation of his last year at the University of Wisconsin Bill drove to Greeley, Colorado, where the Johnsons now lived. "The time has come," he told them. The Johnsons signed up as partners and together they mapped out the next stage of Bill's career switch. While Bill was in school, they would look for a site. They knew precisely the kind of place (an old house near the downtown area to attract the lunch crowd) and the kind of menu (French provincial) they wanted.

Four months before graduation, they had bought an old Victorian relic and Bill's teachers helped to design the plans for the restaurant. While the other students were playing with mock-ups in their courses, Bill was designing the restaurant he would soon own.

Bill had marshaled his career change as if he were masterminding the Normandy landing and so far he had successfully executed his plans. At the precise point that he should have felt the surge of realization, he felt the thud of reality.

By the time the four partners had finished removing the residue of the twelve cats and eight dogs that had once occupied their Victorian house and completed the metamorphosis that would create The French Countryman out of the shambles, Bill was exhausted—and scared. "I had lost a lot of confidence. I found I didn't know as much as I thought I did."

The first twelve months were so bad that they made the year Bill had spent keeping the peace at Urbana seem idyllic. "I would liken it to having a baby that never grows up. It never goes away and you can't walk away from it."

The French Countryman consistently rated rave reviews from restaurant critics in and out of Greeley but the good reviews couldn't pay the suppliers or arbitrate the disputes among four equal partners. When the Johnsons offered to buy back the Andrews' share in the partnership three years later, Bill said yes.

Bill took the money he had made and the expertise he

gained and returned to the drafting board. This time he sketched an entirely different restaurant. Sweet William it would be called and instead of modified Julia Child recipes, it would offer lighter fare. Eggs Benedict and omelets and sandwiches at all hours of the day.

When we talked, Bill was planning the first of what he hoped would become a chain. He had already located a site and as methodical as ever, he had already composed his first shopping list.

"I want to do something that is totally my own and—who knows—some day maybe I will go back and do another French Countryman."

As different as the stories of Bill, Barbara and the Pavloffs may seem and indeed are in details, they are more similar than they may appear at first blush. People bring themselves to the process of changing careers and are imprinted by it, not the reverse. True enough, the people in these pages are a varied group. Their career changes aside, they are little alike. Up to this point I have chosen in many respects to re-emphasize their diversity. The time has come to examine some of those reappearing threads.

Each of the people who changed careers sooner or later reached a turning point. For all of them there was a crisis period when it seemed easier to abandon the notion of changing careers than to go ahead. But for the people who succeeded this crisis was an epiphany which further fired their resolve. In the case of the Pavloffs it came that first ghastly winter in Maine. Knowing then that they would not open their inn for another year, watching their bank account dwindle, they might easily have panicked and given up. And yet George says, "I never thought about getting another (full time) job."

Exceptions they may be but the experience of the Pavloffs is instructive in one respect. They went ahead, often blindly, because they were unaware that they should not succeed. Not knowing that the odds were arrayed against them, they proceeded and surmounted them as so many others did. Any number of career switches might never have been made if the people had known in advance the mine fields that lay ahead. In short, ignorance is not always a liability. Even those who were aware of the odds were convinced that they could beat them. Few business ventures can match restaurants when it comes to bankruptcy. Small restaurants are noticeably doomed to fail but Bill Andrews never thought it could happen to him. "I figured somebody might fail but it would not be me. I was sure that I would survive."

They were a confident group. "When you really want something," said Barbara Wennerstein, "things tend to come together. They work out." This is not to say they were starry-eyed optimists. No one, for instance, would ever accuse Ely Callaway of that. But for the people who changed careers the antonym for optimism is not pessimism but hard-nosed realism. Ely said, "You just make the best estimates you can and go ahead. I think about the possibility of failure but I don't worry about it. I suppose if there were an invasion of locusts it could happen but I know we're not going to have that invasion. I don't worry mainly because I know it is going to work."

This confidence which comes from negotiating our life passages to a successful conclusion may be responsible for the essential solitude of the decision to change careers. To a large extent they kept their own counsel. Professional advice was strikingly absent. Paul Hadley, the Episcopalian priest who is now at the Department of Transportation, briefly consulted a career guidance counselor but found the experience so dissatisfying that he quickly abandoned that approach. None of the others even made the first appointment. Sometimes this help was unavailable or they weren't aware that it existed but the feeling is they would not have sought it in any event.

The amazing thing about these career changers is that they forfeited even the advice that was readily available. Not one person mobilized the support network of family, friends and colleagues. (The impact this had on their families is discussed in the next chapter.) They drafted their own blueprints not just because they had to but also because they were the kind of people who felt most comfortable relying on themselves.

Perhaps in retrospect it was just as well. The support they might have anticipated was not forthcoming. The reaction of friends and associates was uniformly negative. On occasion it was envy and as often it was jealousy masquerading as hostility. There was a general disbelief. This is not particularly surprising. Relationships which last tend to be mutually reinforcing. Married couples and single people seek out friends who are of their own ilk and in a similar life stage. Whole social circles are built around professional associations. The unstated pact is: you ratify my choices because you chose them too. When one party breaks that pact by making new choices, a queasiness sets in. The classic example, of course, is the shock waves which ripple out among a couple's friends when they announce they are getting a divorce. This phenomenon was no less present among the people who changed careers.

The experience of Barbara Wennerstein was typical. When she revealed that she was about to leave her $18,000 a year position and that no other job was yet in sight, her friends and family were horrified. Her friends chorused: "What are you doing?" and "How can you quit your job?" They warned: "Don't quit until you have something else lined up."

Barbara listened and went ahead—eventually. The litany restrained her longer than she would have liked. "The reason I stayed with my job as long as I did," she stated, "was the influence of my family and friends."

This was a familiar backdrop. When Ely Callaway summarized the reaction of his friends, he said succinctly, "Mostly they think I am nuts." To leave the presidency of the largest textile company in the Western world for the precarious life of a small vineyard owner must be madness. How else could his best friends, presidents and chairmen of boards themselves, think of it? Because if they thought of it differently, it might require the admittance of things in their own lives that they would rather not face.

A similar reaction was encountered by Semih Ustun, the editor at the Voice of America who quit to head Vie de France bakeries. What did his colleagues say?

"They thought I was nuts. I was forty-four years old and under the Voice of America regulations I could retire in six more years with a very comfortable pension. I suppose if you look at it in those terms I was out of my mind."

Once again we hear the same refrain from the business friends of Jack Davies who revived Schramsberg Vineyards. When he announced his resignation at Docummun, many of his colleagues were stunned. Some concluded that Jack Davies had gone slightly daft. One said, "My goodness, I couldn't do that. I have to support my family."

"As if," sniffed Jack, "I intended to let my family starve."

To be sure, changing careers requires money but it demands fewer reserves than one might think. Not one of the people in this book had inherited wealth. Even those who had found a secure niche in the upper-middle class like Jack Davies and commodities stockbroker Iver Brook who became a marine biologist had done so by the dint of hard work. A small minority had accumulated money which could be used to subsidize a career switch but if that change were to be unsuccessful, they would have been left with nothing. Ely Callaway had close to $2 million to invest in a vineyard and winery and few of us ever will. But Ely had worked twelve hours a day for thirty-three years to amass that sum and if he had failed, he would have had little to show for a lifetime of effort. As Ely said, "This is my own money. When you work for a company, you don't have to worry that the company will go bankrupt because it's not your skin. This is a different kind of involvement." All these people gambled money they could not afford to lose.

Basically they used the money they had and made the most of it. Some like Bill Andrews and Gary Johnson had spouses who earned enough money to absorb part of the financial shock. A few like Ely Callaway and Semih Ustun launched their new businesses while they were still employed. They, however, were rarities. The overwhelming majority found that it was impossible to straddle their old and new worlds. There were simply too many demands and so little time. They took money where they could find it. They used their savings, sold their houses, signed business and personal loans and borrowed from friends. Most were forced to combine several or all sources.

It is difficult to estimate the cost of changing careers. There are so many variables and just as many imponderables. Barbara Blaes spent only a few dollars for an advertisement in a community newspaper. Callaway invested millions. The range could not be wider. But it is safe to say that the cost must include the money that was never earned as well as the financial outlay. The Restaurant School cost Bill Andrews $1,800 for tuition and part of that was offset by tips in the restaurant. But when his living expenses and his travel costs between Philadelphia where he was in school and Washington, D.C., where his wife was working are added in, the tab is pushed far, far higher. "I figure the whole year cost me $15,000 when you also figure in the $18,000 or so that I didn't make—which I think is valid. It is not only the monetary sacrifice that counts."

All agreed the financial risk was real. They made significant financial sacrifices or risked substantial losses in order to change careers. The risk is even more striking because none of those whose career changes would cost them dearly waited until they had the cash squirreled away in a safety deposit box. Just as they set out before they had finished plotting their entire journey so, too, they left before they knew they could pay their way. They were not dalliers. In general they decided to change careers in a matter of months. (In some cases the incubation period seemed to have been years.) A breathtaking period when they wound up their affairs and made their plans followed. At some point they simply shunted aside their doubts and plunged ahead.

Was the risk worth it? Financially, no.

Second careers in general offer poor returns on investments. There were striking exceptions. Ustun is sprinting
toward his first million and Christi Finch says she is earning
three times her former salary. But theirs are unusual cases.
Much more typical is Bill Andrews. Before he left The
French Countryman he had not earned a salary for four
years. Ely Callaway estimates that the total elapsed time
before he turns a profit is fifteen years and the Pavloffs can't
even visualize when that day will arrive. This is not to say
they are necessarily worse off.

Money loses some of its urgency when people are engaged
in their own pursuits. Carol Anderson, the juvenile probation
officer turned chimney sweep, said, "At some point I decided
I could have money or leisure but not both. I decided I would
rather have the time." Then, too, they found it was easier to
forfeit now when they were building to a self-determined
future. Barbara Wennerstein's income had been halved but
as far as she can see the sacrifice is small and relatively brief.
"I don't feel worse off. I don't see this lasting forever. I feel
it is just temporary. And it is leading to someplace I want to
go."

To which might be added: not one of them suffered
regrets.

Part
FOUR

Family Snapshots 8

Sweet Nancy pushed the remnants of her chef salad back and forth on her plate, forming little hills and valleys, and traced interstate highways through them with her fork.

In the East the autumn leaves were turning the maples and elms into red and yellow torches but outside the only restaurant in Temecula, California, the thermometer still hovered in the 90s in early October. The grapes from the Callaway Vineyards several miles back down Route 15 had been harvested and crushed and were now fermenting, well on their way to premium wines, vintage 1978.

Everything should have been perfect. Nancy Callaway, the wife of Ely and the namesake for his "Sweet Nancy" late harvest Chenin Blanc, wanted to believe that. But the conspiracy between the romantic vision of her life and the nonfiction reality of it was increasingly difficult to maintain. Something which she had difficulty naming was stirring within her.

The problem which she was reluctant to accept is that she has trouble filling up her days. After the "Phil Donahue Show," what?

Nancy Callaway wants to be happy out there in the desert of Southern California. If she isn't, it is not entirely her fault.

Two people rarely grow at the same rate. Husbands and

wives are not shoots from the same plant. At mid-life spouses do not always share the same version of a happy ending. The dream of one can be the nightmare of the other. A radical career change rewrites the existing script. When one person wants to stay and another wants to go, otherwise "perfect" marriages sometimes end up in divorce courts. Some 10 to 15 percent of marriages, according to career counselors I consulted, dissolve when a spouse sets out on a new venture. Some career advisors put the figure even higher up to 50 percent of marriages. This happens more commonly when the wife feels growing pains than when the husband does. Most of the women I studied were single or if they had married were now divorced; most of the men in this book are married. The security of marriage appears to facilitate career changes for men. That same stability impedes sudden departures for women. The explanation is not difficult to come by. New careers are not likely in the midst of child-rearing and when the children are finally grown too many husbands are too comfortable to provide their wives freedom to do their own growing. As it so often happens, women pay a higher price for development. They set off on their pilgrimages alone.

Ely and Nancy Callaway do not conform in every respect to this scenario. In fact, when Ely decided to stop whizzing around the country as president of Burlington Industries and root himself in Temecula, they were not yet married. Their story, however, illustrates the underlying theme. The realization of one dream often entails the denial of another.

Nancy would not say that she fell in love at first sight. That would be overstating the case. She was too old, too sophisticated for that to happen. Blessed with the Mary Tyler Moore, All-American good looks of cheerleaders and Homecoming Queens, she had had more than her share of serious romances but she was still single when they met. She was a model in San Francisco and her then-constant companion was Ely Callaway's cousin.

The two of them flew to New York for a visit in 1971 and The Cousin engineered the fateful meeting. Before they left San Francisco, Nancy was prepped for the coming encounter.

"His cousin gave me a copy of a speech that Ely had made on trade to a Senate subcommittee. Usually, I'm not interested in anything that has to do with politics but to please his cousin I read it. I was very impressed, not only with what he said but also how he said it."

An express elevator whisked The Cousin and Nancy to Ely Callaway's domain on the top floor of the Burlington Industries building. A receptionist ushered them into an office where two-inch carpets muffled all sounds from the street below.

"I remember that she said 'Mr. Callaway' is here to meet 'Mr. Callaway.' "

Ely stood to welcome them. By his sheer presence he dominated the vast expanse of wall-to-wall carpet and the windows to the floor overlooking some of the world's most expensive real estate. Nancy recalls it well.

"I so vividly remember laying eyes on him. He was so vibrant and alive. He was such a positive personality. There was that twinkle, that gleam in his eye. He really is a rascal. It was impossible to overlook him. I felt that I had never met anybody like that in my entire life."

The feeling was apparently mutual.

Several months later Ely Callaway was scheduled to visit the West Coast. He called Nancy and asked if she were free for dinner. On their first date they went to Trader Vic's where they sipped exotic concoctions and watched pineapples float in their drinks.

Nancy and Ely fell in love. A star-spangled courtship, sprinkled with fairy dust and bound in ribbons of New York–San Francisco plane tickets, followed. Cross country telephone calls and transcontinental dates alternated until Nancy succumbed to his pleas and moved to New York. She took her own apartment on West 58th Street right down the street from Burlington Industries and Ely.

"We had a wonderful life. We went to all the plays. We went out to dinner every night. We went to Madison Square Garden. We met our friends in the country. We went shopping together. We walked around the streets at night. There was no way that I didn't feel my romance with Ely reached all the expectations of what it should be. I miss it all very much."

Life was one long dinner at the Four Seasons until Ely announced he was retiring to Temecula. The first time he brought up the vineyard she asked, "Where on earth is Temecula?" and thought it sounded a lonnnng way away. Nancy knew his retirement plans but at the start of their relationship she had never anticipated that it would happen so soon or that she would be part of it. With the provincial passion of an adopted New Yorker, Nancy believed the backwaters began at East 92nd Street.

The change was abrupt. Nancy had fantasized concrete canyons and got real mountains instead. Culture shock!

"I didn't think seriously of not going or of going just as a trial. I knew it was a permanent move. I would have gone to Alaska to be with Ely. I felt very safe. I knew no matter what Ely decided to do he could handle anything and everything and I knew whatever he decided he would be exciting to be around."

They were married in Palm Desert near Palm Springs in 1973. A picture of a radiant Nancy with a sprig of flowers in her hair and a beaming Ely sits in his winery office.

No doubt Nancy believed when they married that love conquers all. The trouble is that love is a very poor companion between 9 A.M. and 5 P.M. Although Nancy willingly, gladly followed Ely, she sacrificed her desires for his dream in order to do so. Women who choose to go may not be making a bad bargain but that doesn't disguise the fact that the terms of the choice are defined by the men they love. Out there in the desert Ely had his vineyard and Nancy had Nancy.

"A fairy tale life is the way I want to think of it. I want to think in terms of everything lovely and happy."

Nancy wanted to play Barbara Stanwyck in a 1950s movie.

She would wear long skirts whose ruffles flirted with the tops of her polished boots and she would always look as if she had just galloped up to the farmhouse door.

Only reality kept intruding. That ranch house door opened into an ordinary tract house and Nancy fit into Temecula as well as a peacock would fit into a canary cage. She and the other women shared few common interests and anyway the boss's wife can never be a real friend to the wives of her husband's employees. "I tried but it didn't work." Ely, sensing her frustration, sought to bring her into the winery. "He wants me to be involved very much but he just couldn't find the right niche for me. He asked if I would be his secretary!"

One day when Phil Donahue was keeping her company again, Nancy confronted an unwelcomed truth. She was alone except for toothy, cherubic Phil and very lonely. "I was totally wrapping myself around the winery and Ely. I had nothing else." She was also very tired.

The weekdays were so empty that she tried to recoup on the weekends cramming all the companionship she craved into the magical times at their condominium in Palm Desert. Only Ely's ideal weekend was several rounds of golf with the president of Citicorp when he could complain about the insufficiency of venture capital for small businesses and demand that something be done about it. That was not Nancy's idea of happiness.

"He goes fast and I go slow. He was going 10,000 miles an hour and I was trying to be a perfect wife and keep up. I was mentally and physically exhausted."

Nancy was struggling to fill the role that Gail Sheehy terms the caregiver, the woman who lives out her life for and through her relationships. "You know when you get married you have certain ideals about what you should do for your husband." Nancy embraced those Mrs. Goodwife notions with a passion. Caring for Ely meant: vacuuming the house in Temecula on Friday so it would be neat and tidy for their return on Sunday night, packing their suitcases, loading the suitcases into the red BMW and then, like a film reel that is being rewound, speeding through the sequence in reverse, unloading, unpacking and cleaning the condominium in Palm Desert for the next weekend. After three years which seemed to be spent in a car that was perpetually coming and going, exhaustion set in. It also became obvious that Ely Callaway could take care of himself. His wife was forced against her will to begin staking out a life of her own.

One of the first steps was an interview program on a cable television station in Palm Springs. With the Callaway entree and the celebrities roosting there, Nancy found she could snare guests with ease. Separate cars to the desert followed so Nancy could stay to tape her television shows early in the week. A second step was to join the Junior League in La Jolla and to lease a studio apartment there.

Now says Nancy, "I lead a very separate life. Which I don't really want to do."

When Ely kisses her goodbye in the mornings these days, he asks, "Sweetheart, where are you spending the night?"

At best a partial resolution.

She still lives a disjointed life, flung out over the empty spaces of Southern California desert. She still travels for hours to the compass points of her world. Ely goes to the dinner parties of her Junior League friends in La Jolla but Nancy continues to find friendship in a place where she doesn't live difficult to maintain. And when she is in Temecula, she is alone except for Ely.

"Sometimes I think if I could just squish it all together geographically, compress it into one place, everything would be all right."

But some ends that are left untied are largely the result of her own internal doubts. She continues to cling to the role of Mrs. Goodwife who has the pot roast in the oven and a freshly baked apple cake cooling in the kitchen when her husband comes home at night. Although Ely is unabashedly proud of her undertakings, misgivings about her course simmer beneath the surface.

"I would like to be with Ely all the time but I can't stand the isolation. I go in spurts, spending a day, a week here and there. Everything is so far away—one hour and five minutes to La Jolla and one hour and 30 minutes to Palm Springs. I'm used to walking to Bergdorf Goodman. I feel split and I hate being gone so much."

Nancy has to assimilate the lesson which most women are forced to learn sooner or later. While a life without love may not be meaningful, love alone is not a full-time occupation. But then that was her dream, not his.

One last cry escapes.

"I feel that I literally do have a fairy tale life, so why am I not relaxing and enjoying it? I feel that I am married to one of the truly great men in America, the one great love in my life, so why am I not happier?"

Nancy is still waiting for the "and they lived happily ever after" to be written to *her* story.

An element of triage exists in these radical career changes. A little bit of the survival of the fittest could be heard amidst the gaps of the individual stories I was told. "It's either her or me," said a man who had decided to change careers but had yet to impart that news to his wife. The response of the men was so consistently uniform to one of my questions that I came to anticipate it. In reply to, "And how did your wife react?" they paused and answered abruptly, "She totally supported me." Period. End of sentence.

Some of the men clutched their wives' hands and together they plodded through the decision-making process that culminated in a mid-life career change. But they were the exception. Lengthy heart-to-heart talks before the fire were notably lacking.

More often the wives were told in a sudden confessional burst well after the fact that left no room for argument, no space for demurring. Gary Cline woke his wife, Marie, in the middle of the night and said, "I've got to go to the seminary." She was flabbergasted. "I had never really discussed it with her. I didn't want to think it was a real possibility so I avoided any talk of it. It was frightening for me—and for her."

The seminary is a three-year program. Marie said, "I'll give you three years and then I am leaving." Gary was committed no matter how long it took. After a fifteen-year recess from college where he had been a marginal C student, he didn't know if he could complete the course work in three years. He went anyway.

At the end of the three years he said, "Marie doesn't have the commitment that we do at the seminary and she resents my involvement there. One of the results of this change is that my wife has become more independent. I could dominate her and did for a long time. After I got immersed in the seminary, I lacked the psychic energy to do that. We have a lot of work to do on our marriage."

Sympathy for their partner's plight was noticeably lacking. Their urgency was such that they could not afford to be diverted. There were men who had identified the lacunae in their own lives and who had marshaled their mental and emotional forces to fill them. They were not to be dissuaded.

Remember Iver Brook, the commodities stockbroker who decided to get a doctorate in marine biology? For months after his decision was firm, he groped for the appropriate words to tell his wife. He never found the right words so in the end he just blurted the facts. He could not have picked a more symbolic moment if he had tried. It was December 31, 1967. New Year's Eve. The start of a new year. Peggy and Iver Brook had invited all of their friends to come celebrate the start of 1968 with them.

Iver figured, "Here we go. I'll just try."

Shortly before midnight he cornered his wife. "I'm going back to school," he said. Peggy thought he was kidding. Then she realized he was serious. It was not exactly a happy new year.

They sat on the bottom stair step and talked until 4 A.M. while their guests swirled around them. Their guests came and finally went. They won no host and hostess awards for that party.

Peggy was forty-six. She had been thirty-one when she and Iver married. For a person of her generation that was late in life. Like her husband, she was a child of the Depression and her attitudes had been molded by her parents' experiences. She, too, had a professional father who went for months without ever collecting a fee. The things she valued most in life—security and stability—were the things that had originally attracted her to Iver because she knew he wanted them too.

Suddenly he didn't want them any more. He was willing to cast aside all the things that were meaningful to her and once to him. The House in the Suburbs. The Congenial Neighbors. The Good Schools. For fifteen years Peggy had been the good trooper. All of a sudden the general said that they were fighting a different war.

Her reaction?

"She panicked."

Iver was sympathetic. He understood. More than the other men I studied, he empathized with her situation.

"Here she was a suburban housewife who is living in the house and community she had always wanted with good neighbors, good schools and two kids and I suddenly announce that I'm going to pull off for six months minimum, maybe a year. I think she was upset real bad. It's not easy to move into entirely new surroundings at that age." His response?

"I don't know what would have happened if she had waged a solid campaign against it. Peggy had always been very supportive. My guess is that I would have gone ahead."

Peggy put on a new uniform and re-enlisted like most of the women. But not all. Wives can remain wives and mothers stay mothers wherever the couple lives. They may have trouble adjusting, the experience may be wrenching but their roles are not threatened. Some women, however, signed up to be helpmates and partners in a joint venture. Their careers are at stake when their husbands announce at mid-life that they are changing directions and that the new course requires a solo flight plan. If she typed his Ph.D. dissertation way back when and poured sherry at faculty teas for twenty years, she is not going to look kindly at his mid-life longings. Too much of her has been invested in that ivy-covered facade. If she stayed up nights alone with the colicky baby while he, the young knight in white, attended other people's infants in the hospital emergency room, she is not going to be willing twenty years later to give up the $50,000 a year income so the now-established physician can indulge himself.

Sometimes the husband's occupation is a critical strand of the wife's identity, in which case his decision to change careers will rupture her self-image.

Gerd Stern was a poet and an artist when he and his first wife married. He was a happening in the art world of the 1960s before the word even existed. His first multi-media extravaganza at the San Francisco Museum of Art in 1963 was an electronic free-for-all that featured television, tele-phone, audio tapes, slide projections and more. The unsus-pecting eyes and ears of spectators were bombarded by simultaneous electronic messages. Gerd and his wife settled down in an abandoned church in Garnerville, New York, where Gerd and other multi-media artists—collectively known as US Company or USCO—collaborated on environments. Their work was celebrated as the future of art by the art critics of such publications as *The New York Times*, *Newsweek* and *Life*. All was well while Gerd was rocketing through the esoteric lofts, galleries and museums of the New York art world. The poverty of those years could be borne in the name of art. Life was exciting. Creative bonfires blazed through the night. Interesting people milled in and out of the church. His wife was plugged in. Through him she merged into the ferment of the sixties.

When Gerd moved to Cambridge, Massachusetts, and founded Intermedia Systems to apply those same artistic concepts commercially, his wife refused to go. "She married an artist, not a businessman," said Gerd.

One of the closest partnerships exists between ministers and their wives. Traditionally a church bought a package deal. It paid one salary and hired two workers. The wife was expected to lend an ever-helping hand. Generations of ministers' wives doused personal desires and ambitions and struggled to keep their lipstick on and their stocking seams straight. They cranked the mimeograph machine, taught Sunday School, sang in the choir, ran the rummage sale, organized the altar guild, tossed salads for the covered-dish supper, paid condolence calls, rejoiced at christenings and smiled, smiled, smiled. Generations of ministerial students sought wives who were willing to subordinate their own lives to their husbands' careers.

When ministers leave the church, their wives discover that their career has ended also. Dr. Robert Foulkes, the director of the Northeast Career Center in Princeton, New Jersey, specializes in counseling these men and their families. I tested this observation on him. He agreed.

"It is murder on the spouse and the family," he said. "Most of the spouses that we see really feel that the church is special. They feel that the ministry is a special career. They approve of that. There is a great deal of family stress."

The husband may have experienced a crisis in values or he may have decided that the ministry was the wrong career to begin with but the wife who has sacrificed for their common calling is suddenly adrift. It is impossible for her to be a minister's wife if he is no longer a minister. The minister finds that in order to change careers he must first wean his wife from the church. The struggle is waged on two fronts and the most intense fighting may occur in his living room.

"Some wives are delighted about hubby," he said. "But many more are hanging on viciously, saying 'You must stay in at all costs.' They are more dedicated than their spouses."

The marriages that seem to fare the best are those that have endured the longest and where the wives have separate interests to pursue. Having a life of their own, they are inclined to grant freedom and space to their husbands. The closed marriages, built on a series of "you do this and I do that" contracts, are the ones that are the most easily threatened. The close embrace is as likely to suffocate as to protect.

Of all the couples I studied Gary and Betty Johnson seemed to have ridden the shock waves of mid-life career changes the best. The mutual friend who first urged me to contact the Johnsons confirmed my feeling. "Theirs," she said, "is a MARRIAGE in capital letters."

Several factors helped the Johnson marriage to survive, even to flourish. Gary confided in Betty from the start. She was on the sidelines, watching, as he progressed from thinking about changing to planning the switch. His decision was not an ultimatum. When he was ready to change, so was she. As a nurse and professor of psychiatric nursing, she could readily understand his attraction to her field and his choice of a second career. In fact, his decision helped to validate the one she had made years before. As he began nursing school, she could understand and sympathize with the problems he was encountering. His studies were another mutual interest which they could share.

And no doubt luck also intervened. Their years together had woven firm but resilient bonds of mutual respect and giving. They could stretch and hold fast at the same time.

Shortly after Gary took his second-year finals, I put my feet under their kitchen table and the three of us talked about the impact of his career change on their marriage.

"I feel we were fortunate," said Gary, "to have as many years together as we did before this happened. We are smart enough to intervene before the stress gets so bad that it could really affect us."

Betty chimed in, "The nursing course is very stressful for a lot of married students in the program. We have an old marriage of seventeen years that is fairly stable. A lot of the kids have young marriages and it is really difficult for the spouses who are not in the program, who have not been through the course to realize that it is really very, very difficult."

None of this means that their marriage has gone on exactly as before.

"I always felt," said Betty, "inferior to the logical and

mathematical side of him. I resented that because it was so foreign to me. Now that he has made the career change, I feel much more self-confident about what I am doing."

"I see that kind of strength," said Gary.

"We've always talked about the things that bothered us," continued Betty. "We really communicated. Nothing has changed there but now we communicate in different ways. I used to be very passive. I would go in my room and cry. Now I yell back."

Perhaps that is inevitable. Not bad, just predictable. If he stays home and she goes to work, the chances are that she will feel a right to complain when things don't go to her satisfaction.

The most obvious change in their marriage as a result of Gary's career switch, however, has been the reversal of sexual stereotypes.

For two years Gary has started Betty's coffee at 6 A.M. and spread mustard on Wonder Bread so their three children will have sandwiches for their school lunches. Gary dusts the bookshelves and volunteers to bake the brownies for the elementary school bake sale. He answers the door when they come home at 3 P.M. and tucks them into bed at night. "It makes getting a Ph.D. seem like kindergarten." Betty luxuriates in all this. She teaches psychiatric nursing at the University of Portland and is delighted to bring home the paycheck that pays the bills. When Gary was offered a part-time appointment in the mathematics department at the school, he said no. "I felt the kids needed me more." So Gary washes the dishes and Betty goes off to work. On weekends they take turns as the parent-in-charge.

The reversal encompasses their roles as husband and wife as well as mother and father. Gary is financially dependent on Betty now and in the process Betty has emerged as his mentor and protector. Her urge is to fight his battles.

"The hardest time I had this year," said Betty, "was working beside an instructor with whom Gary didn't get along. He was really mad at her and it was hard not to intervene. I stayed out completely because it could have been sticky but I had a real temptation. I thought a lot about it but I finally decided 'no, that's not really an okay thing to do.' "

The two have turned inward and their marriage has become more closed. Couples must sacrifice something somewhere if their journey is to succeed. The Johnsons chose to shed friends. Their involvement in the church, once a focus of their life, has declined and there are no longer standing invitations for Friday night dinners to single friends whom Betty is convinced won't eat properly unless they come to her so-called "moveable feasts." Even the spur of the moment, come for coffee after class get togethers have vanished. The steady stream of people in and out of the house has dwindled to a trickle.

"We really haven't made friends here except among the people we've met at school," Betty said. "And we went the whole last semester without inviting any of them over. The time just went zip."

"Our energy has so many demands on it from work and the kids," said Gary, "that we just don't do the things we once did. We don't have space in our lives for other people."

Sometimes those people even include their children, fourteen-year-old Blaise, ten-year-old Rose and five-year-old Johanna. "Betty and I," said Gary, "have so much to share that the kids get short shrift from us these days." Betty added, "This career change is much harder on the kids than on Gary and me. We talk to each other all the time and the kids have a tough time capturing our attention." Over the corn on the cob and the Jell-o dessert Rose yells, "*Stop talking nursing. Quit talking about nursing.*"

The Johnsons had the children in mind when they settled on the University of Portland. Oregon seemed less disruptive, more like Vancouver than some of the other places they considered such as San Diego and San Francisco. Rose and Johanna burrowed in at once but Blaise balked from the beginning.

One night in Vancouver Blaise told his mother, "Why

don't we let him go and we'll stay here. It's what *he* wants to do."

In fact, Blaise who is starting to cope with his first sexual stirrings is not at all comfortable with the notion of my father, the nurse. He misses the security and predictability of a father who offers a traditional vision of masculinity. His friends intensify his discomfort by their teasing. "Hey, Blaise," a classmate called across the schoolyard, "I hear your father is a nurse. Are you going to give him a bra to go with his white stockings?" Blaise lied and said his father was not a nurse. ("Well, he's not—yet," insisted Blaise, twisting uneasily in his chair, as his father related this incident.) Gary is different and if there is one constant in adolescence it is that conformity is all. Blending into the crowd is infinitely preferable to standing out. A father in nursing school is a distinct liability in junior high school.

A majority of the people I talked to had children but relatively few of those children were directly affected by their career change. Some of the men married late in life and had children after they switched careers. Others who had children at home made a conscious decision to remain in the same locality and the children were mostly oblivious to the transformations in their parents' lives. Barbara Goldstein said of her ten-year-old daughter Janie, "She hears us talking late at night but I don't think she really comprehends what is going on." Carol Anderson who changed careers and sexual preferences at the same time was also convinced that her daughter Gillian was untouched. "I don't think Gillian notices the difference. For her it has made no difference at all." Although Carol's switch has made little outward difference in Gillian's life, Carol wonders if it has not influenced her in subtle ways. "I sometimes wonder what she thinks of me. I wonder what I would have thought if I had a chimney sweep for a mother. I can't imagine what my reaction would have been."

Older children who are cultivating their own gardens are singularly enthusiastic. They tend to rejoice in their parents' growth. In the midst of growing up themselves, they unexpectedly find a kindred soul. Barbara Blaes said, "My children were thrilled that I finally got out of the kitchen." Ely Callaway's three children had a similar reaction. "They love the idea of the old man being a little old winemaker. They never noticed me when I was president of Burlington. That was nothing to them. The same thing happened with my cousins. They couldn't have cared less when I was at Burlington. They thought Callaway Mills was much more important. Of course, it's only one-fiftieth the size. Now that they see their name on the bottle they think I'm doing something great."

Blaise may have sulked but Gary's mother was devastated. Gary, after all, was fulfilling her dream. "My mother really wanted a scientist, a university professor for a son." When Gary was denied tenure, she chose to ignore its real meaning. "She kept saying, 'Everything will turn out okay.'" It was patently obvious it would not and when things, in fact, did not work out and Gary announced he intended to go to nursing school, she fought against it. "Frankly, my mother was disappointed. She felt it was very prestigious to be a university professor but a little common to be a nurse. She really enjoyed being taken to lunch at the Faculty Club. Now when she comes to visit me, she has to eat in the cafeteria." The year of Gary's decision was a stormy time in their relationship.

There was another wrinkle. His mother was a licensed practical nurse. In fact, she earned her license in mid-life, returning to school when Gary was a teenager, to do so. In the nursing hierarchy an LPN is near the bottom and the antagonism between registered and licensed practical nurses is often intense. "She has a lot of angry feelings toward registered nurses. She doesn't feel simply because a person is an RN that she or he is competent." Gary seemed to be entering the ranks of the enemy.

Several years passed before his mother was able to reconcile herself to his decision, before she could be happy with her son's version of his life. Yet, finally, she called and said, "If you want me to say 'I let you go,' I let you go."

"From that point on," said Gary, "things got better in my mind. Now she can introduce me as my son, the nurse."

Ironically, Gary's father accepted his son's choice from the start. "He was pretty comfortable with it the whole time. He pretty well lets people be. As long as people are happy he feels it is okay."

The reaction of Gary's mother is fairly common. Parents often erect Maginot lines of resistance when their adult children want to change careers. And they object for many of the same reasons that Gary's mother did.

All too often the message that parents send to their offspring arrives in one of two envelopes. The first says: be exactly like me. Be "like Dad" or, less frequently, "like Mother." The child is expected to grow up and continue the family tradition. If a son, he is to wear the junior proudly and conform to the conventional pattern. Wanderlust, a chafing against prescribed rules, may be understandable in other people's sons. It is more difficult to acknowledge in one's own. If a daughter, she is to bear the grandchildren and perpetuate the next generation. Usually the parental mantle is draped on boys. The phrase goes: he is a chip off the old block. He, not she. But this is not always the case and when the cloak is draped on girls, it tends to confine even more. Women who return to school at mid-life report that they encounter the most strenuous objections from their parents and in-laws.[1] Carol Anderson, remember, was to become the P.T.A. booster her mother had been. "My mother is aghast at what I have done. She wants me to stop being a chimney sweep *immediately*, if not sooner."

The second, more common message says: be everything I couldn't. A clone is nice but most parents would prefer a perfected version of themselves. In an open and upwardly mobile society where this possibility exists few parents begrudge the sacrifices that enable their children to scale the next rung on the ladder whether it is from the working to the middle class or from there to the professional class. The children who have grown up hearing "I never had your advantages" could populate a major state.

Either way parents acquire a tremendous emotional and financial stake in their children's lives. They resent, even fear, change in their adult sons and daughters. Any change threatens their investment. If the forty-year-old son retires the family shingle, the father may feel that he and the life he has led are rejected also. If the grown daughter walks out of the kitchen and into law school, the homemaker mother may feel her choice has been repudiated. And if the professional of either sex packs away the diploma and takes up pottery, both parents will question the wisdom of all those years that the money was squeezed out of the grocery account and deposited in the college tuition fund. The self-image of many parents is linked to the outcome of their children.

Parents hope to transmit their values to their children but the value revolution of the 1960s and 1970s have left parents and their middle-aged children gazing at each other across a new generation gap. Parents who married and had children during the Depression still cling to the notion of one life, one career and a gold watch at sixty-five. The fact that their children could cavalierly discard the very security that they worked so hard to achieve is difficult to accept. The mother who stocks the linen closet with ten tubes of toothpaste and the pantry with canned goods "just in case" is not going to understand the daughter who quits a well-paying job to roam the country as a free-lance photographer.

The story of Dani Emery is a fine example of this conflict. Dani has a high-salaried, high-powered position as chief of the economic research program at the Census Bureau in Suitland, Maryland. After six years in the federal government she is close to the top of the civil service hierarchy. On an eighteen grade scale she is a GS-14. At forty she makes $38,000 a year. But Dani is also planning to leave the civil service and become a management consultant in private industry.

Her parents, Helena and Charles Brzezinski are appalled. They are of the generation that saved and planned and scrimped so that their children could do just a little bit better and so when they retired they might travel to Europe on a senior citizens' tour. The Brzezinskis are first-generation Americans, both of them children of Polish immigrants, who believe that a chicken in the freezer and a weekly paycheck provide the same sort of security that a numbered Swiss bank account offers. Helena was one of nine children. The boys went to college and she went to work as a clerk at the Bureau of Labor Statistics. Charles came from a family of four children. There was money enough to send one of them to college. Since he had a bad leg, his parents reasoned that he would be the most in need of a college degree.

He was graduated from Worcester Polytechnic Institute in Massachusetts in the midst of the Depression. At the commencement exercises, the president stood up and said, "This class has achieved the distinction of not having one graduate placed." Charles Brzezinski went to work in a factory counting screws and considered himself fortunate to have a job at all. Such were the advantages of a college diploma. He eventually gravitated into the civil service and a position as a statistician at the Department of Defense.

But he never lost faith. Work, work, work, he told his two daughters. Learn something practical. You may have to support yourself. Your husband may die. God forbid, you may be divorced. Always be able to get a job.

When Dani fantasized about designing elegant buildings, he said, "Take mechanical drawing." Her junior high school principal refused to admit her to the class. That was a course for boys. Girls enrolled in home economics. Charles Brzezinski took the day off from work and marched into the principal's office. "My daughter," he said, "is *not* going to make apple brown betty." Dani enrolled in mechanical drawing.

The Brzezinskis early on started college funds for their daughters but Dani still scraped plates in the dining hall at the College of Notre Dame in Baltimore to finance her college education. She wanted to major in speech and drama. Her father insisted on economics. "He really kicked my ass into economics. He said, 'Major in economics and you can always get a job.' He always insisted that I should be able to make a living."

Now that Dani is supporting herself and her three teenage children comfortably, they can't believe that she would willingly forsake the security and benefits of government employment. "Do you realize what you are giving up?" they keep asking. A family friend called and said, "Do you know how upset your parents are?"

Like many of her generation Dani possesses the comfort of a belief that her parents are unable to hold. Her attitude is: "I won't go hungry." "I can always sell panties in Woodward and Lothrop's basement. I can be a checkout clerk at Giant and I know that eventually I will become the chief checker. I know I will never starve." The Brzezinskis, who continue to hoard stray carrots and dabs of gravy in the refrigerator against some distant catastrophe, fear they very well might.

Career counselor John Landgraf sees this parental clinging to the gold watch standard all the time. "The parents are scared," he said. "They believe in the gold watch theory. They put the pressure on the forty-year-old sons and daughters to stay put. The family pressure is like the song 'stay as sweet as you are.' People who want to change careers have to buck that and it is hard."

Most of the career changers in this book juggled spouse and family, home and work—or tried to—and prayed that they could keep up the performance. A few, however, chose differently.

For all the talk in this country about children, for all the *Good Housekeeping* magazines sold, for all the popularity of such family shows as "Eight Is Enough," we are noticeably willing to sacrifice our spouses and our children for our careers. Frequent moves, 6 A.M. rides into the city and 7 P.M. trains out, hastily grabbed dinners before a quick retreat into the den to prepare tomorrow's sales report, weekends on the golf course to snare a client leave little time left for families. Of readers who responded to the *Psychology Today* survey 21 percent said their work schedules interfered with their family lives. Some 24 percent complained about excessive hours and 13 percent said they worked excessive overtime. Another 28 percent felt they had to start work too early or leave work too late.[2] But they never said no. At the end of the daily maze lies total exhaustion and one more night spent plopped in front of the television set.

If the majority of career changers had a propensity to let their families pay the price, several couples deliberately changed careers in order to weave a different fabric for their lives. All married and had children late in life. Unlike couples in their twenties who assume that the clash between work and family is inevitable, these couples who are in their late thirties and early forties were unwilling to accept this schism. They rebelled against the pattern of Daddy Who Goes to Work and Mommy Who Stays Home and sought wholeness.

Undoubtedly, this reflects the various meanings that family and work hold when people couple at different ages. In studying the timing of the life cycle, sociologist Bernice L. Neugarten found that certain ages are generally considered correct for major life events.[3] People who conform, who finish school, marry, raise children, reach their career peaks and retire at the appropriate ages are said to be on track. Once a person switches gears and veers off on a different path, the intrinsic meaning of those events changes, mutates into something entirely different. The emotions are not the same and the experience is modified. It may be better or worse depending on the person but it will be something else for the individual who listens to his own cadences than it is for the individual who conforms to convention. The person who marries at thirty-five will not have the same kind of marriage as the individual who says "I do" at age twenty-two. The couple who waits until their late thirties to have children will not form the same family unit as the man and woman who become parents in their mid-twenties.

So it was with these couples. Their families and their marriages were of noticeably more importance to them. They were the sparks that ignited their desires to change careers.

Up in the Napa Valley the grape vines are stirring again. The first gray-green tendrils are curling themselves around the barbed-wire arbors. The bottles of champagne from last fall's harvest are asleep in the caves at Schramsberg Vineyards. On the kind of Saturday morning in April that inspires thoughts of Robert Browning, the Davies keep a leisurely pace. Jamie is transplanting marigold seedlings on the front lawn. Jack is reviewing the accounting books. Their three sons wander in and out of the two-story white clapboard house. Chickens scratch in the driveway and ducks and Rosie, the dog, chase each other through the flower beds. Browning would say all is right in their world. Which is exactly the way they intended for it to be.

Jack was thirty-seven and Jamie was thirty-five when they married. Shortly afterward they left behind the romantic wind-tossed sea glimpses of San Francisco where they courted and moved to Los Angeles.

Southern California was a different world and that meant a different life. Jack rode the freeways and Jamie hung curtains in a little tract house and got pregnant. On Saturdays Jack often disappeared to the airport for another week-long tour of Docummun branches, impressing on plant managers the necessity of keeping costs down. While he was gone, Jamie played pick-up-toys with her sons. They settled in but they weren't ready to settle.

Unlike many men, Jack saw clearly through his Harvard Business School trained eyes where he was heading. "I knew that in ten years I wouldn't be able to talk about anything except the intracacies of refracting metal components." He knew something else. "That's not too terribly interesting to anybody else." Like his wife.

Jamie was willing to go along—for a while. "I knew when we went down to Los Angeles that I didn't want it to be forever. I felt it was the right thing for Jack to do at the time. I felt those years had a purpose but I didn't want to stay there permanently."

Jack spent a lot of nights in empty hotel rooms thinking about Jamie alone, swabbing Gerber's Baby Food off dimpled chins. "I gave some important thought to my wife's attitude. I thought if she could have a career, something she could involve herself in, she would be happier and it would be better for all of us."

Back in the tract house, alone in front of the television set after the babies were tucked in bed, Jamie was thinking similar thoughts. "I felt we definitely needed a change. I knew he did and I was ready to move from the city. I felt we needed something we could share but, of course, we had to make a living at the same time."

Their future emerged like the picture on the cover of a jigsaw puzzle box. A circular piece here, a triangular shape there and suddenly it all takes shape. Both still loved the San Francisco Bay area. Jamie grew up there and was graduated from the University of California at Berkeley. Jack spent his bachelor days in Marin County when San Francisco still claimed to be the only cosmopolitan city in the United States. During those years Jack joined the San Francisco Wine and Food Society and his palate learned to distinguish a beaujolais from a bordeaux. Jamie loves cooking. And the two of them are fond of sitting around the dining room table after dinner, sharing a good bottle of wine with friends. It took a year for the outlines of a small family-owned vineyard and winery to take shape.

"There was none of this light flashing, going off in our heads, ever," said Jack. "It all sort of evolved. We found that this was a way of making a living that we could like in a personal sense. A winery seemed to satisfy all of our criteria."

The first years were rough. Especially for Jamie.

The days never ended. Three children under the age of five clawed at her skirts. The roof of the house was rotted and needed to be replaced before it was really inhabitable. There was no help. And the winery was as demanding as a fourth child.

"I must admit that the first few years when our boys were still babies, with the difficult condition of the place and the difficulty of help, I had to constantly remind myself that this was a long-range proposition and that it would not last forever like that."

But the Davies knew where they were headed and they were determined to get there. They knew what they wanted and they steeled themselves to create it. And they did.

Their marriage is a union in the fullest, truest sense of the word. Their business is a merger of their two selves. When Jack travels through the wine country of France, Jamie is beside him. When noted food writer Simone Beck visits, Jamie sets the picnic table in the vineyard while Jack opens the champagne. And in the Napa Valley she is not Jack Davies' wife but Jack Davies' partner.

"I don't know a single wife in the valley who doesn't work side by side with her husband every day. I feel there is a real place for a woman in each of the wine ventures up here. A small winery is a very personal business. You have to develop a following of individuals who are interested in the wine and part of that interest is the people behind the wine. As part of our public relations program, we entertain people from all over the world who are interested in wine. We invite them into our family circle. Having a woman involved is a very nice thing. I think we have a certain sensitivity, an under-standing of people that helps. Up here I am not considered to be Jack Davies' wife. People think of me as an individual and I like that."

Jamie thrives in the Napa Valley. She wears her life as if it were a talisman. She knows her destiny and thinks it is just fine. The outcome could have been very different. But Jamie had the good fortune of marrying at an age when she wanted to be a partner as well as a wife and of finding a husband who was at an age when he valued his wife and family as much as his career.

Their sons and their sons' wives may eventually be the biggest beneficiaries of their luck.

"We are definitely very close now," Jamie says. "There is no separation between what he does and what I do in certain parts of the business. People don't believe it but if I end up with a sinkful of dishes, Jack is the first to help. I want the children to observe that. I don't want them to grow up with the idea that there is a woman's role and a man's role."

The Davies have woven a life which is of a single cloth. There is no distinction between their work and their play, their private spaces and public places.

As their vines sent down roots and prospered, they sprouted their own connections in the community. They have a rich, multi-dimensional life. All of the vineyard owners are proud of their valley and committed to defending their way of life against encroachments. Socially that requires maintaining a spirit of cooperation and friendship. Jamie's a mover and shaker, a pivot around which the social life of the valley revolves. A lot of wine is drunk at that picnic table in the redwood groves. "People have friends in and you want them to meet other friends and somehow we always end up with grandparents and children at the same party and no one minds." In fact, it creates a life style that people whose relatives are strung out across the United States would envy. Economically that means keeping out the tract suburbs and urban problems that continue to creep north from San Francisco. Jack has emerged as a community leader.

When he lived in Los Angeles, the sheriff and chairman of the board of supervisors were names on an election day ballot. In Calistoga they are personal friends who work together in common causes. "I've never before been involved in things of fundamental importance to the community but here there are many, many issues which touch all of us directly. They are not things you merely read about in the newspaper. Everybody is involved day in and day out."

Not long ago Jack led the fight to kill a four-lane superhighway which the state of California proposed to build through the center of the valley. He is largely responsible for the strict zoning laws in the area.

"People ask," said Jack, "what do you *do* up there. Finding things to do is the last problem we have. We never feel that we are living out in Boonesville. By and large it is a very interesting life."

In the end it is a question of scale.

Jack Davies was schooled and trained to rise to the top of the corporate hierarchy. Undoubtedly he was headed there. His about-face flew in the face of conventional wisdom. He chose to draw a tighter circle around his life and to concentrate his influence in his own backyard. To do so takes a strong man and one who values people over things.

"Sometimes I look at some idiot up there [at the top of a company] and say to myself I could do it so much better. So why didn't I stay in a big business? I guess the answer is because I don't have to be in the big arena to prove myself. My impact has been on our small world right here in the valley. Some people may think this is small potatoes but I don't think so. I'm committed to making fine wine and the Napa Valley is the greatest asset the United States has for this purpose. Therefore, if I can protect it, I think that's accomplishing something."

Once upon a time Jack thought about life after work and Jamie anticipated the day when grandchildren would bounce on her knee. Those days are gone forever. There is no retreat from the life they have created.

"We don't think in those terms any more," said Jamie. "How do you ever retire from something you have created?"

The answer is: you don't.

In the End a Beginning 9

Well over a hundred years ago Thomas Carlyle, the English essayist and philosopher, wrote, "Blessed be he who has found his work, he needs no further blessing." To which the people in this book might very well add, "Amen."

Work is supposed to be the salt that flavors our days but we all know that it is often the ingredient that sours our lives.

A paradox this. Side by side on the library shelves sit studies that say the majority of people would choose to work even if they didn't need the money and studies that conclude people are more dissatisfied than ever at work.

Productivity, a simple word for a complex concept that calculates the amount of goods produced per hour of work, falls and contributes to the decline of the dollar abroad and trade deficits. Government bureaucrats spend a lot of time trying to understand the reasons people aren't working as hard as before and Congress even creates a center to study the problem. Just a few blocks away from these government buildings, a near riot occurs when the transit authority announces it will pay $5 an hour to workers who are willing to shovel snow off the railway tracks and cannot provide jobs for all who come to claim them.

The unemployment rate was about as high as it ever has been in 1979 and that fall *U.S. News and World Report* ran a cover story on the unhappiness of well-educated and successful young professionals. Fully 60 percent of these workers, according to the article, would prefer a different job.[1]

Perhaps the mystery should be expected. All of the relationships which animate our lives contain contradictions and those that surround work run no deeper and are no more perplexing than those that envelop sex or love.

The stories of the people who populate this book offer a clue to a resolution. Their lives embody the distinction between "work" and, to use E. F. Schumaker's felicitous phrase, "good work." A tidy definition would be this. "Work" provides a livelihood. "Good work" enriches the soul as well as the wallet.

This harkens back to the "Me Generation" and has echoes of the growing up that we do after thirty-five. It also says a lot about the social climate that we all live and work in.

The people who started to come of age around 1945 and the generations which have taken their place in the work force since, represent a revolution of rising expectations. Simply put, few people today have to work very hard simply to survive. That is true despite the rising cost of living which began in the 1970s and threatens to continue through the 1980s. Even the national malaise that finds Americans for the first time in the history of national polls saying that they believe their children will not enjoy their standard of living does not obscure the fact that most people are better off than their parents.

Hedges exist now which were missing a few decades before. A goodly number of people who are now in command posts in the country have no personal memories of the Depression, have never experienced real economic hardship or been threatened by economic insecurity. This is a new phenomenon. Social Security benefits, disability payments, unemployment compensation, food stamps and welfare erect barriers on behalf of people who cannot work and sometimes people who will not work.

The rights that labor organizers fought for in the early part of this century are now presumed. A clean work place, safety and a decent day's wage for a day's labor are expected. Technology has eliminated much drudgery and the blessings of automation have nearly eliminated physical effort in many fields and substantially reduced it in others.

All of this is profoundly liberating but like most liberation movements a whole new set of problems has been created in its wake. These advantages are now called entitlements and like most things we have been born to, they are not enough. Labor relations analyst John R. Browning has said, "Today's workers want much more. They want nothing less than eight hours of meaningful, skillfully guided, personally satisfying work for eight hours' pay. And that's not easy for most companies to provide."[2] If people no longer need to worry about starvation, they will brood about meaninglessness. If they no longer fear the prospect of death or injury on the job, they will fret about the lack of challenge.

And so we do. When *Psychology Today* asked its readers to rate some eighteen job characteristics in order of importance and satisfaction, they found almost no linkages between the two. Job features which were most satisfying were of little moment. "Friendliness of people you work with" was number one in satisfaction but only fourteenth in importance. "The respect you receive from people you work with" was third in satisfaction and eighth in importance. "The amount of job security you have" ranked fifth in satisfaction and eleventh in importance. The reverse was equally true. The aspects of jobs which people consider most important generated little satisfaction. "Chances to do something that makes you feel good about yourself" was number one in importance but twelfth in satisfaction. "Chances to learn new things" was picked third in importance but tenth in satisfaction. "Opportunity to develop your skills and abilities" appeared fourth in importance but nineteenth in satisfaction. Significantly, some of the closest correlations were found among the entitlements. "Amount of pay you get" was twelfth in importance and sixteenth in satisfaction. "Physical surroundings of your job" was eighteenth in importance and thirteenth in satisfaction.

"The assumption that work should have significance both in its performance and its product is one of the dictums of the decade," says Mainstream Associates. This is the impulse that sparks mid-life career changes.

They sought intimacy and closeness. Therein lies the mid-life lure of the helping professions. Lawyers and ministers, nurses and image-makers have all peopled these pages. Certainly this kind of emotional sharing produces intimacy but frequently the closeness is defined in physical terms. Perhaps the benefits of technology and labor-saving devices have been sprinkled too liberally through our lives because the desire here is for the direct engagement of hands and the more of the six senses the better.

People who love their work are also apt to love the physical dimensions of it. (Conversely, if you don't like the tools you use every day, there is a better than even chance that you are in the wrong job.) Actors vibrate to the smell of greasepaint and writers conduct love affairs with battered typewriters. The people who changed careers often found this sort of bodily contact was a new-found joy in their work. Several learned that a pyramid of peaches, ripening in the sun at an open air market, could quicken the pulse rate. Carol Anderson discovered the perverse satisfaction of muscles and limbs that ache with exhaustion after a day of manual labor. The smell of grapes permeates the Callaway winery and Ely is never more than a few steps away from it. Jack Davies twists and clips his vines himself. The physical element is an important and welcomed aspect of their second careers.

They also pursued occupations where it was easy to see the relationship between their work and the results. Bill Andrews commented, "No one when I was at the University of Wisconsin ever came up to me and said, 'I really liked what you did today.'" Most likely because no one was absolutely sure what he had done. Concreteness was equally important in these second careers. This characteristic tends to disappear in the forms of one sort or another that most people spend their days processing. George Pavloff said, "I loved my experience at the institute. I worked with fine, fine people. But the work became increasingly abstract and removed from reality and from real life. This is not to say that the work doesn't serve a purpose but the purpose seemed so remote." There is nothing even slightly remote about toting breakfast trays up and down back stairs or making twenty beds a morning.

Throughout all these second lives immediacy was abundantly present. Bill Andrews summed up his rewards by saying, "The satisfaction of restaurant cooking is that you get immediate feedback. Someone says, 'That's good,' and that's the nutshell. (Of course, if it is bad . . .) I don't have to wait at all. There's pride in doing a thing well and having people say they like it. It's all ego in the restaurant business." Others would say the same for owning an inn or producing a fine wine or passionately arguing a client's case before a jury.

In slightly differently phrased fugues of the same theme, most career changers spoke of the thrill of knowing: "This is my work and I am responsible for it." They adopted occupations in which there was no refuge from final acceptance for success or failure, where responsibility could not be diffused. They were clearly the final authorities. If Gary Johnson bungles a patient's medication, he has no place to flee. When Iver Brook publishes an article, he accepts the fact that it will be subjected to rigorous examination by the authorities in his field of marine biology. David Goldstein knows that he will be held accountable if his firm's potential client buys elsewhere.

Concreteness is more readily available on a small scale. One of the underlying themes of these career changes is the drift from large to small. This occurs as our motivations change course in mid-life. Bureaucracies and institutional frameworks where most of us start our working lives are ideal settings for fulfilling power needs and making money which are our objectives then. They are poor incubators of self-development and growth which gain ascendancy after forty. Not by chance, then, have so many people in this book become self-employed or maneuvered themselves into positions where they set the terms of their days. These people are most apt to receive periodic report cards on their efforts.

Intimacy and concreteness. Intimations of both could be heard in the conversations I had with Ely Callaway. At fifty-three Ely undoubtedly had everything most people seek and at the same age deliberately chose to relinquish power, influence and a six-figure salary to seek a different set of rewards. He had no difficulty enumerating them.

"Two things give you satisfaction in the wine business," he said. "One is the taste. You know that you started it and you did it and it's your personal influence. You know you're pleasing the people who drink it and that's pretty fabulous. The second is making money. If you make money, over the long haul that's a pretty good sign that you are a success."

Perhaps the optimum would be that all of us who find our enthusiasms waning and interests flagging at mid-life would be able to establish second careers. Certainly there are no lack of occupations in the offing. Ruth Osborn, director of the Center for Continuing Education at George Washington University, pointed out, "There are all kinds of careers that didn't exist ten years ago." But that is the ideal.

If we are constrained by emotional, social or financial considerations from switching careers, we can still hope to rekindle the meaning in our working lives. The lives of the people who changed careers are signposts that point in the right direction. By definition the ingredients of "good work" are present within them.

The most readily available synonym for this concept may be craftsmanship. That has a distinctly old-fashioned air to it but spruced up in the love beads of the flower children and the Woodstock mythology, it became the underlying theme of the archetypical book of the 1960s, *The Greening of America*.

"Work," wrote Charles A. Reich, "can be pleasant,

satisfying and free, without making man feel that he has done anything worthwhile with his life—that he has lived greatly. And so the ultimate question concerning work is this: how can it be heroic? What does it mean to be heroic, and how can this be translated into contemporary terms?"[3]

Two decades before, C. Wright Mills, the chronicler of life in the modern bureaucracy, had already proposed an answer.[4] No one before or since has summed up so succinctly the qualities whose presence can make work redeeming and whose absence can make it de-humanizing. All of the characteristics which the people who changed careers achieved are detailed here:

1. Good work is concerned, first and foremost, with the quality of a product and the skill that product requires. Money, fame, status, prestige come second and sometimes not at all. To be sure, as Ely Callaway pointed out, money can be an indicator that a product is well done and for that matter so can fame and prestige. But for craftsmen these by-products of work hold little allure. The craftsman is attracted to work he loves and can do well. Most of us will find that this stage of sublime indifference is difficult to reach before the fourth decade of life. To get there, it helps, as these career changers demonstrate, to have achieved a measure of success in the first half of our working lives.

2. In good work we can see the relationship between the part and the whole. We can "own" the product of our work. If we can't stamp our names on our products in the form of by-lines and brand names, we can possess them psychologically. In some of the more enlightened businesses that have dispensed with assembly lines, the pay-offs in terms of reduced absenteeism and higher productivity have been remarkable. Identification is easier when we produce not widgets but automobiles that our friends may drive.

This is not to say that good work never entails drudgery. It does and often in more abundance than we would like. But as Mills writes, "If work, in some of its phases, has the taint of travail and vexation and mechanical drudgery, still the

craftsman is carried over these junctures by keen anticipa-
tion." As glamorous as some of these second careers may
appear, all of them offer their fair share of tedium and
frustration. Kitchens where the temperatures top in the
steamy nineties day after day. Turning thousands of wine
bottles by hand. Long hours spent reading the garbled prose
of court opinions in search of the one right case. But these
career changers endured such drudgery because of the bond-
ing between them and their work.

3. Good work provides challenges. It is not ease that
makes work good and hardship can be a prod to growth.
Reich talked about heroism but in mid-twentieth century
America opportunities to quest for the Golden Fleece are
noticeably absent. Adventures of all kinds are few and far
between. For many of us navigating the freeway each morning
may be the closest we come. The lack of excitement in our
daily lives is probably the reason that amusement park owners
report their biggest attractions are those that whip riders
around upside down at 70 miles per hour and that travel
agency owners record an upswing in the number of people
who wish to go on dangerous expeditions to remote places.
Good work can fill that lack.

Challenges offer the opportunity to pit ourselves against
"the recalcitrance of materials and the malice of things" and
prevail. In a push-button, touch-tone world that is not so
easily found. For spirited people this testing of the self seems
to be the essence of work. When work becomes mechanical,
it loses its lure. Mastery is a signal that the time has come to
move on. Such people find that switching careers is a spiritual
version of the redoubtably physical Outward Bound.

4. As craftsmen we are free to stop and start work as we
please. Leisure has grown in importance in the not-so-distant
past. (Most likely this growth reveals a lot about the character
of many jobs.) According to a recent survey, only 21 percent
say that work means more to them than leisure and another
60 percent say that although they enjoy their work, it is not
the major source of their satisfaction. In labor negotiations
unions have offered to trade more time off for raises in hourly

pay. In good work deadlines are always present but we can
exercise control in meeting them. If we choose to work at 3
A.M. on Sunday morning and take Tuesday off, so be it.
Control is the key word here and it was one that the people
who changed careers often mentioned. Carol Anderson can
elect to lower her income and increase her leisure and no
boss will mention the strain that puts on the probation
department.

As craftsmen we are also free to shape the outcome of
our work to our own specifications. We can add, subtract and
modify at will. Jack Davies can age his champagne for as long
as he pleases and no corporate hierarchy will urge that he
hurry production so the profit margin will grow.

5. Skill is a necessary component of craftsmanship,
essential in fact but good work allows for the development of
the self as well as technique. The technical skills do not exist
apart from us but grow out of the intermeshing of our lives
and personalities. As we perfect our craftsmanship, we have
the chance to furnish new rooms for our inner life. Gary
Johnson learned about medicine in nursing school but he
discovered as much, if not more, about previously neglected
aspects of himself. To work well is to grow as individuals.

6. Craftsmanship integrates work and play. As Mills
points out, "Play is something you do to be happily occupied,
but if work occupies you happily, it is also serious, just as play
is to the child." Some forms of artistic creation most readily
demonstrate this. No one who has ever stood in awe before
an Impressionist painting or heard Arthur Rubinstein play a
Chopin sonata can doubt that these artists received pleasure
in their work. Although artists may grab the attention, the
same combination exists in the lives of people whose closest
link to the art world is painting the garage.

The long hours that successful people invest in their
work is not always the result of neurotic compulsion as some
psychologists would have us believe. The love of work is also
a compelling urge that keeps people in their offices until
midnight and drives them back on weekends. The love of
work and success comes close to Siamese twinship. Not

everybody who loves his work achieves stardom but it is difficult to imagine an individual who is acclaimed for work he truly dislikes. This kind of affection for their work was a hallmark of career switchers and the people who changed, remember, were chosen from the ranks of the successful.

Christi Finch illustrates these points and to the precept that work should be fun she attributes her success. "I think the reason why we have succeeded is that we started out to do something we enjoyed doing and ended up making money at it. Too many people reverse the process. They try to figure out a way to make money first and end up failing."

7. A corollary of this is that good work is companionable. It provides company for our hours away from the office or studio. Associates are an extended family. Shop talk is the most pleasurable conversation. The craftsman in fact may rarely disengage from his work even when he is physically distant. A writer once said that he could always recognize a fellow author with a book in progress. A certain preoccupation, he said. "There's something funny going on behind the eyes," he mused. But the same could be said for the doctor who has a patient on the critical list and the entrepreneur whose sales curve is going down when it was projected to go up.

Leisure may only be the space that is necessary to get on with the work. "As he brings to his leisure the capacity and problems of his work," says Mills, "so he brings back into work those sensitivities he could not gain in periods of high sustained tension necessary for solid work."

Good work has an easy rhythm to it. An ebb and flow, a contraction and expansion—all the cadences of the world around us.

Two decades of adulthood later, we may feel that we have doubled back to the starting point. The end of the teens and the end of the thirties have an agonizingly lot in common. The same questions that we wrestled with before return to haunt us. Both periods are marked by identity crises and career doubts. But at forty we possess advantages that we lacked at twenty. We do not have to create ourselves from scratch. The task is of renewal and rejuvenation. The same past decisions that constrain us also offer a structure within which we can grow. We have a better understanding of our strengths now and also of our weaknesses. If we have more liabilities, we also have more resources. Freed from parental pressures and the demands of small children, we can plant our feet in the soil of our own choosing.

All of the students of adult development from Carl Jung to Daniel J. Levinson have written of the importance of the forties. The "noon of life" was the phrase that Jung used for the time when we can see back to what we were and forward to what we may become. Levinson spoke of "full fledged adulthood" when we can rejoice in our individuality and our humanity. At forty we take our place in the link of generations.

For once F. Scott Fitzgerald was wrong. There are second acts in American lives. The people who switched careers changed the scenery and got on with the play.

Chapter
Notes

Chapter 1

1. Tom Wolfe, "The Me Decade and the Third Great Awakening," *New York*, August 23, 1976, pp. 24–40.
2. Daniel Yankelovich, "The New Psychological Contracts at Work," *Psychology Today*, May, 1978, pp. 46–50.
3. Patricia A. Renwick, Edward E. Lawler, and the Psychology Today staff, "What You Really Want From Your Job," *Psychology Today*, May, 1978, p. 65.
4. Dale Tarnowieski, *The Changing Success Ethic* (New York: The American Management Association, 1973).
5. Quoted in Henry Still, *Surviving the Male Mid-Life Crisis* (New York: Thomas Y. Crowell Co., 1977).
6. Judson Gooding, "The Engineers Are Redesigning Their Own Profession," *Fortune*, June, 1971, p. 72.
7. From a survey by the Episcopalian church reported in Laile E. Bartlett, *The Vanishing Parson* (Boston: Beacon Press, 1971).
8. Subsequent statistics are drawn from an analysis by Dixie Sommers and Alan Eck, "Occupational Mobility in the American Labor Force," *Monthly Labor Review*, (published by the United States Department of Labor) January, 1977, pp. 3–19. I have rounded the figures off to the nearest whole number.
9. Betty Holroyd Roberts, "Middle-Aged Career Dropouts: An Exploration," unpublished doctoral dissertation for the Florence Heller School at Brandeis University, Waltham, Massachusetts, 1974.

Chapter 2

1. Richard Louv, "The Grapes of Ely's Wrath," *San Diego*, September, 1978.
2. Judith Bardwick, "The Dynamics of Successful People," *New Research on Women*, (Ann Arbor, Michigan: The University of Michigan Center for Continuing Education, 1974.)
3. The Harris survey of 1,502 adults was reported by *The Washington Post* on August 8, 1977.
4. Virginia Crandall, W. Katkovsky and Anne Preston, "A Conceptual Formulation of Some Research on Children's Achievement Development," *Child Development*, 31: 787–797.
5. Margaret Hennig and Anne Jardim, *The Managerial Woman*, . (New York: Doubleday, 1977), p. 47.
6. Paula I. Robbins, *Successful Midlife Career Change* (New York: AMACOM, 1978).
7. Daniel Levinson, *The Seasons of a Man's Life* (New York: Alfred A. Knopf, 1978), particularly pages 97–101 and 147–149.

Chapter 3

1. Elliott Jaques, "Death and the MidLife Crisis," *International Journal of Psycho-Analysis*, October, 1965, pp. 502–514.
2. In Levinson, *The Seasons of a Man's Life*, pp. 260–270.
3. Erik H. Erikson, *Childhood and Society* (New York: W.W. Norton & Company, 1950).
4. A good popular rendering of these studies is Lucille K. Forer's *The Birth Order Factor* (New York: Pocket Books, 1977).
5. In Hennig and Jardim, *The Managerial Woman*.
6. The articles are compiled in F. Scott Fitzgerald, *The Crack-Up* (New York: New Directions, 1945). The quotes are taken from pages 69–90.

Chapter 4

1. Will Clopton, "Personality and Career Change," *Industrial Gerontology*, Spring, 1973, pp. 9–17.
2. For insights into the midcareer crisis of blue-collar workers, *see* Harold L. Sheppard and Neil Q. Herrick, *Where Have All the Robots Gone?* (New York: The Free Press, 1972).
3. Charles Harris, *One Man's Medicine* (New York: Harper & Row, 1975).

4. *Social Indicators 1973*. Undated paper prepared by the Office of Management and Budget and published by the Social and Economic Statistics Administration, U.S. Department of Commerce.
5. C. Wright Mills, *White Collar* (New York: Oxford University Press, 1951), p. 236.
6. Else Frenkel-Brunswik, "Adjustments and Reorientation in the Course of the Life Span," in *Middle Age and Aging*, edited by Bernice L. Neugarten (Chicago: The University of Chicago Press, 1968), p. 84.
7. Paula I. Robbins and David W. Harvey, "Avenues and Directions for Accomplishing Mid-Career Change," an unpublished paper.

Chapter 5

1. Dale L. Hiestand, *Changing Careers after Thirty-Five* (New York: Columbia University Press, 1971).
2. Bernice Neugarten, "Adult Personality: Toward a Psychology of the Life Cycle," in *Middle Age and Aging*, edited by Bernice Neugarten, (Chicago: The University of Chicago Press, 1968), p. 140.
3. These figures are based on the responses of nearly 500 middle-class men. John Clausen reported his findings in "Glimpses of the Social World of Middle Age" which was presented at a meeting of the Gerontological Society in Portland, Oregon, on October 31, 1974.
4. Harold L. Sheppard, "The Emerging Pattern of Second Careers," *Vocational Guidance Quarterly*, December, 1971, pp. 89–95.
5. Seymour B. Sarason, *Work, Aging and Social Change* (New York: The Free Press, 1977), pp. 245–250.
6. Roger Gould, *Transformations* (New York: Simon & Schuster, 1978), p. 230ff.

Chapter 6

1. Raymond G. Kuhlen, "Developmental Changes in Motivation during the Adult Years" in Neugarten, *Middle Age and Aging*.
2. In Robbins, *Successful Midlife Career Change*, p. 49.
3. A sampling of 400 people chose this as "the best age" for a man to have made a final career selection. A similar question about

women was not included. Bernice L. Neugarten, Joan W. Moore and John C. Lowe, "Age Norms, Age Constraints and Adult Socialization," in Neugarten, *Middle Age and Aging*, p. 24.

4. In Renwick, Lawler, "What You Really Want from Your Job," *Psychology Today*, May, 1978, pp. 53–65.

5. Reported in *Life Magazine*, January 9, 1970.

6. *Social Indicators 1976* (Washington, D.C.: U.S. Department of Commerce, 1977), p. 353.

7. Harold C. Lyon, Jr., *Tenderness Is Strength: From Machismo to Masculinity* (New York: Harper & Row, 1977), pp. 68–69.

8. Jacqueline Kennedy Onassis, "Jacqueline Kennedy Onassis on Working," *Ms.*, March, 1979, pp. 50–52.

9. Neva Nelson Sachar, "The Real Story Behind the Bell Jar," *Mademoiselle*, March, 1979, pp. 112–113.

10. Colette Dowling, "Beyond Liberation: Confessions of a Dependent Woman," *New York*, August 8, 1977, pp. 30–34.

11. Judith M. Bardwick, *Psychology of Women* (New York: Harper & Row, 1971), p. 145.

12. Harry Levinson, *Executive Stress* (New York: Harper & Row, 1970), p. 38.

13. This survey of working women from the age of eighteen on up was undertaken by Axiom Research Bureau and reported by *Working Woman* in their November, 1978, issue by Ann Casey under the title "Career? Just a Job?," p. 58ff.

14. Quotes in Arlie Russell Hochschild, "Inside the Clockwork of Male Careers" in *Women and the Power to Change*, edited by Florence Howe (New York: McGraw-Hill, 1975), pp. 47–81.

15. See "Occupation, Employment and Lifetime Work Experiences of Women" by Larry E. Suter of the U.S. Bureau of the Census, an unpublished paper presented at the American Sociological Association in 1973.

16. Rhoda Baruch, "The Achievement Motive in Women: Implications for Career Development," *Journal of Personality and Social Psychology*, January, 1967, pp. 260–267.

17. The statistics are drawn from Ruth Helm Osborn and Mary Jo Strauss' *Development and Administration of Continuing Education for Women 1964–1974*, prepared for the College of General Studies, The George Washington University, Washington, D.C.

18. The statistics were supplied by Mainstream Associates and are based on a study of some 500 clients.

Chapter 7

1. Reported under the title, "Satisfaction II: Changing Attitudes," *Working Woman*, October, 1978, p. 64.

Chapter 8

1. In Osborn and Strauss, *Development and Administration of Continuing Education for Women 1964–1974*.
2. In Renwick, Lawler, "What You Really Want from Your Job," *Psychology Today*, May, 1978, p. 60.
3. In Neugarten, Moore and Lowe, "Age Norms, Age Constraints and Adult Socialization," in *Middle Age and Aging*, pp. 22–28.

Chapter 9

1. "New Breed of Workers," *U.S. News and World Report*, September 3, 1979, pp. 35–38.
2. Ibid., p. 35.
3. Charles A. Reich, *The Greening of America* (New York: Bantam Books, 1971), p. 407.
4. In Mills, *White Collar: The American Middle Class*, pp. 215–223.

Bibliography

Judith M. Bardwick, *Psychology of Women* (New York: Harper & Row, 1971).

Judith M. Bardwick, "The Dynamics of Successful People" in *New Research on Women*, edited by Dorothy G. McGrugan, published by the Center for Continuing Education for Women, University of Michigan, Ann Arbor, Michigan, 1974, pp. 86–105.

Laile E. Bartlett, *The Vanishing Parson* (Boston: Beacon Press, 1971).

Laile E. Bartlett, *New Work/New Life* (New York: Harper & Row, 1976).

Colette Dowling, "Beyond Liberation: Confessions of a Dependent Woman," *New York* magazine, August 8, 1977, pp. 30–34.

Lucille Forer with Henry Still, *The Birth Order Factor* (New York: Pocket Books, 1977).

Rhoda Baruch, "The Achievement Motive in Women: Implications for Career Development," *Journal of Personality and Social Pscyhology*, January, 1967, pp. 260–267.

Rhoda Baruch, *The Interruption and Resumption of Women's Careers*, Harvard Studies on Career Development, No. 50, Cambridge, Massachusetts, 1966.

Fred Best, editor, *The Future of Work* (Englewood Cliffs, N.J.: Prentice-Hall, 1973).

Don Biggs, *Breaking Out . . . of a job you don't like . . . and the regimented life . . .* (New York: David McKay, 1973).

Orville G. Brim, Jr., "Theories of the Male Mid-Life Crisis," *The Counseling Psychologist*, vol. 6, No. 1, 1976, pp. 2–9.

Richard Nelson Bolles, *What Color Is Your Parachute?* (Berkeley, Calif.: Ten Speed Press, 1977).

Ann Casey, "Career? Just a Job?" *Working Woman*, November, 1978, p. 58ff.

Peter Chew, *The Inner World of the Middle Aged Man* (New York: Macmillan, 1976).

John A. Clausen, "Glimpses of the Social World of Middle Age," prepared for the symposium "Middle Age: Some Early Returns," annual meeting of the Gerontological Society, Portland, Oregon, October 31, 1974.

Will Clopton, "Personality and Career Change," *Industrial Gerontology*, Spring, 1973, pp. 9–17.

Virginia Crandall, W. Ratkovsky and Anne Preston, "A Conceptual Formulation of Some Research on Children's Achievement Development," *Child Development*, 31: pp. 787–797.

Wayne Dennis, "Creative Productivity between the Ages of 20 and 80 Years," in *Middle Age and Aging* edited by Bernice L. Neugarten (Chicago: The University of Chicago Press, 1968), pp. 106–114.

Else Frenkel-Brunswik, "Adjustments and Reorientation in the Course of the Life Span" in *Middle Age and Aging* edited by Bernice L. Neugarten (Chicago: University of Chicago Press, 1968), pp. 77–84.

Barbara Fried, *The Middle Age Crisis* (Revised edition), (New York: Harper & Row, 1976).

Eli Ginzberg and Associates, *Life Styles of Educated Women* (New York: Columbia University Press, 1966).

Judson Gooding, "The Engineers Are Redesigning Their Own Profession," *Fortune*, June, 1971, pp. 72ff.

Roger Gould, *Transformations* (New York: Simon and Schuster, 1978).

Roger Gould, "The Phases of Adult Life: A Study in Developmental Psychology," *American Journal of Psychiatry*, 129 (1972), pp. 521–531.

David Gutman, "Individual Adaptation in the Middle Years/Developmental Issues in the Masculine Mid-Life Crisis," *Journal of Geriatric Psychiatry*, volume 9, Number 1, 1976, pp. 41–59.

Charles Harris, *One Man's Medicine* (New York: Harper & Row, 1975).

Philip Harsham, "Do-Your-Own-Thing Careers," *Money*, July, 1978, pp. 32–35.

Margaret Hennig and Anne Jardim, *The Managerial Woman* (New York: Pocket Books, 1976).

Lisa Hobbs, *Running towards Life* (New York: McGraw-Hill, 1971).

Arlie Russell Hochschild, "Inside the Clockwork of Male Careers" in *Women and the Power to Change*, edited by Florence Howe (New York: McGraw-Hill, 1975), pp. 47–81.

"Jacqueline Kennedy Onassis Talks about Working," *Ms.*, March, 1979, pp. 50–52.

Elliott Jaques, "Death and the Mid-Life Crisis," *International Journal of Psycho-Analysis*, October, 1965, pp. 502–514.

Gerald J. Jud, Edgar W. Mills, Jr., Genevieve Walters Burch, *Ex-Pastors: Why Men Leave the Parish Ministry* (Philadelphia: Pilgrim Press, 1970).

David L. Krantz, *Radical Career Change* (New York: The Free Press, 1978).

Raymond G. Kuhler, "Developmental Changes in Motivation During the Adult Years," in *Middle Age and Aging*, edited by Bernice L. Neugarten (Chicago: University of Chicago Press, 1970), pp. 115–137.

Daniel J. Levinson, *The Seasons of a Man's Life* (New York: Alfred A. Knopf, 1978).

Harry Levinson, *Executive Stress* (New York: Harper & Row, 1970).

Richard Louv, "The Grapes of Ely's Wrath," *San Diego*, September, 1978.

Harold C. Lyon, Jr., *Tenderness Is Strength: From Machismo to Manhood* (New York: Harper & Row, 1977).

Abraham Maslow, *Motivation and Personality* (New York: Harper & Row, 1954).

C. Wright Mills, *White Collar* (New York: Oxford University Press, 1951).

Bernice L. Neugarten, Joan W. Moore and John C. Lowe, "Age Norms, Age Constraints and Adult Socialization," in *Middle Age and Aging* edited by Bernice L. Neugarten (Chicago: The University of Chicago Press, 1968).

Bernice L. Neugarten, "The Awareness of Middle Age" in *Middle Age and Aging* edited by Bernice L. Neugarten (Chicago: The University of Chicago Press, 1968).

Ruth Helm Osborn and Mary Jo Strauss, *Development and Administration of Continuing Education for Women*, a report prepared for George Washington University, Washington, D.C.

Charles A. Reich, *The Greening of America* (New York: Bantam Books, 1971).

Patricia A. Renwick, Edward E. Lawler and the Psychology Today Staff, "What You Really Want from Your Job," *Psychology Today*, May, 1978, pp. 53–65.

Paula I. Robbins, *Successful Midlife Career Change* (New York: AMACOM, 1978).

Paula I. Robbins and David W. Harvey, *Avenues and Directions for Accomplishing Mid-Career Change*, unpublished paper, March, 1977.

Kenn Rogers, "The Mid-Career Crisis," *Saturday Review of the Society*, February, 1973, p. 38ff.

Diane Rothbard Margolis, "Back to College at Middle Age," *Change*, October, 1974, pp. 34–37.

"A New Breed of Workers," *U.S. News and World Report*, September 3, 1979, pp. 35–38.

Betty Holroyd Roberts, *Middle-Aged Career Dropouts: An Exploration*, unpublished doctoral dissertation, Florence Heller School, Brandeis University, Waltham, Mass., 1974.

Neva Nelson Sachar, "The Real Story Behind the Bell Jar," *Mademoiselle*, March, 1979, pp. 112–113.

Iris Sangiuliano, *In Her Time* (New York: William Morrow and Co., 1978).

"Satisfaction II: Changing Attitudes," *Working Woman*, October, 1978, p. 64.

Seymour B. Sarason, *Work, Aging and Social Change* (New York: The Free Press, 1977).

"Second Careers as a Way of Life: A Symposium," *Vocational Guidance Quarterly*, December, 1971, pp. 87–118.

"Second Careers/A Selected Bibliography," compiled by Carol H. Killeher (Washington, D.C.: The National Council on the Aging, Inc., 1973).

Gail Sheehy, *Passages* (New York: E.P. Dutton & Co., Inc., 1976).

Harold L. Sheppard, "The Emerging Pattern of Second Careers," *Vocational Guidance Quarterly*, December, 1971, pp. 89–95.

Harold L. Sheppard & Neal Q. Herrick, *Where Have All the Robots*

Gone? Worker Dissatisfaction in the 70's (sic) (New York: The Free Press, 1972).

Social Indicators 1973, prepared by the U.S. Office of Management and Budget, published by the Social and Economic Statistics Administration, U.S. Department of Commerce.

Social Indicators 1976, Selected Data on Social Conditions and Trends in the United States (Washington, D.C.: U.S. Government Printing Office, 1977).

Dixie Sommers and Alan Eck, "Occupational Mobility in the American Labor Force," *Monthly Labor Review*, January, 1977, pp. 3–19.

Gloria Steinem, "Dear God, Why Do They Work? (Without Apologies to Freud)," *Ms.* magazine, March, 1979, p. 45ff.

Henry Still, *Surviving the Male Mid-Life Crisis* (New York: Thomas Y. Crowell Co., 1977), p. 240.

"Studies on Problems of Work and Age," *Industrial Gerontology*, Spring, 1973.

Larry E. Suter, "Occupation, Employment, and Lifetime Work Experience of Women," an unpublished paper prepared for the U.S. Bureau of the Census.

Dale Tarnowieski, *The Changing Success Ethic* (New York: The American Management Association, 1973).

L. Eugene Thomas, "Mid-Career Change: Self-Selected or Externally Mandated," unpublished paper, no date.

L. Eugene Thomas, "Why Study Mid-Life Career Change?" *Vocational Guidance Quarterly*, September, 1975, pp. 37–40.

L. Eugene Thomas, Richard L. Mela, Paula I. Robbins, David W. Harvey, "Corporate Dropouts: A Preliminary Typology," *Vocational Guidance Quarterly*, March, 1976, pp. 220–228.

George E. Vaillant, *Adaptation to Life* (Boston: Little, Brown and Company, 1977).

Lindsy Van Gelder, "Why Women Work: Five Good Motives (Besides Money)," *Ms.* magazine, March, 1979, p. 52ff.

Patrick Walsh, "Occupational Mobility of Health Workers," *Monthly Labor Review*, May, 1977, pp. 25–29.

Nancy Weber, *The Life Swap* (New York: The Dial Press, 1974).

Tom Wolfe, "The 'Me' Decade and the Third Great Awakening," *New York* magazine, August 23, 1976, pp. 24–40.

Work in America, Report of a Special Task Force to the Secretary of Health, Education and Welfare (Cambridge, Mass.: MIT Press, 1973).

Daniel Yankelovich, "The New Psychological Contracts at Work," *Psychology Today*, May, 1978, pp. 46–50.

Anne M. Young, "Going Back to School at 35," *Monthly Labor Review*, October, 1973, pp. 39–42.

INDEX